Would the Real Gerry Ryan Please Stand Up

Gerry Ryan was born in Dublin and studied law at Trinity College. His love of radio saw him abandon his legal career to become a pirate station DJ in the late 1970s. He joined RTÉ Radio 2 as a DJ when it opened in 1979, but his talent for talk saw him emerge rapidly as one of Ireland's top radio and television broadcasters. His daytime radio show, *The Gerry Ryan Show*, attracts more than 400,000 listeners a day.

Would the Real Gerry Ryan Please Stand Up

GERRY RYAN

PENGUIN
IRELAND

PENGUIN IRELAND

Published by the Penguin Group
Penguin Ireland, 25 St Stephen's Green, Dublin 2, Ireland
(a division of Penguin Books Ltd)
Penguin Books Ltd, 80 Strand, London WC2R 0RL, England
Penguin Group (USA) Inc., 375 Hudson Street, New York, New York 10014, USA
Penguin Group (Australia), 250 Camberwell Road, Camberwell, Victoria 3124, Australia
(a division of Pearson Australia Group Pty Ltd)
Penguin Group (Canada), 90 Eglinton Avenue East, Suite 700, Toronto, Ontario, Canada M4P 2Y3
(a division of Pearson Penguin Canada Inc.)
Penguin Books India Pvt Ltd, 11 Community Centre, Panchsheel Park, New Delhi – 110 017, India
Penguin Group (NZ), 67 Apollo Drive, Rosedale, North Shore 0632, New Zealand
(a division of Pearson New Zealand Ltd)
Penguin Books (South Africa) (Pty) Ltd, 24 Sturdee Avenue, Rosebank, Johannesburg 2196, South Africa

Penguin Books Ltd, Registered Offices: 80 Strand, London WC2R 0RL, England

www.penguin.com

First published 2008
1

Set in 12/14.75 pt Postscript Monotype Bembo
Typeset by Rowland Phototypesetting Ltd, Bury St Edmunds, Suffolk
Printed in Great Britain by Clays Ltd, St Ives plc

A CIP catalogue record for this book is available from the British Library

ISBN: 978-1-844-88187-1

www.greenpenguin.co.uk

CONTENTS

WOULD THE REAL GERRY RYAN PLEASE STAND UP

I've always been guilty of adapting my persona according to what people expect of me. It's very difficult to figure out exactly who I am – if I'm real at all, or if I'm just a collection of different attitudes and postures and survival suits. I think I'd have been a very good deep-cover spy. I would have absorbed another identity very quickly and lived out another life very effectively.

My real friends get it; my real friends see through it.

Siobhan Hough, for instance, and Deirdre McGee, both of whom have worked on *The Gerry Ryan Show* from day one. They know exactly when the alias is there and when it's not. They can second-guess in a heartbeat what I'm going to do or say or how I'm going to react . . . I know they get pleasure out of watching people think they know what I'm going to say and I can see them standing there going, *You fucking idiots, he's not going to agree to that! This is exactly what he's going to say . . . and . . . Oh! There he is saying it now!* They know me intimately.

I think my family have been generous in dealing with this. I think that they're able to go, 'OK, he's a bit weird sometimes, but you know what? He's a good guy, he takes care of us, he's funny, he's entertaining.' And the thing is, I turn up. I am the guy who will materialize in Mogadishu to bring you home.

There is a very small number of people who understand me. My wife understood me better than anyone else in the entire world.

Harry Crosbie is an extremely close friend of mine, and Harry can second-guess me very quickly. David Blake Knox, who directs *Ryan Confidential*, is very close to me and he can, without a word from me, understand what I'm feeling or thinking. He'll know how I'm going to react. I see Bono sometimes and when I say something he gets this kind of smirk on his face, like he knows I'm not being entirely real . . . So it's a very small number of people.

A woman, a friend of someone who ended up working on the show, was commissioned by a newspaper to follow me for several weeks to look for dirt. She was introduced to me afterwards, long afterwards. She told me she had to give up the job. She told the newspaper, 'Well, it's impossible to try to figure out what this guy does – if he does anything. He goes down to have his lunch at the Four Seasons, so unless you're prepared to shell out for lunch in the Four Seasons, you can't get in there. Then he was going away for the weekend, and I thought maybe it might be a dirty weekend. So I followed him over to Paris, and he's in Paris in the Hôtel Meurice with somebody much younger than him. And it actually turns out to be his wife. And you can't get in there unless you pay a grand at the door. There's a limousine waiting for him outside. He's ushered to the limousine and goes to a restaurant that we can't afford to get into. Then he goes to a nightclub. There's two women with him. One turns out to be one of his best friends, the other is his wife. I can't get into the nightclub because you have to have your name on a special list or pay a grand to the guy at the door.' So she said, 'I just gave up. Unless you guys are willing to pony up huge amounts of money for me to follow this guy, it's not going to happen. All his private parties are held inside hotel suites. God knows what they do, but I certainly don't.'

How much of this book is the real me? Well, I haven't lied about anything. What's the real me? What's the real anybody? What are you going to do? Are you going to bed with me? Meet me at breakfast? Listen to me coughing in the morning? Watch me going through self-doubt before I go on the radio? Then transform myself into a psychopathic zealot, or deplane from that into some sort of reckless adolescent?

You want to know what I'm like? Come and live with me.

SHOW ME THE MONEY

My father used to say to me, 'Money isn't everything. It's just 99.9 per cent.'

If you're sick, if you're in difficulty at work, if your relationship is breaking down, if your life is falling apart, it's much better to go through those experiences with money. He was a middle-class, post-Second-World-War boy who graduated from the Royal College of Surgeons and was driving a Jaguar, a brand new Jaguar, in the mid-sixties. I remember sitting beside him on the number thirty bus into town. He had a brown-paper bag on his knees and in the bag was two thousand pounds in cash. He opened it up and showed me the money.

'What's that for?' I asked him.

'That's the money for the car,' he said.

The bus went down the Howth Road, swung round Fairview Park, then into town, and we walked the rest of the way, from the terminus up to Georges Street. You could have got a second bus, but There Was No Point Wasting Money. Cavey's shop on Georges Street was an Aladdin's cave, chock full of the most fabulous cars. Ours, the one that would be ours, was a pale blue Jag XJ6, with all the trimmings. Very few people in Ireland were buying cars of any kind at this time, much less Jaguars, so this was really exciting. We were treated like a potentate and his son. We were brought in and given what Harry Crosbie would call a meat tea. We were given a tour of the shop.

Sitting there, with these men in their suits, selling you these cars, was a rite of passage. My father was saying to me that the whole reason he brought me with him was to show me that This Is What It Is All About. Having this means You Have Succeeded.

Now, his family was hugely important to him. His status as a community dentist was hugely important to him. This was a man who towards the end of his life didn't take money from his patients. This drove my mother insane. He had no receptionist at this point so she used to send out the bills, then make the threatening phone calls: Pay Up Or Else . . . It would transpire that my father had told them not to worry about it, because these were people who had either reduced circumstances or no circumstances at all. He believed that he'd had such a good life from the community that he ought to give something back, so instead of money, he'd come home with chickens and tins of Ambrosia. There was a deeply humanitarian side to the man. He was also officially rated, in the final years of his practice, the cheapest dentist in Ireland, so this was not a greedy man. He was saying, that day in Cavey's – and this was a masculine thing, 'I have that car, and that car says I Have Succeeded. I'm even going to enjoy just sitting in it.'

He worked in London for a short while after he qualified, then came home, converted his old bedroom into a surgery and built up a practice from scratch. The drive from Kincora Avenue where we lived, to his parents' home on Clontarf Road where he worked, took about three minutes, but the statement that car made was huge. But it was much more than a materialistic thing. The car was beautiful. It bestowed tremendous status. At a time in Ireland's history that was pretty bleak, culturally, socially and economically, it showed that its owner had risen above it. I remember sitting in the car with him on numerous occasions. In fact all the serious conversations I had with my father were conducted in the car, driving somewhere, and I still recommend it as a great place to talk to your children, because you've got a captive audience.

CAR TALK

I remember him saying to me, 'What do you want to do when you get older? Do you want to work on a building site?' Nowadays, of course, if you worked on a building site, you'd own two Jags, but back in those days you had to go to Cricklewood or Boston to get a job.

'I don't want to do anything that's physically too hard,' I said, 'and I want to make my mark.'

'Well, then, you have to get an education. You've got to go to university and get a profession.'

'What do you think I should do?'

'It doesn't matter, to be honest. You don't have to love what you do. It would be good if you did love it, but it must be well paid. And it must single you out from the rest of the community because you'll get tremendous satisfaction from that.'

He asked me, 'What's different between you and some of the boys in your class?'

I said, 'Well, there's no difference between me and the other boys in my class.'

'There is,' he said. 'What happens in the summer?'

'Well,' I said, 'we go to Donabate.'

We had a mobile home down in Donabate – not a caravan, mind, a mobile home. That, believe it or not, was a major extravagance, a huge status symbol in those days. The mobile home, the Donnington, was brought down from the North of Ireland. It was hooked up to the Jag, and my father hauled it into the field in Donabate like Caesar entering Rome. Can you imagine two more polarized objects? A mobile home and a Jaguar?

At the time it made perfect sense. My father was a competent handyman; he could do plumbing and carpentry, he was a good sparks, so he did quite a bit of work on the mobile home over the years. To circumvent the endless trudge to the pump for water, he sank an artesian well. He laid a patio. It sounds ludicrous now, but the fact that the mobile home had a working bathroom transformed it into a major status symbol. He even added an extension, a Barna building, and piped it for running water. We called it the Atrium.

He said, 'What do we do then after that, after Donabate?'

I said, 'Well, we go to the Isle of Man for a week or two. We stay in Douglas.'

'And do you like that? Is it good? Do all your pals do that?'

I said, 'Well, one or two of them have . . .'

'And what do we do after that?'

'We go to Spain for a month, maybe . . .'

He said, 'How many people that you know do that?'

'Not very many people,' I said. 'In fact, none.'

'Well,' he said, 'that's because your father has money. That's how we're able to do that. And you really love being able to do all those things, don't you? You love flying, you love eating different food . . .'

I remember, distinctly, walking past a restaurant in Spain and smelling food. It was paella, but I didn't know that, there not being much call for paella in Clontarf at the time. My father, it has to be said, wasn't too keen on food produced by foreign nationals. He used to bring suitcases of Galtee rashers and things like that with him so we wouldn't be poisoned by Franco's regime. We didn't know or understand at the time that these people had a hugely sophisticated cuisine that left Ireland in the Stone Age when it came to food.

As we got older, we began to be brought to restaurants because we demanded it. My mother used to prod my father out of the apartment. We used to go as a big team, ourselves and the O'Keefes. Ray O'Keefe was the chairman of the Irish Permanent Building Society. He was another Jag driver, and was hugely influential because he would talk about stocks and shares. He was responsible for lending money to people to buy houses. Houses! You can't get more powerful than that. When we got into the restaurants, I began to realize there was another world out there. The wonderful experience of being in an exotic restaurant. The smells, the tastes, the atmosphere . . . and, once again, how did you get it? How? You got it by having money. There was no other way.

We were never given pocket money. The message, I suppose, was that the money itself wasn't the issue: it was what it could do for you.

Every single Friday, my father would bring my mother into town and she would get a new outfit. This was at a time in Ireland when most housewives would buy maybe two dresses a year. My father always had what I thought was far too much input in the choice of her dress but, then, he was paying for it, and she seemed happy enough with the arrangement. He'd often take us out of school on a Friday and bring us into town. We would have lunch maybe in the Metropole Grill, which, as far as I was concerned, was America. Afterwards, we'd go down to the Adelphi cinema, where we'd be greeted by the manager, who was a friend of the family. Then we'd have our tea in the Hollywood-style grill in the Adelphi. All of this was achieved not just because my parents liked going to the movies or shopping, or because they wanted to give their children a Disneyland experience once a week. They were able to do this because they had money. This, all of it, was building an unarguable case. You needed money to get a bicycle, you needed money to go on holidays, to get those hipsters, to buy that record, to travel on a plane.

THE BALLYHAUNIS-MEETS-LA LIFESTYLE

Travel on a plane! As far as I was concerned, air travel was the crack cocaine of life experience.

When we went out to Collinstown, as Dublin airport was called, this art-deco environment was so utterly removed from the world that normal people existed in. The checking in, going up to the lounge and maybe having something to eat before the flight, the whole ritual of getting on to the plane: walking across the Tarmac with . . . the smell of aviation fuel. Aer Lingus had a perfume they used to spray in the aircraft before the passengers got on and that to me was the essence of travel: foreign places, people with different voices, different skin colours . . . Swimming in the sea without freezing your nuts off. It was hugely exciting. We always, always flew first class and, once again, this couldn't be done unless you had money.

My father, our family, had all of these contacts, all of these people we used to hang around with. And they had money too. Maurice Keating was a senior captain with Aer Lingus, one of their leading lights and one of the first men to fly jumbo jets for the airline. He occasionally piloted the Viscounts we went on holidays in, and I remember being brought up to the cockpit to meet Captain Keating. That's how he was referred to, at home around the dinner table. Captain Keating. Here again was a man of great status and influence, highly paid, in a highly responsible position. All of this, the life, the contacts, was achieved because we were professionals.

I bought into it from a very early age. This is absolutely fantastic. This is What I Want: the G-Plan furniture, the colour television, the aerial . . . Long before we had a television, we had an aerial. This was middle-class Ireland at its most surreal. We had a 120-foot-high aerial erected in our back garden and my father brought all the neighbours in to look at it. They were absolutely mesmerized. My mother ferried out tea and sandwiches and people stood around drinking the tea and eating the sandwiches and chatting and looking at the aerial and going, 'Isn't it absolutely fabulous?'

It was, of course, a complete eyesore, and if you put one up today, the planning people would be all over you in a flash, but it was what it was, which was an icon of success. In flashing lights down its length, it said: I Have Made Enough Money To Buy An Aerial (And Who Knows? We Might Even Get A Telly One Of These Days).

So much of it seems incredible to me now, the gaucheness of it, the naïvety of it, that Ballyhaunis-meets-LA kind of life, but I spent my life looking forward to those milestones – the foreign travel, the trips to town, the purchase of a new car, going to O'Connor's jeans shop to be decked out in Wranglers. Until I was fifteen or sixteen, my mother came with me to buy clothes, and when we got home, she'd make a point of saying, 'Go and thank your father for this. It's his money that bought those jeans.' And I would, I'd thank him but he'd be uninterested. He wouldn't want to talk about that.

PROBLEMS WITH THE ACCOUNTS

Then came the fateful day when I arrived home from college and asked for my father. He was in bed. My mother explained, in very sombre tones, that there were Problems With The Accounts. At the time, I suppose, I had a fairly cavalier attitude to money. I believed that we were much more wealthy than we actually were. I thought, Well, we're fine, we're rich. I don't have to get a student job like everyone else. Jobs were for halfwits and people on grants. Why would I be getting a job? Sure we've millions. But now the taxman had come calling and there was nothing for

him. In response, my father did a very Irish thing. He took to
the bed. I went up to the bedroom to talk to him and he told
me simply that we had no money. I remember thinking, Christ!
How the fuck did that happen?

'Sure you're wealthy. You've a Jag.'

'That's all I've got. This house and a Jag.'

Dad's approach to tax was basically not to pay it at all. I was a
law student, and went to see his accountant with Peter Lennon,
a colleague and friend of mine.

'Chris,' I said, 'what the fuck is happening here?'

'Look,' he said, 'this doesn't have anything to do with me.
Your father will not return the documents.'

Dad had gone into complete Revenue meltdown. He was
obsessed, obsessed, with Revenue intrusion. Anything to do
with paying taxes was beyond unfair. It was immoral and deeply
aberrant of the government to try and take his money from him.
He had the same approach to rates. In fact, a guy on the city
council recently sent me a copy of correspondence that my father,
late in his life, had had with the council. This was when he still
had a private dental practice. He had refused, basically, to pay
water rates. The council said something like, 'You have to pay
commercial water rates because you're running a business, and
you're obviously using water for your business because you're a
dentist, Mr Ryan.' My father replied that he used bottled spark-
ling water that he purchased himself, and that he would rather
have the water cut off than pay commercial rates.

So there were several taxation periods where not only had he
not paid any tax, but he hadn't even sent in any returns. He
took to the bed, and wrote a very long letter to the Revenue
Commissioners in which he threatened to go on hunger strike.

This was in the days of The Deal.

I understand that Charles Haughey had some involvement at
this point. Charlie made overtures to the Revenue Commission,
saying that it might be better to try to come to an arrangement
with this man. And, eventually, a deal was done. My father agreed

to pay off the tax over a period of time and he emerged from the bed, fully clothed, showered, shaved and smiling, in spite of himself. We never heard another word about it.

Not for one minute was I disappointed with him. I just realized that the guy had spent the dough. He'd just spent it. Life went on, albeit in much reduced circumstances. And I will never forget the sad, sad day when I arrived home from college and, instead of the Jag, there in the drive sat an Opel Corsa.

This is it, I thought. We're normal.

I should have known things were going wrong. There was this kick-down facility on the Jaguar, which allowed you to knock it into a lower gear so you could accelerate faster. When it broke, I remember saying to my father, 'When are you going to get this fixed?'

And he said, 'Ah, we don't need it.'

Thinking about it afterwards, I realized that funds had been drying up for two or three years before the crash. The foreign trips stopped, the shopping sprees stopped and his lifestyle became simpler. He continued to practise and he became a community dentist, really. I think, in a way, he was happier, at the end of it all. But what did I carry away from all this? The message, the money message, was stronger than ever, except that it carried this health warning: having it on Wednesday didn't mean having it on Friday.

All of which made me ultra-determined that, whatever I did, I was going to put myself in a position that offered what I called 'animated earning ability' – to be in a job where you would start off earning a lot of money, but you would have the potential to earn even greater money.

OBSESSIVE COMPULSIVE DISORDER

I'm not quite David Beckham, arranging the Pepsi cans in the fridge, but I'm not far off it. I do find myself arranging the magazines in the tray, I do find myself putting the CDs in alphabetical order. I'm new to iTunes, and I'm very methodical about downloading the album artwork, a practice, I suspect, restricted to a nerdy few. I've one other friend who's got OCD and he recognizes it in me. The two of us are very comfortable together. When we go to restaurants, we're very freaked out by cutlery out of place, dirt on the table and things not happening in the correct sequence.

He does a lot of the stuff I do. I arrange my shirts according to style and get really upset if they're not all front-of-collar facing towards the centre of the wardrobe. At the moment I've got these wonderful wardrobes that are like something out of James Bond. The whole system pulls out and you have all your suits and your trousers and your shirts perfectly in place. I love having everything perfectly in place. I have cleaners come in and shampoo the carpet twice or three times a month because I need the place to be immaculate. I sometimes try and mess things up a little bit before my kids come over so I don't appear too kind of Dr Goebbels. So I can't be *that* obsessive.

The car always has to be perfectly clean. The only place I'll wash it is in the Topaz in Killester because I'm convinced it's the only one that delivers an effective soft wash. I send it off to get valeted. I cannot abide being in a messy car. I can't go to work until the bed is made. When I lived with Morah, she would probably have wished I was a bit more like that than I am now, but she was usually in the bed with my daughter when I left for work.

My father used to hoover an awful lot, and I used to be really embarrassed by it. I mean, a man hovering? Shameful. Why isn't my mother doing it? I now hoover compulsively. Today I was looking at an ad in the Debenhams catalogue for a top-of-the-range Dyson. Now I feel myself tantalizingly close to getting into the car and driving to Debenhams to get it. I'm *sooo* looking forward to putting its dust-mite-busting features to the test.

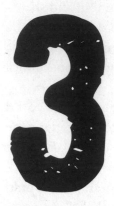

AT HOME WITH THE RYANS

Performance was a natural thing in our house. It was also a way out of difficulty, a way out of having to answer questions or explain yourself. I remember with Mum and Dad, if they had a row, myself and my two brothers would instantly get into performance mode. We would retreat into a fantasy world. That really is what performance is.

There were three of us in the family. I'm the oldest, and there's a year between me and my brother Vincent, whose nickname is Mano. Michael arrived as a sort of afterthought five years after Vincent. I was born in Tudor House, which was this pseudo-Gothic pile in Clontarf where my parents had a flat. My dad was sick before I was born so he and my mum lived there with my maternal grandmother. I was still a baby when they bought 108 Kincora Avenue. This was in an emerging estate, very typical of the kind of baby-boomer sixties estates that were being built then in Ireland.

They gave us a very happy home, Mum and Dad. They were an unusual match, I suppose, my theatrical, expressive and sometimes explosive mother, and my academic, considerate and reserved father. It was a mix that worked well, and made for a lot of robust debate around the dinner table

I think my mother was frustrated in her role as a housewife. I mean, she was a good mother and a good wife, but I believe she would have liked to stretch herself a bit more. As a younger woman she had been involved in her family's theatrical business. She had costumed and staged shows for musical societies all over the country and she really enjoyed doing that. I think not doing that any more and living with a guy from a much more subdued background than hers was difficult for her. Her married life didn't provide much of an outlet for her theatrical side, so it burst out on occasion in blazing arguments with her sons. I don't know whether that's a fantastic introduction to womanhood for three boys, because it probably gave us to understand that women were fascinating, beautiful, desirable . . . but unbalanced. If I'm honest, I've always had that opinion. I'm constantly fighting the deep-seated sense that women are wildly unpredictable and come from another planet.

The Bourkes, my mother's family – this was where all the performance came from. Her mother was a Kearney and was related to Kathleen Behan, Brendan Behan's mother. Peadar Kearney, who wrote the English-language lyrics for the national anthem, he was a relation too. My maternal grandfather Paddy Bourke was a classic touring fit-ups entertainer. This combined old-world circus, excerpts from the classics, vaudeville, turns from the audience. They'd rock up to a town, put up the tent or squeeze into what passed for theatrical accommodation and put on everything from *Hamlet* to whatever was in the Top Forty. Paddy was also involved in providing extras and finance for some of the very first Irish cinema productions.

My maternal grandmother, Paddy's wife, was a great business-woman. She had ten children, and the majority of them went into the theatre in one way or another. Together, they built up a hugely successful empire of theatrical enterprises. At one stage the Bourkes provided you not only with costumes for your play or your musical through Bourke's Costumiers, they also sorted out the theatre and the staff. My mother would help choreograph and stage-manage shows. They provided lighting and sound equipment, as well as advice and finance for touring the show. Later on, they branched into television rentals.

VELVET CLOAKS AND LIMELIGHT

The most compelling thing about the Bourkes, however, was not their business acumen. They were an incredibly glamorous family at a time when Ireland was otherwise monochrome. The women were sexy and sophisticated; the men were sharp-suited and drove classic cars. My uncle Lorcan Bourke, the senior impresario of the family, was responsible for a huge amount of the development that took place in musical theatre in Ireland. He wore expensive Italian suits and handmade shoes. He coloured his hair, an affectation that was inconceivable outside the theatrical profession. All of this, not to mention the velvet cloak he sometimes wore, made a huge impression on me.

Growing up in a family like that, you couldn't but get a taste for the glare of the footlights and the smell of the greasepaint. These women were on stage perpetually, even when they weren't, and their houses, when we visited them, were always incredibly vibrant and dramatic. My mother was a dancer, along with her sister, my godmother Grainne, who married Eamonn Andrews. She was a complete sexpot. My aunt Patsy, who's still alive, I knew better than any of the others. She was another statuesque and strikingly good-looking woman. I can remember being absolutely fascinated to see her in the shortest miniskirt I'd ever imagined. They kept a very close eye on what film stars were wearing and, for a republican family – that was essentially how they painted themselves – they were inordinately interested in what Princess Margaret, Princess Anne and the Queen wore.

They all did a stint at Bourke's Costumiers, which meant they were in daily contact with people who were putting on shows, whether Shakespeare or Gilbert and Sullivan. All of them would perform at the drop of a hat. Any time, any place, anywhere. I remember my mother and Aunt Patsy spontaneously breaking into a song from *Annie Get Your Gun* in the middle of the Angelus. Anyone who came into contact with my aunties was shocked, intrigued, amazed and turned on by them. They were just super-different from everyone else. For my own part, I was beguiled and bewitched. More than any other influence, it was those women, their style, their flair, their taste for the limelight, who had the greatest impact on my evolution as a performer.

And, of course, there wasn't just glamour on its own. There was money, plenty of money. On a Sunday I'd often go with my parents to lunch at the Andrews house. Grainne and Eamonn had a house designed by an architect. Actually designed by an architect! And no less an architect than Sam Stephenson, who had designed the Central Bank. Instead of gutters, it had chains running down the outside for the water to trickle off Japanese-style. There, you might meet guys like Bruce Forsyth, Max Bygraves, Dickie Henderson and Morecambe and Wise. At the same time, my father was cultivating friendships with powerful and wealthy men, so you might also run into the likes of Charles Haughey.

THE IONOSPHERE IS BOUNCING WELL

While my mother's genes might have given us the desire to perform, my father provided us with the tools of the trade. He was as into gadgets and gismos as I am. There were always recording devices in the house, whether it was a Chicago Webster wire-recorder or a Sony tape-recorder. So not only was there the ever-present Victorian parlour temptation to put on a show, there was also the opportunity, tragically for the listener/victim, to replay it endlessly. Of course, in my teenage years, I seem to have recorded over everything. Hopefully history will record that as a lack of vanity rather than a lack of foresight.

When my father was working in London shortly after the Second World War, he bought an R11 100 radio. These were the radio receivers and transmitters that had been used in Lancaster and Wellington bombers. A valve radio with a really warm sound, it took a minute or two to heat up after you'd flicked the switch, and there was ritual, and ceremony, in switching it on, listening to the heterodyne, then watching its light collapse and expand as you tuned in. I remember getting to know all the different stations, I remember the thrill of suddenly discovering Radio Free Athens or something even more exotic. There were unidentifiable stations, there for a week and then gone. There was Radio Prague, Radio Moscow, Radio Bhutan, then all the English-language services of the Iron Curtain countries – these were propaganda vehicles. All of the programmes seemed to be presented by a Soviet version of Lord Haw-Haw, extolling the virtues of the worker and boasting that fifty million tons of grain had been harvested in the Urals that day.

The R11 100 radios had been used as pathfinders by the guys flying the bombers; the crew's last mission was still etched on ours in pencil. The frequency location of each of the seven or eight radio beacons was marked on the dial; the radio operator would turn to each, and the heterodyne would increase or decrease the tone, indicating whether you were to the left or the right of the beacon. I was always very careful not to rub those markings off because I felt it was a kind of a connection with the boys – and they must only have been boys. It was hugely grounding to sit listening to 'Across The Universe' by the Beatles on Radio Luxembourg, mindful of the fact that boys of the same age had originally used that radio when they were flying over Berlin, with their lives in the hands of the pilot. I had it restored recently by a group of wireless enthusiasts, and having it, using it, still connects me with my dad.

Once the ionosphere was bouncing well, as my father used to say, you could pick up almost anything, even on the other side of the world. The quality was usually pretty atrocious but that only added to the exoticism, to the feeling that you were eavesdropping on some secret broadcast, particularly if you were listening on the headphones. These were the same ones that would have been worn by the radio operator on the bomber. They were incredibly comfortable moleskin headphones that fitted perfectly, excluded all external sound and had a beautiful timbre. Of course, as a teenager, I cut them up and used them for something else. If I'd only known what I was doing! But with these on, you couldn't hear anything else, you were utterly immersed in this static-filled world, waiting, always waiting for that coded message to come through . . .

Slowly but surely that world telescoped into Radio Luxembourg and BBC Radio 1, but even after I had developed a full-blown interest in pop radio, I still went back like an old lover to the original stations, because I felt that leaving them was a kind of betrayal.

DOWN WITH THAT SORT OF THING!

My father and I made Airfix models together. I probably made every single fighter plane, bomber and coastal seaplane from the First and Second World Wars with him. It was a fantastic experience. Either late in the evening or on a Sunday afternoon, I sat and made those planes with Dad. He would explain their significance and the roles that they had played in the various campaigns that were fought.

He was, it has to be said, incredibly fastidious and also very mean-spirited about his recording equipment, but only when it came to my mother. He had no problem with me or my brothers using it from an early age – but a woman? Down with that sort of thing! Unfortunately, he was proved entirely justified in this. One of her pals persuaded her to play a wire or a tape, and foolishly – because she should have anticipated how angry my father would be, and how much of a sulk he would get into and how long that sulk would last if his sacred equipment was damaged – she tried to work it. Whatever she did fucked the thing up completely. From that moment on, she never put a record on, never turned on a tape, never put a video into a VCR.

He had the same attitude to teaching her to drive. And here again, unfortunately, he was probably right. My mother didn't understand the concept of opposite lock while reversing, so she couldn't park. She didn't get the difference between the brake and the accelerator either. I've wondered if this was an affectation for women of her generation. Did it just suit them not to know how to do it? Did it suit them just to let the men take care of that sort of thing?

They were tremendously affectionate towards each other, my mum and dad. My father was an incurable romantic. He had been writing poetry for my mum from the beginning of their courtship. They were very physically affectionate in our presence, something I didn't see a lot in other households. My father would embrace my mum and hold her for what appeared to be an unseemly length of time. You're always embarrassed by the idea of sexuality in your parents' relationship. My mother wasn't afraid to say that she enjoyed the sexual attention of my father, which was absolutely mortifying and really something to run a thousand miles away from. And then, in later life, to watch them walking along the promenade in Clontarf, hand in hand, was an amazing thing. What an achievement to get to that point in their lives. I know that when my dad was dying, my mother found it extremely upsetting that he was unable to be like that with her any more.

HOW TO RUN THE COUNTRY: 1

I grew up in a world where corporal punishment was part of everyday life, where you started off as a child getting your ass tanned whenever you did something bold. If you stuck your finger into an electric socket, not only did you get an electric shock, you also got a hiding from your mother or father. That discipline went right through your preschool, your primary-school and your secondary-school experience. If you were out of order, you could encounter physical combat with a teacher, and there was only ever going to be one result.

Only once did I see a boy hit back. In primary school Charlie McCauley famously stood up. It was one of those extraordinary *Spartacus* moments, in which Charlie, at nine years of age, seemed to be bigger than the teacher. He stood up, drew back and boxed him square in the stomach. This wild act did not, however, incite open rebellion, such was the level of respect for the authority of the teacher. And why? Because if you stepped out of line, you might get a hiding.

Although it was only a handful of teachers who engaged in corporal punishment, I recall one particular episode where a boy was thrown, by his collar and the seat of his pants, out the back door of the classroom and hit the outside wall of another. He was quite badly injured, but did anything come of it? No, it did not.

All of this was appalling but it kept us in check. We were under control. Even at Leaving Certificate level, there was still the possibility that if you stepped out of line, if you were aggressive, abusive, cheeky or failed to step up to the mark in terms of your classroom responsibilities, you'd end up engaged in physical confrontation with a mature adult male, and inevitably you would not win.

Now, none of this is to be recommended. Neither UNICEF, nor Amnesty International, nor any parenting group would suggest that this is the right way to go, and it's not, but it did have the right effect. You were controllable at a time when your potential for violence was enormous. Society was protected.

In *States of Fear*, the documentary series on the abuse of children in state schools, we saw what happened when corporal punishment goes out of control or when it becomes an entertainment for the person delivering it. That was the moment that, as a State, we realized there was no going back, that the physical sanction was gone. But the problem is, when we rid ourselves of it, at home and in school, we put nothing in its place. There was a vacuum. The level of sophistication required to deal with young males in the absence of that sanction, the psychological resources and time needed to control a child in an efficient and effective way are vast. When we did away with corporal punishment, nobody had the faintest idea how to replace it. Nobody had even thought about it. That's the great sin.

So I believe that all the complaints being levelled against parents, against schools, against the guards are hollow because, as a society, as a community, we didn't come up with a plan. I'm absolutely amazed that within the Department of Education, within An Garda Síochána, within our mental-health system nobody thought, Well, what are we going to replace this incredibly powerful sanction with? So, now we have young men outside nightclubs fighting to their deaths. We have young people running home to get tooled up, and killing and maiming one another with guns, knives and screwdrivers. There's a complete lack of respect for human life. People are terrified that we're rearing a generation of smart, sophisticated, sexy killers.

We have come only so far from the cave. Young men were designed to go out and kill things and bring them home for someone to eat. They were designed to defend women and children from the tribe across the hill who wanted to come and take the women away. Those instincts have not gone. You can disenfranchise men by telling them that they are in fact proto-women or that they're the same as women or that they are redundant. That won't change the fact that young men want to fight, they want to burst out of the nest, they want conflict. They thrive on it. They love it.

Other communities have recognized this. The policy of zero tolerance that was employed during Mayor Giuliani's time in New York worked very efficiently. This sounds like Fascist thinking, and it is. But Fascist thinking has a place, if it's used for the betterment and protection of society. Before zero tolerance, New York was known universally as one of the most dangerous cities in the world. Today you can walk from one end of Manhattan to the other and feel safe, and it isn't any less sexy, it isn't any less cool, it isn't any less vibrant. It's no less a hub of cultural exchange and excitement; it's still the epicentre of everything. It has not been diminished by the fact that they have brought street violence under control. We need to remember that, or we will become what New York was like in the sixties and seventies: a no-go area.

What we really need is to be honest: we've failed. Start at that point. The economic advances we've made are wonderful – no one has to emigrate any more, as a culture we're much more sophisticated and this is a much better Ireland to live in, but we have failed to control the vicious instincts of a lot of our young people.

AN ERECTION AND A COMPLIANT WOMB

I believe that as a society we need to train ourselves from a very early age to parent. I mean you need to start training children in primary school about the responsibilities of parenting. We need to develop parenting schemes so that by the time you come out of school, it should be second nature to you – like being able to spell or to count. You should understand your responsibilities because, after all, all you need to bring children into the world is an erection and a compliant womb. We have to develop an aggressive attitude to people who are crap parents. We have an aggressive attitude to the neighbour who dumps their refuse in our front garden, we've an aggressive attitude to someone who steals our car, we've an aggressive attitude to someone who attacks us in our home. We should have an aggressive attitude towards people who are creating delinquents. We shouldn't tolerate them. They should be censured and sanctioned. They should know: if I fuck up here, people are going to notice. We have to let everyone know that parenting is a really sophisticated job.

I'm very impressed with the Juvenile Liaison (J-Lo) system. The object of the exercise is to keep the child away from criminality. One of the things we've learned is that getting into the criminal-justice system can operate as a badge of honour for some kids. We need to keep our children out of it. Do not let them get a taste for it. That means the J-Lo groups need to be really well supported. I often worry that they are the thin end of the wedge, and in Irish policing that some see it as a pansy's posting. In actual fact, I think it is one of the most critical areas of community policing: those are the guys who, with the right training and support, can intervene and divert a child away from a criminal life – not even that, divert them from getting killed. It only takes one act for someone to lose their life.

I'm a big believer in restorative justice – meeting the victim of your crime, whether it's someone whose bike you've stolen, somebody you've beaten up, or somebody whose home you've broken into, and know that if you don't cut it with this person and show you understand why they're upset and why they're hurt, if you don't apologize fulsomely, and mean it, you're going down. You're going to have a criminal record, you're never going to Australia, you're never going to the US. I think it's a fantastic coming-of-age for a child to face the person they've injured, away from the alcohol, away from the darkness of the night, away from the blind alley where the crime was committed. If you can bring somebody to that moment, you can effect real and lasting change.

YOU NEED A MAN

I think the lack of a man at home at a certain time, in both boys' and girls' lives, is a huge risk factor. I've talked to many women who have no problem with the toddler, with the older child, but then, as he or she becomes an adolescent, they're suddenly impossible to deal with. Your boyfriend at nine years of age becomes your implacable enemy at fifteen. He has no interest in talking to you and you've got little or no influence over him.

You need a man there to make him understand there's a sanction here, buddy. You need the baritone voice to deliver the threat and make it clear that this woman is protected by me.

I'm a really strong believer that there is a moment when you need the bloke going, 'You fucking do that, sonny, or I'll fuck you out the window. Don't speak to your mother like that.' Because there's a terrible window of opportunity for abuse of mothers by their daughters and their sons, and it must be a horrible time. Can you imagine what it's like? You've devoted your entire life to these people and suddenly they're going, 'Fuck off.'

I'm absolutely convinced that women can manage most of it on their own. Most of it, not all of it. Sure, there's huge positive potential in having a man around if he's a good man, if he's a man who shows he's willing to immerse himself in the process of parenting, if he's willing to help out with the housework, if he's willing to be entertaining and engage, if he's willing to get up in the middle of the night and help with the feeding. There are hugely powerful messages in this, particularly for boys, that this is a good thing to do: it's a good thing to help out, it's OK to give succour and comfort, to do things you may think are girls' jobs or girls' responsibilities. These Things Make You a Better Man.

POLICE BY CONSENT MY ARSE

If you were to sample the mood on doorsteps across the country, you would find a society that's not just living in fear but that's grossly dissatisfied with the level of protection it's given. People need to be absolutely convinced that the police force is proactive. An Garda Síochána refer back to this Free State idea of 'policing by consent', that zero tolerance would be unacceptable to the Irish people. Well, I think that needs to be thrown in the bin. We need to reassess the values of our police force. I believe that many of our new young guards, understandably, see themselves not serving the community but in combat with it. We are faced with all the threats of any modern and international cosmopolitan society. We need a police force that enforces the protections of the constitution.

Right now, people are saying, 'We are not protected, we do not feel safe, we do not feel that response times are quick enough, we do not feel that everyone is treated the same by the guards, we do not feel that crime is fully and sufficiently prosecuted through the courts.' I also believe that the community does not respond appropriately or sufficiently passionately to requests by An Garda Síochána for support.

We already have communities in this country where only armed members of the Gardaí can go. We've Moyross, where for months and months armed detectives did nightly battle with the community and nobody knew about it. This is a community that's beyond policing. Police by consent my arse. You can't police there without paramilitary-style force. Now, how did that happen? Where did that come from? Is this the Warsaw Ghetto under Nazi occupation? No, it's not. How did those people develop this mentality, this level of aggression? Because nobody, from cradle to primary to secondary school, gave them a clear understanding of what was appropriate and inappropriate, of the benefits of doing the right thing.

When police arrive on a given scene, they must arrive first of all as a responsible, credible force that is willing to listen to the community. Then they must be able to assess the threat and respond appropriately to it. All too often now two or three guards have to face down fifty or sixty rabid, drugged-up male youths ready to stone them into the sea. What solution do they have if they're not armed? Reverse gear, that's what they've got.

IF THEY END UP DEAD ON THE FLOOR, THAT'S THEIR PROBLEM, NOT YOURS

I find it absolutely mind-boggling that we can live in a country where the Department of Justice, An Garda Síochána and legal opinion tells us that the man lying in bed with his wife is less protected by the law than the gouger standing over him with the gun, threatening to kill him and rape his wife. In my opinion, the intruder loses all of his rights when he steps across the threshold. You should be able to use appropriate force safe in the knowledge that the law will protect you, that the guards will not turn up and take you away in handcuffs, that the courts will not tolerate a civil action for damages by somebody who came into your house to rob, murder or rape you or torture your family.

But there are all these pious voices: 'You need to understand that only appropriate violence can be used and you're better off using no violence whatsoever. You must also understand it could be construed that these people were invited in some bizarre way on to your property.'

This is bullshit. If someone comes into your home with a weapon, in my opinion they have no rights whatsoever. If they end up dead on the floor, that's their problem, not yours. If it happened to me, if someone came into my home uninvited and I had a weapon, I'd kill them. I'd warn them first, then I'd kill them.

Otherwise I'm a liberal.

MULTICULTURAL SOCIETY

In primary school, I believed that by putting a penny in a cardboard box for several months, I would eventually take delivery of a small black boy, one, perhaps, who might be useful around the house. Maybe he could carry my schoolbag for me. Isn't it incredible that we've moved on from there to the point at which not only do we welcome all sorts of different racial influences on our society but the new Irish have become essential to our economy? It was so exciting to watch Brazil playing Ireland and to see that there were enough Brazilian schoolchildren to walk out on to the pitch holding the Brazilian flag with the Irish children holding the Irish flag.

The Polish community is especially welcome – I think of them as parallel Irish. They have come here in their tens of thousands and we owe them such a debt. We must make sure that these people understand that they're welcome.

I believe, though, that we need to take a stance in terms of those who come to our shores. We do not want them to bring in a value system that goes against our constitution or our democracy. I feel particularly that we need to be very careful about how the Muslim community develops and how its members integrate. We have a lot to learn from what radical Islam did to young, disenfranchised Muslims in the UK. The idea of setting up a Muslim parliament as an alternative to the legally constituted parliament in Britain was preposterous. I believe those people should have been deported immediately.

When you come to someone else's country, you should be respected, you should be celebrated and protected, but you must understand that you are now in a new place. If you're in a western constitutional democracy, you have to accept that certain key principles are unassailable. If the rights of women are not supported by your culture, don't come here. If human rights are not supported by your culture, don't come here. If one racial group is cherished over another, don't come here. Otherwise, the cultural vibrancy brought by Eastern Europeans, Africans, Arabs and Chinese is something to celebrate.

CÉAD MÍLE FUCK OFF

I don't ever remember the Irish welcome. I don't ever remember Ireland being the land of a thousand welcomes. I think Irish service is generally delivered grumpily, often by people who are badly paid and don't have a natural inclination to service. We're a post-colonial people who've always hated the idea of getting a cup of tea for anyone else. We despise the idea of turning down another man's bed, we get sick at the very notion of taking an order. We're not a service-oriented nation, so this land-of-a-thousand-welcomes thing is absolute bullshit. The Irish have nothing but scorn for the American 'Have a nice day'. What's wrong with saying, 'Have a nice day,' to someone? Can you imagine an Irish person wishing someone a nice day? Here, it's 'Fuck off – get out of my face. I'm not being paid enough to have to deal with you.'

When the Disney Organization was setting up in Paris, there was one group who could not come to grips with the idea of wishing someone a nice day, who could not differentiate between the loud, blustering client and the quiet, compliant one: the Irish don't want to serve anybody. They want to get pissed, get up late and tell everybody to go fuck themselves. Even the Serbians have a better attitude to service than the Irish.

The Irish are naturally racist. People should remember that the biggest opponents of the civil-rights movement in the US were white Irish Catholics. The most vocal opponents of busing as a means of racial integration were white Irish Catholics. There is an instinctive racism inherent in the Irish. I don't know whether it's part of our post-colonial experience or whether it's because we have been utterly isolated from any other ethnic group. The very best you can hope for from the Irish is that we have a sense of humour about it.

'Ah, sure your man from Lithuania, great crack altogether, can't understand a word he's saying but he's great crack. The Chinese, fair balls, they're great little workers and sure the grub is lovely.'

When the economy is buoyant, that'll get us by, that'll be fine. We have a fantastic paddy-whackery fake approach to tolerance. But at the end of the day, it doesn't matter as long as we can carry it through. Then maybe the next generation can take it to heart and actually deliver real tolerance.

A GENERATION OF PERVERTS

The decline of the Church has been an absolute disaster because the Christian message has always been very positive. I genuinely think that, whether or not you believe in the hereafter and the rest of the dogma, the moral code is good. Unfortunately, it would seem that the Catholic Church in this country became infected by a virus. For a time, the worst of humankind seemed to see the Church as a place where you could indulge your inclination for sexual depravity and torture. This totally destroyed a fraternity that had been based on the teachings of a Palestinian revolutionary, who preached peace and love, tolerance and understanding. These men – and some women – took this teaching and used it to create a platform for abuse. And that virus spread around the world. It's like we went through a period in which some kind of subterranean invitation was issued to the dysfunctional, the perverts and the malcontents to dish out violence, intolerance, sexual aberration and viciousness. What happened that an organization based on love managed to attract a whole generation of perverts? But why, for example, did we run Eamonn Casey out of the country? What wrong did he commit? He had sex with a consenting female, drove a BMW and drank brandy.

Sounds pretty good to me.

There is only one shade of paedophilia, and it's red. I believe that those guys are a threat to the community. I think they are psychopathic. They only learn not to punch you in the face because they know that the consequences will discommode them. They have no understanding that what they're doing is wrong. They are hugely threatening and their actions can be immensely damaging to the victims. We do not want these people to be given any sort of access to children. I know that there are those who believe that a certain level of risk in dealing with others is inherent in democracy. I don't believe that should extend to the welfare of children. So, then, if the only solution is to lock them up and throw away the key, lock them up and throw away the key. Now if there's a better solution to that, if there is a therapy that will get us to no risk – and I mean *no* risk – well, sure, reintegrate these guys. But until we come up with that, I say throw away the key. Who would have wanted Brendan Smith living next door to them? Our legal system says, 'Yes, he's entitled to do that. And, as a matter of fact, if you defame him, we'll actually take you to court. You're not entitled to know anything about his activities or his whereabouts.'

Our database for sex offenders is a joke. I mean, sex offenders and paedophiles from all over the world can enter and exit the Republic of Ireland with impunity. You just wave a passport as you go through Immigration. In the US, you go to a website, you put in your address, and it gives you a list of the offenders who have been released into your area.

It doesn't tell you to go round and burn their homes down, but what it does tell you is to be on your guard.

DON'T TROUBLE TROUBLE
AND TROUBLE WON'T
TROUBLE YOU

I was hugely intimidated by primary school. I found the corporal punishment side of it very difficult to deal with. The relationship that existed between some of the teachers and the children was hugely unsettling. As was the case with most schools at the time, money was in short supply so we passed our years there in these tiny claustrophobia-inducing Nissen huts.

I lived for the holidays.

My life was utterly different from the lives of all the other boys. My dad drove a Jag. Theirs didn't. He was a professional and had been to college. Theirs hadn't. My mother came from this exotic showbiz family and there was nobody, literally nobody, in my class who had anything like that in their background. I was a fish out of water.

I've spent my entire life affecting a personality that I thought would suit the occasion, an alias appropriate to any given moment, but I couldn't find an alias for the classroom in Belgrove.

I don't have lots of memories of my primary-school years, but a few in particular stand out. There was one teacher who had a stick he used to call 'Trouble'. Every morning, he'd stand at the top of the class and deliver this delightful little recitation: 'Don't trouble Trouble and Trouble won't trouble you, and don't give trouble to Trouble or Trouble will give double trouble to you.'

What a way to start the day! The good thing was that he was too old and feeble to beat us efficiently. Though he sometimes did use the stick, another of our teachers had a very positive impact on us. He made us go off and watch movies, read books and, most important of all, he made us think. He would suddenly drop what he was doing – Peig or Jimín Mháire Thaidhg, what a poxy, crap, stupid, ridiculous story; both of those texts made me believe there was no literature in the Irish language. He'd drop whatever he was reading and go straight to James Joyce. I remember him reciting Kavanagh to us. Half the time we didn't know what he was talking about but it didn't matter: the passion of his delivery was captivating. But we dreaded those occasions when, for one reason or another, he reached for his stick.

What a strange world for boys to live in! I remember sitting in a desk and looking out at the rain coming down the window-pane. I remember the damp smell of the timber . . . I remember looking at a crack in the window and watching the raindrops slide off it . . . I remember watching that for a year, thinking, What kind of a shithole country do I live in at all?

I'm not going down the *States of Fear* route, but once this teacher caned me quite severely. Now, I actually didn't give a shit about it, but whether I deserved it was another matter. Later that week I was having a bath at home and my mother saw the marks across my backside. She called my father upstairs and he went ballistic. Unlike a lot of other fathers at the time, who would have added a few extra ones and said, 'You must have done something to deserve this,' my father said, 'Nobody should be doing this to my son. This is not acceptable.'

My father rarely resorted to corporal punishment. You'd really have to push him to get a slap. So he went down to the school. He was very vocal – almost threatening – in his complaint. This resulted in me effectively not having any engagement with the teacher *at all* for about nine months. No communication whatsoever. For a while I thought it was fantastic. I wasn't involved in any of the questioning or any of the punishments. But then I began to – I know this sounds ridiculous – sort of miss the cut and thrust of battle. It was a love–hate relationship between us and our teacher. I mean, I admired him hugely, perhaps even loved him, but we were also a little afraid of him. Half the time you wanted to dodge him and the other half you craved his approval.

I remember thinking at the time, This guy fucking hates me and he's never going to speak to me ever again. I toyed with the idea of doing something really bad, get him to chase me around the classroom, just to bring the relationship back to the way it had been. But before I could put the plan into action, I ended up going to get my appendix out.

This was a big, big operation back in 1910. I remember while I was recuperating from the surgery, I was sitting in the bed one day, staring listlessly out the window, and I saw this teacher coming up the driveway. Jesus! It's Sir! Oh, my God, what's going on here? What really blew me away was that when he arrived into the ward, he had a present for me and a bottle of Lucozade, all wrapped up in that yellow cellophane. And he was a completely different guy from the one I knew in the classroom, laughing, joking, taking the piss out of me and himself. He sat beside the bed, and eventually, after about two hours of very entertaining banter, he said, 'Now Ryan, you come back to school soon. Let's get everything on track again.'

It was an amazing gesture for the man to make.

OH, CAPTAIN, MY CAPTAIN

I was a creepy little fucker in secondary school. It wasn't until much later that I got a taste for being at the centre of things. I had none of that in school, none whatsoever. I was incredibly shy, and quiet. A lot of the teachers really didn't know what to make of me. I did a lot of peculiar things; I'd be late for class, or I'd wear odd clothes, and my hair was halfway down my back by third year. I was never chastised. I believed you could create a light round you that would protect you. I believed you could send out a signal that (1) you were not a threat, and (2) you were good to have around, so I almost never got into trouble. I'd say I was leathered three or four times in my entire experience of school.

St Paul's had been a private school, but by the time I got there, it had become part of what is euphemistically referred to as the free education system in Ireland. It was a Vincentian school, run by a group of extremely sophisticated, enlightened priests. Latin was still part of the curriculum. It was an immensely exciting place to be at an immensely exciting time. I can't say that there was one bad moment when I was in St Paul's because, from day one, I was introduced to wonderful things.

Father John McCann had a film club where we were exposed to the works of people like Orson Welles. He never forced an art-house movie on us unless it was the kind of thing that teenage boys could watch and be excited by. Then we'd have debates afterwards and there'd be plenty of robust argument. I remember watching *Citizen Kane* on one of these evenings and Father McCann likening Kane to Charles Haughey, and asking us could we draw any comparisons. That was absolute genius. We had these fantastic evenings where cigarettes were smoked openly by boys and you could see the wisps of smoke rising up through the projector light.

There was a good sporting ethos; I played rugby. Badly.

But what was more important was the exchange of knowledge between the students. We didn't just swap albums. It wasn't just Kieran O'Connor bringing in *Goodbye Yellow Brick Road* and me bringing in James Taylor's *Mudslide Slim*; we were also beginning to read books like Jean-Paul Sartre's *Nausea*. I remember my French teacher one day bringing me in a brown-paper package with Sellotape hanging off it. Inside it I found *The Autobiography of Malcolm X*, the radical black leader. I remember taking it home and reading it. A few weeks later she gave me Richard Neville's *Playpower*, which was all about personal liberation and the legalization of marijuana. This kind of stuff was happening all over the school. It wasn't that the place was in any way revolutionary, it was more that they seemed to understand the essence of education. We were listening to extraordinary music, we were reading incredible books, we were watching wonderful films. The debating society was second to none. And why? Because of the Vincentians. It was during the long-hair days and they had this unwritten motto: It's not what's on your head, it's what's in your head.

Now, this was not 'Oh, Captain, My Captain'. This was not all inspirational leadership and boys and teachers united in a spirit of fellowship and camaraderie. You got the shit beaten out of you as well.

The way it worked was that you had deans of discipline: if you transgressed you were given a chit or a docket, and you went to the dean of discipline and you were leathered six, seven, eight or ten times. It was a clever way of doing it. The guys who were leathering you were not the guys you were regularly involved with. They were not the guys who sought to inspire you.

Father Harris taught us science, and I was obsessed with it. But it was during his valency tests that I began to realize there was something different about my brain because I could never get the figures quite right. The calculations evaded me by just a half micrometre and I remember thinking, Fuck it! I'm really interested in this but I can't get the calculations right. It was only when I was having tests done on my own children – I really believe in having all your children checked for their natural propensities and problems – that I discovered I had a form of dyslexia. I've always been a terrible speller, but I can't imagine how bad I'd be if my mother hadn't spent so much time with me when I was young. Everything she'd see, she'd spell out for me. I remember getting the bus into town and her spelling out 'Granby Pork Sausages' – this was the ad running across the side of the bus. I still do that today. Everything I see, I spell.

DROPPING THE HAND?

My first sexual experience was with a girl in St Anne's Park in Raheny. A girl, now a woman, who wrote me a letter a couple of years ago, asking – no, *commanding* – me never to mention her name in public again. I had cited her on the radio a couple of times as the object of my first conventional sexual encounter. Subsequently, she said, she had almost had to give up her teaching position, so I'm not going to mention her name here – but she was incredibly cute. Very beautiful. I remember being paired off with her by some other girlfriend and heading off into the long grass of St Anne's Park. I was fifteen years old.

What did you do? What on earth were you supposed to do? I had no idea. I remember thinking, French kissing, that'd be it, that would be the thing to do, wouldn't it? And so we got stuck in, and I remember thinking, Well, this is awful, this is terrible, this is just – this is just Dental Collision. I can't imagine that she was particularly enthralled by the experience either but we kept going through the motions. And that was it. Nothing more than a bit of feverish slobbering, but it was very, very exciting. It was, of course, a rite of passage. Coming back out of the long grass, I remember thinking, Well, that's it. That's that started. Her friends grabbed her and brought her round the corner.

I overheard them asking her, 'Well, did he drop the hand?'

Drop the hand? What did that mean? Was that what I was supposed to do? Drop the hand? Did it mean putting your hand down your own trousers? Or somebody else's? Bear in mind here that things would have been much easier if girls were going through a period of fashion history when they were wearing dresses. They weren't. This was an era of skin-tight Levis. There was no possibility of getting anywhere near their nether regions because they were locked up.

Then there were the jumpers. In my opinion anybody who ever got close to a bra deserved the Freedom of the City because you had to get through two or three jumpers, and possibly a duffel coat. I mean, I'm sure women's bodies were as beautiful as the bodies of women have always been. You did not, however, get to verify this for yourself. The closest I came to it was spending three hours listening to a repeat performance of *Close to the Edge* by Yes on the record-player as I attempted to bypass a three-and-a-half-inch plastic belt buckle, inevitably getting nowhere.

Recently, I talked to a girl I knew from when I was at school. At the time she was part of what we used to call the Drumcondra Set. These were Protestant girls. We had all kinds of notions of what they might be capable of and willing to do. Maybe they didn't wear underwear. Who knows? Maybe they didn't even wear duffel coats. But she told me she remembered an evening with herself and myself, with her pal and a pal of mine. Her friend had a free house and invited us up. In an attempt to send some sort of signal, they had undone their blouses, just two or three buttons from the top. But we insisted on playing some ridiculous rock album, Arthur Brown's *Journey*, explaining it track by track to the girls and subsequently wondering why the blouses got buttoned up.

'You know, you guys were pathetic,' she said, 'you were just useless!'

And we were, we were.

A couple of my pals claim there was a lot of scx going on at the time, but I don't recall it. There was always this elaborate dance that took place. One guy would sit on the couch and wink, nod and twitch furiously to the other fella, indicating that he should take the other bird off to another room whereupon everybody would be having full-blown porn sex a few minutes later. Of course, nobody got anywhere. As soon as you touched the girl, she'd be jumping around the place, before heading off to the far end of the couch – the polar end.

There was an awful lot of 'Do you respect me? And if you do respect me you're not going to try to do that.'

So then you'd go, 'Course I respect you,' though what you wanted to say was, 'Will you please take off all your clothes and writhe around on the floor?'

For some bizarre reason, we couldn't bring ourselves to ask for what we wanted. We tried to pretend we were better than beasts, that we were men who wanted to get into the minds of these women and not their knickers, and that we were willing to sit for eight years waiting for their bra straps to be undone. It might have led to nothing, but do you know what it did lead to? Fewer problem pregnancies, less venereal disease, and I suppose at the end of the night when, with your sovereigns jingling in your pocket, you made your way home, lay alone in bed and pulled your own wire, you said to yourself, 'Well, I've done nobody any harm tonight anyway.'

HELICOPTERS DO NOT
WANT TO FLY

If you look at me during a radio broadcast or when I'm on television, I appear to be relaxed. I appear to be completely in control. The reality is that I'm stressed out all the time. It's the nature of the job. We conducted a test once on the programme. I wore a pulse monitor and sweat detectors on my palms. At about half past eight, my heart rate began to increase – not much, just a little. By one minute to nine, it was racing. Racing. And it pretty much stayed up there for most of the three hours, before slowly coming down in the half-hour afterwards. I suppose I've learned to sublimate the physical symptoms of stress. I know that that can have a fairly negative effect on you in the long term. You can become extremely anxious without understanding why. It can lead to depression. Luckily, that hasn't happened to me. Yet.

There was one period in my life – and I'm sure this is going to happen again – when I found it very difficult to sleep. I couldn't relax. I couldn't read for pleasure. I couldn't concentrate on a full film. I was drinking too much. The late Brian Carpenter, a wonderful pilot, suggested flying helicopters, partly as a means of publicizing his helicopter training business, partly as a stress-buster.

'It's so difficult,' he said, 'that you will not be able to concentrate on anything other than flying.'

I was highly sceptical at first, but quickly discovered that he was 100 per cent right. Flying works because you simply cannot concentrate on anything else. If you concentrate on something else, you will die. The thing about helicopters is, they don't want to fly. Aeroplanes do. The wind hits the wing and it rises. Helicopters would much rather crash.

I took to it straight away. I loved it, and I loved it from a pure aviation point of view. I wasn't interested in what the helicopters symbolized. I loved the idea of being able to fly somewhere there wasn't an air strip, the idea of being able to control this thing that really wanted to spin round and tip over. I loved conquering the machine's desire to smash itself up when I switched it on. That was fantastic. To this day, when I lift a helicopter off the ground, stabilize it and orientate to head off, it's still for me one of life's great experiences, and I include sex, the birth of children, being given awards in that. But it is fantastically difficult. I mean fantastically difficult. You use your feet to control the lateral movement of the helicopter through the tail rotor, you use the cyclic to control the main rotor to give you a stable orientation into the wind, and you use the collective to keep the correct power setting. Your limbs are doing different things and your mind is trying to co-ordinate it all. It's basically like trying to iron, play the piano, masturbate and stir porridge at the same time. But that moment when you transform it from a rocking, falling, jumping, bucking, out-of-control suicide machine into a stable aircraft, that's just incredible. Absolutely incredible. I remember the day I first got it right out in Weston aerodrome. I was sitting there, covered with sweat, utterly intent on the helicopter. Hovering.

When we were in South Africa with the radio programme a few years back, I got to fly a restored 1969 Huey, the helicopter that the US forces used in Vietnam. Even just climbing into this aircraft was incredible; the resonance of every Vietnam movie I'd ever seen. Then, when I switched it on, the noise, the blade slap was so intensely familiar. I took a selection of my colleagues, most of whose hairstyles were blown from here to Johannesburg, on a trip up the coast. There's one great thing that you can achieve with low-level flying in a helicopter and that's ground effect. You may be travelling at 100 m.p.h., but it feels like you're going at 500 m.p.h. when you're fifty or sixty feet above the deck. We travelled up the shoreline like that, then turned inland before heading back to base. It was one of the great, great experiences of my life.

I AM A COMPLETE PUSSY WHEN IT COMES TO HEIGHTS

It's true. I can't handle standing twenty feet up on a ladder. I'll get sick, I'll get vertigo. As a child, I once climbed to the top of a tree in Clontarf, and as soon as I looked down through the branches, I became paralysed with fear. The fire brigade had to be called. I also have that weird thing where you're standing at the edge of a dizzy height and get an almost irresistible urge to jump. That's probably the end of anyone flying with me again, but I don't experience any fear whatsoever when I'm at the controls of an aircraft. Which is not to say I haven't had the odd scare.

In the very early days, I was under the tuition of a guy called John O'Donoghue in Westair. I had begun flying solo at this stage, taking short trips out of Weston aerodrome.

This particular day, John said to me, 'Go out, pre-flight the aircraft, crank it up by yourself and do a small walk around.' Basically, take the helicopter on a few circuits of the aerodrome, three or four feet above the ground.

I didn't do the checks I should have done, looking to see whether the smoke from chimneys was moving fast and low, I didn't look at the treetops to see if they were shaking. I didn't take into account that the aircraft was parked beside a hangar; there would generally be a lot of turbulence coming off its wind shape.

These omissions amounted to incredible recklessness.

I cranked it up, lifted it a few feet above the ground, and immediately things went very badly wrong. I moved my body forward to try and bring the aircraft back under control, but it only pitched forwards, which made me over-control the stick, which put me into a forwards–backwards oscillation. This meant my body was moving up and down so, without realizing it, I was pulling on the collective, which affects the power to the aircraft – I was inputting power increases and decreases, which meant that in addition to the forwards–backwards oscillation the helicopter was also hopping up and down. Now in a blind panic, my next attempt to correct things had me lurching left and right, so the cyclic, which controls the power that's coming from the disc above you, came in on the action and I began to pitch left and right as well as up and down, forwards and backwards. My wife, meanwhile, was sitting in the reception area looking out at me, and waving happily, thinking this was some sort of display. To cap things off, for reasons that were completely beyond me, I was also gaining altitude and was now nearly thirty feet above the ground. Plenty high enough to kill yourself very quickly and efficiently.

I was very, very lucky. I spotted the horizon for one millisecond, downed the collective to kill the power and managed to get the lurching and pitching under control long enough to smash the helicopter down on to the deck, splaying the skids, but not, crucially, destroying either myself or the aircraft.

MAKING THE RIGHT IMPRESSION

Helicopters have another side to them, of course. They indicate wealth, prestige, position. *The Gerry Ryan Show* went through one period in its history when helicopters were used very frequently, and would land in the grounds of RTÉ to pick up *Ryan Show* staff to take them off for lunch. This is a great lesson for anyone who wants to create an exalted impression of themselves. Gay Byrne tells me that he would sometimes look out his window, see a helicopter landing and watch Siobhan Hough, now the producer in charge of the programme but then a broadcasting assistant, making her way head down into the wind of the helicopter blades with various bits and pieces flapping behind her. This image, he said, warned him that there were New Kids On The Block.

I went through a phase when I would fly into work. One day, I decided – I don't know why I decided this, probably for wind reasons, or maybe I was just out of my mind, I don't know – that I would fly along the RTÉ road entrance as if I was in a car, at about a hundred feet or so. The idea was to fly up to the administration building, either go over it or turn left, then land on the other side of the radio building. As I got to the end of the avenue, I realized I was actually facing the director general's office, and there inside the director general's office, staring out of the director general's window, was the director general. In that moment, I knew my helicopter days were over. Later that day, I got a very polite note from the head of security asking that I file proper flight plans and make proper requests through the correct channels if I intended flying to work in the future. The subtext of the note was that any such requests would be instantly refused.

We've worked very hard on the radio programme to give the impression that the show comes from the Jules Verne restaurant in the Eiffel Tower, and that I turn up in a helicopter and only work with supermodels, but at the end of the day it's much more normal and mundane. There's far more graft in my life than people realize. Than I realize myself, even. I delude myself into thinking my life is a lot more exotic than it is. I mean, I do have a great life, but some of my friends are able to jet off on a whim to their home in Barbados. I'm not. I've to be on the toll-bridge at seven a.m.

That's not a complaint, it's just a fact of life.

CHARLIE WAS A ROCK GOD

One of my earliest memories is of Charles Haughey arriving at our house in Kincora Avenue in Clontarf. He was with Eoin Patton, his political adviser and assistant. They were there because my father had some of the best recording equipment in the country, and Charles Haughey wanted, in discreet and secure surroundings, to record a message that would be sent to the US Congress, pleading for help in dealing with the burgeoning crisis in the North. Attacks against Catholics were on the increase and Haughey believed we were abandoning Irish men and women by failing to help in their hour of need. I listened to that recording recently – it's now in the RTÉ archive – and you can still hear the passion in his voice. At the time – this was long before the arms trial – he was, more than anyone else, prepared for war. As far as he was concerned, we were approaching the second phase of the 1916 Rebellion.

This would be the first of my many encounters with Charlie,

the sum of which left a deep and lasting impression on me. If my father was influential in describing the importance of money to me, Charles Haughey was turbo-influential.

Conor and Ciaran Haughey – Seán was only a baby at the time – were good friends of my brother Mano and me. They went to the same school as us and we used to take turns staying in each other's houses at the weekend. In that regard, Haughey's was always a bit of a no-brainer because Kinsealy was like Evelyn Waugh's Brideshead, it was so far removed from the reality of ordinary, regular Ireland. As we now know, there is a selection of explanations for how Charlie Haughey funded his lifestyle but if somebody had suggested to me when I was fourteen or fifteen that he hadn't earned his money, I would have found it utterly irrelevant. I would probably have applauded him. The Haugheys had a mansion, a swimming-pool, rolling gardens, a hunting area and a lake. A whole gang of us well-heeled upper-middle-class kids used to hang around together in surroundings that exuded privilege and wealth.

I understood that Charles Haughey was a very important individual in the life of the country. He had been a minister, though when I got to know him he was going through his time of perdition in the aftermath of the arms trial and had disappeared into the hinterland of political life. And yet he still seemed to be surviving extremely well. When we were in Kinsealy at the weekend and he saw Conor and Mano, Ciaran and myself together, he would come over and ask us how we were getting on. He would talk about his hopes for the country. How are things at home? How are you getting on at school? He talked about art, culture, history, politics, women. I was impressed that he was willing to devote time to talking to us about sophisticated adult matters. And, of course, he was incredibly articulate and witty.

But more than anything he actually said, the real influential factor lay in simply looking around and seeing the stables filled with horses. This was a man who basically had South Fork Ranch on the north side of Dublin, between Clontarf and Malahide. He seemed to have hundreds of people working for him. I mean, besides the rolling parkland and the swimming-pool, there was Mr Tommy to teach you how to shoot. There were always glamorous women around, and there was even a pub.

There was this guy in our wider circle of friends called Tom. He was from a working-class background. I don't know how he ended up hanging out at the Haugheys'. In that group of privileged children this young man stood out like a sore thumb. But he was a great guy. He brought a particular dynamic to the group because he was honest, forthright, funny and charming. But, bit by bit, he was marginalized because he didn't have the financial wherewithal to do a lot of the things we were doing – the trips we'd go on, the nights out. And he couldn't wear the same kind of clothes we did because his family didn't have the money. Slowly but surely, I noticed he wasn't showing up for social events as much as everyone else. Now, teenagers don't pay much attention to stuff like that. It's the nature of the beast that they don't really care. Mr Haughey, however, saw what had happened. And he did something about it. He sat us all down and, in no uncertain terms, he told us that by letting this friend go because of his financial circumstances, we were being utterly and cravenly immoral.

This was mortifying. We went away from that dressing-down deeply embarrassed. It had a gigantic effect on each one of us. I still remember the tone of his voice, the delivery, the buttons he pushed and the sensitivities he addressed on the way you behaved towards friends and your peer group.

BLOODY SUNDAY

I was in Kinsealy on Bloody Sunday. It was January 1972, when the first battalion of the British Parachute Regiment entered the Bogside in Derry and shot dead fourteen unarmed people. That night, we were all listening to *Jesus Christ Superstar*, with Ian Gillan, from Deep Purple, in the role of Jesus. Eimear Haughey had bought the album, and we were all pretty amazed by it. The thing rocked beyond belief.

The next morning we went downstairs to the kitchen. Mrs Haughey was making breakfast. There was the usual conversational hubbub. We were trying to decide between horse-riding and shooting. And although the house was palatial compared to the homes of the average Irish person – I mean, it was Blenheim Palace compared to where I lived – Mrs Haughey was the same as the rest of the mums. She was pottering around, making breakfast, when Mr Haughey came down. He was always immaculately dressed, and favoured the smart-casual, open-neck look when he was off duty. But that morning he was extremely agitated and spoke to us about what had happened in Derry. I had no idea what he was talking about. I had no political allegiance to anyone. If anything, I leaned more towards the commonwealth. I mean, I loved the Beatles, so I thought maybe it might be better to be English. But he stood there in the kitchen and he made this speech about what had happened to Irish men and women, about how this couldn't continue, and that we could not stand by idly, that we must do what it took to protect ourselves. Mrs Haughey was going on making the breakfast while he, one of the most important men in Europe at the time, stood there, making his speech to teenagers. We might not have understood fully what he was talking about, but by God, did we understand the passion. And at that moment I remember thinking, There are things upon this island that I don't understand and I must find out about. And that was a defining moment in my life.

Was he corrupt? I think Charlie was given money by guys who liked him and who had identified him as somebody who would keep the ball in play. I genuinely do not believe that anybody ever received a political favour as a result of giving Charles Haughey money. And I'll tell you why I believe that. I got to know Charles Haughey at a very impressionable time in my life.

Haughey was aloof and removed in his dealings with a lot of people. Not all people: he was connected and generous and gentle with those he was close to. Charles Haughey was as sussed as the smartest fox in the factory that makes smart foxes. If anybody for one minute thought he could nail Charles Haughey by giving him a couple of grand or even a couple of million or a free Charvet shirt, they were utterly deluded. That was not what he was selling: Charles Haughey was selling the same thing Bono sells, that Mick Jagger sells. He was selling stardom. He was selling being close to the man. He was High King, and I think people like Ben Dunne just couldn't stop themselves in his presence. There was a vibrancy. There was a resonance. He didn't need to give favours. He just needed to give his presence. Charlie was a rock god.

I believe he is the quintessential study for how we should reward our public servants, the senior executives of Ireland Inc. Charles Haughey was a cultured merchant prince put in charge of a country that he felt deeply about. He was a Republican through and through, much more so than any other Taoiseach. Charles Haughey would have got on to a horse, ridden over the border and engaged the British Army on his own. This guy was utterly committed to the Irish story – utterly committed to it. He was also committed to living well, to fine wines, beautiful women, big houses, private jets, first-class travel, limousines – and do you know what? Rock on, Charlie Haughey. He was right. I want the main man to be like that.

FINE DINING

My canteen is the restaurant of the Four Seasons Hotel. What a fantastic life! It's just unbeatable. I have all my meetings in that restaurant. I know Louis Walsh does the same thing. They make an exception for him: he seems to be able to order the full Irish at any time of the day.

Recently, my favourite meals have been in fusion restaurants. There's a place down the road from here called the Chill Out Café. A couple of years ago, I wouldn't have considered going to a place called the Chill Out Café. My wife often used to laugh at me. I always felt she liked mid-range funky bistros and I liked fine dining. Now I'm beginning to come closer to her way of thinking. The Chill Out Café is very simple. It's not particularly decorous, but the food is astonishing. It's just astonishing.

When I do takeaway, it's inevitably from somewhere like the Bombay Pantry because their murg chutney is impossible to beat. If I was asked to choose between that and Michelin stars,

I'd probably prefer the Bombay Pantry. I wouldn't have said that a couple of years ago. I'd have been too embarrassed to say it. Out of all the Michelin stars, Derry Clark's L'Écrivain is maybe my favourite because his sommelier is wonderful. She's an absolute gem.

That's another thing. I think Irish people still need to wake up to the joys of sommeliers. If there's an expert at the restaurant you're in, tell them how much you've got to spend on the wine, tell them roughly the kind of thing you like – and you can be as bog inarticulate as it's possible to be just to get across the idea of what you like, even if it means saying something along the lines of 'I like diluted Ribena.' My favourite sommelier was Pascal in Dromoland. He's now selling wine for a living and is a great loss to the restaurant business because he was shockingly good at giving you good value and fabulous wines. What Pascal did was entertain you. He told you stories about the wine, stories about the château it came from, stories about the maker – who they were shagging, who they weren't – and the wine always tasted spectacularly different. He never brought a bottle of wine to the table that I'd heard of. And I just loved that. I think Irish men in particular have a huge problem with somebody telling them what wine to order, but that's what the guy's there to do. You're meant to say, 'I've only twenty euro. Get me something fantastic. Surprise me.' One of the great pleasures in my life was sitting in the Thomond restaurant and listening to Pascal hold forth. The *expectation* as the bottle was brought from the cellars. What was it going to be like? 'Oh, it's the last bottle. Tony O'Reilly was here last week, but I lied to him. I told him it was all gone, and I kept it for you, Mr Ryan . . .' And, you know, whether that was true or not was irrelevant. It was the theatre of the thing that was so wonderful. And then, when you got the bill, you saw that you hadn't been fleeced. The guy actually had found something that was astonishingly beautiful and fantastically presented and not that wildly expensive. I just so love sommeliers. Next to rock stars, they're my favourite people.

GOING OVER TO SAY HELLO TO GERRY

I don't go to receptions. I don't go to big parties. I tend to hide myself away in good restaurants. I think that's really where my whole fine-dining thing came from. People who are paying a lot of money for their wine and their food are less likely to intrude on your privacy. In the early years of my success, with marriage and kids, that was very important. People don't want to make fools of themselves by Going Over To Say Hello To Gerry, whereas in the mid-range funky bistro, that's more likely to happen. I don't have a problem with that, but I did make a decision early on in my career not to have a high-profile social life. The newspapers have always been obsessively curious about what I do . . .

WHEN YOU BURST A SEAM ON YOUR TROUSERS BECAUSE YOUR ARSE HAS GOT TOO BIG

When I was growing up, my mum insisted that we knew how to cook four meals: a fry with all the standard things – you had to include boxty or potato cakes; the Sunday roast; at least one Italian dish (I don't know whether it was something to do with the pope but she showed us how to make a very simple Bolognese sauce); a chicken chow mein that bore no resemblance to chicken chow mein, but you could still live on it. She also insisted that we learn how to sew and darn, and how to iron. When I went to university and became an itinerant in terms of my accommodation, that really stood to me.

She always said, 'One day, Mum will not be here. You should be able to put a button on your shirt. When you burst the seam on your trousers because your arse has got too big, you should be able to sew it back.' So I am able to do that.

She said, 'You should be able to iron your clothes.' Of course, I have the OCD super-meticulous ironing technique, which means I don't have enough time to iron because it takes far too long. That's why I love laundries and dry-cleaners. And in terms of cooking, her attitude was, 'You'll never starve, and women love it.' She was absolutely right. Women do love a man who can cook. If you're in a family environment, feed the children once or twice a week. It makes a big, big difference.

These days I still cook Sunday dinners. I'll do either a leg of lamb or a filleted roast, with all the old-fashioned trimmings. Get the Roosters, peel them, boil them, let them cool down, put the goose fat on, let that solidify, make the batter for the Yorkshire puddings. When I lived at home, there were occasions when people joined us for Sunday lunch, and I tried to sort of add in something extra in the vegetable department to make it look a bit different. But most people just want a really high quality piece of meat, really good roast potatoes and Yorkshire puddings. Basically they're happy if you can get that right. And getting that right is not easy. Anybody can switch on the oven and put the things in, but I can make a bloody good roast, and I've enjoyed doing it for a long time.

I used to cook a lot of Indian and Oriental food. I do almost none of that now. To cook Indian and Oriental food, which my wife did very well, you need a lot of time, and I just don't have it. And am I actually going to make a better, you know, murg chutney than the Bombay Pantry, who will deliver to my door for three euros? Am I really going to be able to do anything that even vaguely comes near it? No, I'm not. I've got over the satisfaction of making something that looks and tastes vaguely ethnic, and now I'm happy to leave it to the experts. But I did enjoy the flirtation I had with it for a number of years. I made curries that used to blow my children's heads off. My wife developed a fantastic palate for curry. I think she could probably eat Sellafield.

In the bachelor world of separation, you tend not to cook as much. Men in my situation often find they end up drinking more of their calories than eating them, so I'm very careful about that. I do have a decent meal. But I've always gone out for meals, so my life hasn't changed that much. And I'm very lucky. I'm blessed. I have enough money that if I want to trot down to the Four Seasons for my dinner, I can do that. If I want to go down to Derry Clarke at L'Écrivain, sit at the bar and have a nice glass of Pomerol with whatever he wants to surprise me with, I can do that. As David Bowie said, it's one of the nice things that fame brings you. It can get you a good table in a restaurant. Won't bring you happiness, but it'll get you a good table in a restaurant.

MY LAST MEAL

Recently, I've become less enamoured of European cooking and more drawn to Asian. I think the starter I would like is shredded chicken, which is available in Furama in Donnybrook. One of the best meals I've ever had was in a restaurant called Shula's at the Dolphin and Swan Resort in Florida. It's a licensed Walt Disney property, and one of the finest steak houses in the world. I had the American equivalent of a T-bone steak. Aged, air-dried and hung for three weeks. No seasoning. Cooked to perfection. So, I want Shula's T-bone, with the Four Seasons' spring onion and mashed potato. It's not on the menu, but you can ask for it. And then there's a fantastic dessert they used to do in Shanahan's called the Chocolate Volcano. In Patrick Guibaud's recently, I had one of those little things they give you before you start the meal, the *amuse-bouche*. It was a gin jelly with ginger in it. And it was mind-bogglingly good.

I've lost interest in restaurants that serve foam and froth. My pal Harry Crosbie told of an extraordinary experience recently. His wife persuaded him to go to this place in the UK that was all foam and froth. The dessert came out, and it was a giant bubble. And they prick the bubble and you're asked to inhale what's inside. That's your dessert. He said he had to have a dozen.

PADDY GOES TO LONDON

London, 1979. I'd just finished the Leaving Cert.

'Dad . . . Dad? It's me. It's Gerry.'

'How are you, son? How are you getting on?'

'Grand. Fine . . . Ah, look, there's a bit of a problem here . . . I'm down to my last ten pounds.'

'Christ. That's dreadful, isn't it?' (Good! Good! He's biting! We're going to have funds wired over. This time tomorrow I'll be eating curry and drinking beer.)

'Yeah, it's pretty bad.'

'You know my advice?'

'Yeah?' (Western Union! Find me the address of the nearest Western Union!)

'Get a job.' (Excuse me?)

'Yeah, yeah, yeah, but besides that . . .'

'Get two jobs. I'll give your regards to your mother. Bye.'

I lived in Notting Hill, which was pretty awful at the time

because we were the only white people there. The Jamaicans used to chase the Dublin guys out of Arundel Gardens up to the high street every day. This was my introduction to multi-culturalism. I was there with my friend Peter Murray, and my girlfriend, Patricia Murphy. We were doing a line, as they called it in those days. In the seventies, all my contemporaries had these little pretend marriages. Patricia was a wonderful, inspirational girl and had no problem getting work. She went off and got a job in a place on Oxford Street that sold copies of Picassos and Monets and the like. She seemed to be able to get it together. I couldn't get it together. I was down to my last tenner, but unless someone was going to ask me to advise the British government on constitutional law, I would obviously be wasting my great intellect.

I used to hang out in the house in Arundel Gardens, staring out at the rain, listening to Lou Reed's *Transformer* and day-dreaming about what I was going to do in life. Would I become a filmmaker? A poet maybe? A lawyer? Or maybe I'd go into the army. Horseshitting around, really, while Patricia supported the pair of us on her income. I had convinced myself that I was Special and Different, and that somehow or other, if I thought in those terms long enough and strongly enough, some-thing would happen – that I would, miraculously and overnight, become a rock star or a filmmaker or a very successful actor. See, my whole thing was that I didn't want to get involved in manual labour. I certainly didn't want to live the artist's life, you know, starving in a garret. I wanted to be artistically and intellectually credible, but have loads of money. Now, in seventies Ireland, that was a bit of a tall order. And also I was a borderline halfwit. I didn't really know how to do anything. Eventually Patricia said to me, 'I think you should consider getting some extra money.'

I said, 'No, no, no. No need for that. I'll ring up my father.'

The Manpower agency had plenty of jobs, but they were all sort of sweeping-the-floor kind of jobs. I sat down at the inter-view and the guy said to me, 'What do you think you can do?'

I said, 'Well, I'm a legal practitioner.'

'Yeah?' he said. 'What's that mean?'

I'd signed up for a legal apprenticeship just after my Leaving but I hadn't actually done anything even remotely related to legal science. Didn't stop me presenting myself as a qualified lawyer, though.

'Look,' he said, 'there's a job in a Rolls-Royce engine factory. Turn up here tomorrow at seven o'clock.'

I remember going and being so depressed. The first day I was there, a Pakistani guy had his arm sawn off by a lathe and there were all these middle-aged Alf Garnett types giving you plenty of advice: keep away from the Pakis. I'd never met a Pakistani. What do they know that I don't? Maybe they've something against the Irish. *This is ultra depressing*, I remember thinking. Not only am I having to do manual labour but I'm with maybe the most horrible people of all time.

DISCOVERING I WASN'T LORD SEBASTIAN FLYTE

But I was earning a decent salary and I started going out to the theatre and cinema, I began visiting the Victoria and Albert Museum. London had opened up. I had money. I discovered Indian food, I went to see *The Rocky Horror Show*. I'd been there for weeks and weeks and weeks and I'd seen nothing but the Jamaicans of Notting Hill. But this was during one of the big IRA bombing campaigns in England, and that made things a bit difficult if you were Irish. This was odd, because I hated everything to do with Ireland. I hated the Irish language, I hated the fact that the economy was so dilapidated, I hated the control the Catholic Church had over the country – I hated everything about grey repressive Ireland. I mean, I loved the Beatles and the Rolling Stones, I loved English poets and the BBC, but one of the first times I opened my mouth in a pub to order a drink, the whole pub turned round and looked at me and the guy said,

'What do you want with that, Paddy?' And I realized I wasn't Lord Sebastian Flyte any more. I was Paddy from Dublin.

As the summer wore on, I knew the Leaving Certificate results were getting closer. I remember the day they came in. Everyone had done really well: Patricia had enough to do social sciences in UCD; Peter had enough for architecture. The fact that I'd heard nothing from home was not a good sign. I rang my father again and asked him how I'd got on.

'Oh, you mean how did you do in your Leaving Certificate?'

'Yeah.'

'Not so good.'

I remember thinking, Why didn't they ring me up and tell me this?

My mum had been very sick in the run-up to and during the exams, suffering from pancreatic cancer. It had nearly killed her. The day before my English exam, my dad sat down with my brother and myself and told us that Mum was going in for a revolutionary operation on her pancreas and that, in all likelihood, she would not survive it. It sounds fairly stark now, but he instilled in us a degree of fatalism and courage; that didn't make it OK, but it did help you get on with what you were doing. But when I look back on it, I actually sat through the Leaving Certificate in a complete fog.

I remember going with Peter Murray to visit Mum after the operation. The two of us arrived into intensive care in the Mater. She was hooked up to this bank of grey machines and seemed to have lost half her bodyweight in about three days, but she still managed to speak to me, briefly.

Cycling home, Peter said, 'Your mother doesn't look great.'

'No,' I said, 'no, she doesn't. She looks like she's going to die.'

And the next day, I sat English and I remember nothing about it. I can remember absolutely nothing about any of the Leaving Certificate. I fabricated memories about it, from other people's recollections about what a beautiful summer it was. I've imagined myself outside the exam hall in the sun. I've imagined myself talking to my girlfriend about the papers. But I was so shocked by what was going on, I can't actually remember any of it.

Mum staged a complete recovery, and thrived afterwards because my father totally devoted himself to her at that time.

When I left for England just after the Leaving, I went under a cloud. Mum was only a week out of hospital when I said, 'OK, I'm off to London.' But I had to go. I absolutely had to. My parents had been extremely reluctant to let me or Mano go anywhere. Because there was only a year between us, he and I were, and still are, very close. At that time we hardly ever went away on school trips, and even when it came to staying over at friends' houses, my father didn't like it. In the last two years of school, he and I forced the issue as much as possible, but my dad was not happy about it at all. I've never really figured out why, but that summer, I knew that if I didn't go with Peter and Patricia to London, I'd never break free into the world.

I remember going for a walk the first day I was there; I don't know what I was looking for, milk or something. This was in the days before mobile phones, and I got lost. Lost without a phone or a phone number, and having forgotten the address of the place we were staying in. I remember breaking down in tears and thinking, I am hopelessly under-qualified for this expedition. Eventually, like a blind man, I felt my way along the railings of Notting Hill and arrived back several hours later, to the bemusement of my now drunk friends who couldn't figure it out at all.

'What do you mean you got lost? You were only five hundred yards away from the house!'

This turned out to be true.

But London was the beginning of growing up for me. Sharing a tiny room way up in the back of that house in Arundel Gardens, going to the Victoria and Albert Museum, Hyde Park, going to see concerts – I remember seeing 10cc play at the Rainbow, Finsbury Park. Eating Indian food for the first time! I'd sampled Vesta at home, but it was nothing compared to the real thing. This was the beginning of my education, the preamble to breaking out of my family and making my own way.

I thought I'd go home, get a flat and start college, but of course when I got back, I'd no money, and I had to wait a year for college because I didn't get enough honours to get into Trinity.

I DRINK TOO MUCH

The deal I've done with alcohol, right, is this: I'm going to die anyway. What I'm still trying to work out is what condition I want to die in. Am I going to risk cirrhosis of the liver? I interviewed Larry Hagman recently. Here's a guy who, from the outside, you would have thought was maybe a bit eccentric, but you would never have taken him to be an alcoholic. Larry Hagman used to start drinking champagne at five in the morning and got through between five and seven bottles before ten that night. OK, I don't start drinking at five in the morning, but I do drink whiskey. Eventually, Larry got to a point where he was suffering from encephalopathy and full-blown cirrhosis. There's no real going back from cirrhosis. It's very, very difficult to halt or even slow down. Your only real options are either to die or get a new liver. Larry got himself a new liver and, unlike George Best, he stopped drinking. But I'm still like, you know, why did you do this? Why were you drinking at five in the morning? And he said it was because he liked the effect. He had a gentle buzz going by five thirty, and for the rest of the day, it was just a matter of topping that up.

I certainly like the effect of alcohol but I'm fairly discerning in what I like and don't like in taste.

I've tried to figure out the role that alcohol has played in my life in terms of getting me into trouble, making silly decisions, or being sick. I generally don't suffer from hangovers that much any more. I certainly did when I was younger. Does that mean I'm drinking less? I don't think so. I've drunk spirits since I was about seventeen. I started with gin and tonic, but I felt that was sort of effete. I didn't really like the taste, but I quite like certain types of gin now, in particular Tanqueray. But whiskey, I think, fulfilled several roles for me. One, I thought it looked good. Dean Martin's a big hero of mine, and I used to watch him on television. Of course, now we know he was pretending to be drunk – I think he'd tea in the glass – but at the time I was absolutely convinced by his performance. He would hiccup and meander around the set, bumping into things, telling stories with that affected slur, and he always had a bourbon in his hand. Dave Allen always had a drink by his side and he looked pretty cool as well. The message these guys were sending out was that a drink was a kind of badge of honour. So I drank a lot.

There was a lot of binge-drinking when I was in school. It's wrong to say that it was invented by the current generation. We drank every weekend, wildly to excess. I grew up in a drinking society. My family drank. Well, my father didn't. My mother drank, but very moderately. If she had more than two or three sherries, she'd have a violent hangover. That should have been a good indicator to me, but the reality is that you don't always end up doing what you see your parents doing. I never saw my father drunk, ever.

My children have certainly seen me drunk, though less so in recent years. They tend towards conservatism. Both of my eldest are now old enough to drink and both are disapproving, very disapproving, in fact, of excessive alcohol consumption. And they'd be pretty quick to point it out to you if they thought you'd had too much. You can tell from a slight stiffening in their body language that they're thinking, Right, a couple more drinks and people will be saying stupid things. They're very uncomfortable in the company of adults who are drunk. And they're not rude children, they're immensely polite. Usually they'll just extricate themselves from the situation. Adults often don't realize just how uncomfortable children can become in that environment.

I CAN'T BEAR HANGOVERS

I tended mostly to be an affable drunk, though maybe those who came into contact with me would dispute that. I was always more of a go-quiet-and-fall-asleep drunk, I think. And at this stage of my life I still really, really enjoy a good whiskey. For a lot of my life I drank Bushmills. I liked the taste. The effect, though I liked that too, was secondary. It's not that I needed drink to become more articulate or more voluble. I just liked the feel of it. It's a narcotic thing. I like the buzz. Now, today, it's all about knowing when to stop, and it's only at this stage in my life, in my fifties, that I'm beginning to understand that if I have another drink, I'm going to be in bad form tomorrow. I can't bear hangovers, so I make sure to get them very, very rarely. But I still drink. I read today that binge-drinking is six or seven units in a row. I might have sixty units in a week, so am I binge-drinking every night?

Of course, nobody tells the truth about that kind of thing. A doctor asked me once, 'How many units would you have?'

I said, 'Well, I don't know, what do you think?'

'Would you have, like, seven or eight units?'

I thought he meant in a day, so I said, 'Oh, yeah, easily.'

'OK,' he said. 'We'll put that down. Seven or eight units a week.'

And I remember just going, 'Oh.' So, technically, I didn't lie.

Alcohol, of course, causes huge problems in this country. But does that mean that you say, 'Right, we've got to get rid of alcohol?' No, it doesn't. It means you try to educate people. I feel very strongly that when it comes to using things like alcohol, we should tell people about it. It's like sex. The one thing they never told us about sex when I was in school was that the reason people did it was that it felt fantastic. They should have said at the very beginning, 'By the way, you'll be compulsively driven to do this because it's so enjoyable. You will swim rivers of snot to do this because it's so much fun.' If that had been admitted, we might have had a better handle on unguarded sexual activity. The same goes for alcohol. Start off telling the truth: 'It's great fun, but it can kill you.' People don't do that. The 'Just Say No' thing is ridiculous. The average psyche is not designed to just say no. The more you try and cod an Irish person into making the noble and correct decision, the more likely they are to go on the piss. So, yes, you can enjoy this, you can have a good time, but there is a point beyond which you should not go because you will damage yourself or others.

I think I'm probably pretty close to that point myself. I'd say that if I drank much more for much longer, I'd be sick. Right now, I'm below the danger level. For the last couple of years, I've had elevated enzyme levels in my liver, which means it isn't metabolizing alcohol as efficiently as it should; this is something most Irish guys of my age tend to discover is happening to them. The way I think about my drinking nowadays is basically this. I need to be in my full senses at this moment in my life. I couldn't get up and go to work, I couldn't continue to take care of my family in any credible way unless I was mostly there. Don't have to be completely there, but mostly there. If you drink too much, it compromises you, especially the next day. You're intellectually slower, your decision-making capacity is not good. And I notice, the older I get, that after an evening of heavy drinking, there are periods when I don't remember what happened or what was said.

That doesn't matter too much because I'm generally very careful about what I do and say. And I'm not a violent person, so there's no trail of destruction behind me.

Without doubt, I drink too much. I mean, I look at a bottle of whiskey after I've been socializing – and it's only when you've poured the whiskey yourself and you've got the bottle that you know where it's gone. There could be a third of it drunk, and you're perfectly fine, it's grand, you're getting on with your life the next day. But you look up at that bottle and you say to yourself, 'My God, a third of a bottle of whiskey? That's a lot.' It would be enough, according to the experts, to have you certified as borderline, you know, alcoholic – if you were doing it on a regular basis.

There've been several points in my life where I was dependent on alcohol to get through stressful times, or where I just got into a social routine. With me, it's mostly a social thing. I'm very auto-suggestive. I sit down to watch a movie and somebody's having a chicken burger – I want a chicken burger. They're having a drink so I want a drink. I have to watch that very carefully.

WHAT'S THE POINT? YOU'D ONLY FALL ASLEEP AGAIN

Alcohol has definitely made me less healthy than I should be. It's stupid to say that I have the exact same physical health I would have if I didn't drink or if I drank less. Emotionally, would I be better off? I don't think it's played much of a role in terms of that part of my life. I've been lucky there. Of course, there are loads of things I regret doing after a few drinks but, luckily, they're not very big things. They're more stupid things. I don't do it now, but there was a time when I would fall asleep socially. I used to believe that that was acceptable because I was Gerry Ryan. I mean, I do recall being at dinner one night at Le Frère Jacques on Dame Street, and I woke up with my face in the plate. I asked why no one had roused me and they said, 'Well, what's the point? You'd only fall asleep again.' At the time I thought that was hilarious. If it happened to me now, I'd be deeply concerned. First, it would be on the front page of every newspaper because somebody would take a picture with their phone. That's the other thing: all it takes is just one phone picture of Gerry Ryan with his trousers falling down and drool coming out of his mouth. That's now available for publication in a heartbeat. That has had a huge effect on me. My behaviour is much less adolescent than it used to be. When I first came into this business, the likelihood of that happening was very slim. Now all you need is a hard day on the tiles with your pals, and you're falling out of the Four Seasons, you trip over your shoelace, puke and fall into it and there's your front page. How Low He Has Fallen.

My favourite tipple is Jameson twelve-year-old. I like Gold Reserve. And, in moderation, do you know what? It's pretty good in terms of the brain state the next day. You can't say that of all of them. I don't know how the Americans, God love them, put up with bourbon. It's one thing about the United States that I've always found bewildering. How can such a sophisticated people be so primitive in their choice of whiskey?

I used to spend a lot of time collecting single-malt whiskies. I did a tour of all of the Scottish Highland distilleries with Willie O'Reilly, good friend, one-time producer of the show and now head of Today FM. We drank our way, basically, through northern Scotland and, of course, Scottish and English measures are much smaller than Irish ones so we were able to outpace almost everybody we met. But I'm less interested in that dimension of it now. It was the same when I used to smoke cigars and I was a member of the Decent Cigar Society. They had these evenings when guys would come over and talk about how Cohiba made their Siglo or something like that. I had a fairly nerdy collector's attitude towards cigars, whiskies and wine. It's very much in my character to learn a lot about something I like. At one stage I had a big collection of whiskies, fifty or sixty, and I would delight (in an obsessive compulsive way) in lining them up.

My eldest son Rex, who was eight or nine at the time, was in charge of the two big humidors, and he had the business of keeping the cigars at the right temperature down to a fine art. He kept the whiskies' labels all turned out front too. On Saturdays I used to take him into town, into Guy Hancock's Decent Cigar Emporium on Grafton Street, where – this was before the smoking ban – this fantastic selection of guys used to get together: Cubans, Americans, embassy workers, with a cast of disparate characters like myself. We'd drink whiskey or brandy and coffee, and smoke cigars in the back room of the Decent Cigar Emporium, and it was absolutely fabulous. I loved it. And young Rex loved it as well. He'd just sit there listening to the conversation. It was really the last example of something like that and its demise is to be lamented. I know that the clean-air argument is very persuasive, but in that smoky back room, there were things to be learned from listening to those men.

I don't think I've paid any price professionally for my drinking. A lot of what I do is kind of a bit rock 'n' roll anyway, and the one thing I'm well able to do is my job. I don't think you could say that I'd have done it better if I didn't drink. The drinking was part of it. It's what defined me, in a way, and for better or worse, the Gerry Ryan you listen to on the radio or watch on the television is a guy who drinks too much. That's part of the package. I don't think it's possible to say that I would have done things better. I might have done them differently, but I think the evidence shows that most of what I do turns out to be pretty good anyway.

IN TROUBLE WITH THE LAW

My friend Peter Murray and I were in the Palace Bar one evening when Peter introduced me to John Rodgers, a future attorney general, then a junior counsel. Both Peter and I had a notion of studying law, and John, an acquaintance of Peter's, was our contact. He agreed to sort me out with an apprenticeship. I remember thinking, OK, good, I'm sorted. The overall plan remained as before: to evade the labour market for as long as was humanly possible. It wasn't exactly that I was lazy, I just didn't want to do anything that would take lots of time for little return. Law appealed to me because it offered ample scope to earn more than a basic salary. I was interested in science, but I couldn't seem to master the computational side of it — I knew from a fairly early stage that there was no possibility of following my father through the Royal College of Surgeons.

Law, however, was tailor-made for me because I was interested in language, argument and debate, and it had all of those things.

In my interview with the Law Society before the law preliminary exam, I was asked what kind of law I was particularly interested in. Pompously, I said constitutional and family law. In those days, they were two dead certs for making no money whatsoever.

'Oh, really?' said the guy. 'And tell me, are you interested in cars?'

'Yeah!' I said.

'And what kind of car does your dad drive?'

'A Jag.'

He snorted. 'Family and constitutional law, eh? Right.'

At the time, the accepted route into law was through a combination of apprenticeship and college, but because I'd missed out on Trinity, I spent that first year after the Leaving working exclusively as an apprentice. I believe now that that was a good thing, because in that year after I returned from London, I was amazingly immature. I still had a highly delusional idea about my place in the world, and remained caught between my desire for the high life and the dreadful necessity of doing something constructive to achieve it. Though not everybody in my life would agree that this happened so early in the story, I believe I grew up in that year.

Apprenticeship itself was a very old-fashioned arrangement whereby you signed a document that more or less confined you to the firm. You were paid nothing. I was apprenticed to Frank Malone, of Malone and Potter, who had an extensive and unusual practice that mixed political and criminal cases. It was Dudley Potter, Frank's partner, who took me under his wing. He, in large part, was responsible for much of the growing up I did that year. He had an enormous influence on the way I viewed politics and law, the way I viewed the interaction of the civil authority and the citizen.

But I was incredibly lonely. All of my friends had started college. My girlfriend had started in UCD and was building new friendships of her own. I spent most of the day with Dudley and was still living at home because I'd no money to live anywhere else. When I was alone by myself in the office, it was crushingly boring. Sometimes I'd have to walk to the Four Courts to lodge or search for documents, and have to pass the drug-dispensing clinic on the quays, with all these guys smacked out of their heads on the pavement. Heroin was a rampant problem in Dublin at the time.

Slowly, as I began to find myself around the Four Courts, I got to know people and started to enjoy the time I was able to spend reading texts and law reports. Because it was a year out, I had no exams so I could let myself be distracted and go off on flights of fancy, reading texts that had no relevance to first-year law students. I also discovered that a lot of the barristers and lawyers, particularly those who used the library, were quite open to being interrupted and asked questions. Not that I made any real friends down there – unlike in college, where I found people naturally gravitated towards me. Because there was nothing else to do, I immersed myself in the law reports, and began to develop a fabulous sense of what law was about. I fell in love with jurisprudence. I loved the idea of delving into old cases, dusting off a report from the eighteenth century and submerging myself in something that had as much relevance then as it had had on the day it was tried. I knew I'd made the right decision and that this was the place for me to be.

Time with Dudley was extremely informative. He was constantly explaining things to me, constantly explaining politics, about which, I quickly realized, I was incredibly naïve. My understanding, for instance, of the republican struggle in the North of Ireland was that a bunch of bastards was basically trying to wreck everything for everybody. I really had no real understanding of the link between the armed struggle in the late seventies and the ambitions of the state's founding fathers. I thought they were just destroying tourism. We frequently defended guys who were in the process of being extradited to the UK, and I have to say that, more often than not, Dudley was highly effective at preventing it. Slowly but surely I began if not to respect at least to understand the republican point of view, because I came into contact with it through Dudley.

A PSYCHOTIC CLANCY BROTHER IN THE FOUR COURTS

Dudley was a highly convivial character. Over coffee between court appearances, he would tug you into an understanding of what was going on and the relationship between law and political struggle. He wore grey suits instead of the more conventional black, and was tolerant of the fact that I didn't own one. I was among the few apprentices who didn't. There was no protest in that, but I did stand out a bit, with the shoulder-length hair and Aran sweaters in the midst of all these sombre suits. I looked more like some kind of psychotic Clancy brother than a solicitor, but Dudley never mentioned my appearance, although he would have been well within his rights to do so.

His interest in and understanding of the pure science of law was exceptional and he imparted his love of it to me. He taught me about using the language of the law to obscure and obfuscate, to hide things you didn't want others to see, all for the better cause. He taught me about the balance of justice and what it really meant. The question I badgered him with all the time was, were we defending innocent men?

'That's irrelevant,' Dudley would say. 'That's not a question you need to ask. You just need to present an equal opportunity for this person to be defended before the courts. You're not in the business of deciding whether they're guilty or not guilty. In fact, you have to say goodbye to the case if they tell you they're guilty.'

I suspect that we represented few who were completely innocent. That alone should have given me a pointer that this just wasn't the business for me.

A lot of the guys we defended were serious criminals. They, of course, had no interest in the legal-science end of what we were doing, though some of it was highly sophisticated. I remember there were a couple of guys who were very big underworld names and the only thing the guards could arrest them under was the Vagrancy Act, which says, basically, you can't be a vagrant. We challenged that constitutionally. Meetings with these guys were always intriguing because they had no interest in the minutiae or the ambition of the project, other than its capacity to delay their case in proceeding to trial. The object of the exercise was to keep them on the streets, running their businesses, whatever those businesses were, drug-dealing, gun-running or whatever. I was *so* removed from them. Hugely removed. But Dudley, this very middle-class guy with a college education, he managed to relate to these guys with consummate ease.

One case sticks out in my memory. A man had been accused of raping this old woman – she was in her late seventies – in the company of a number of other men. It was an absolutely horrific case. He and the other men had broken into her house and terrorized her. It's the kind of story we're familiar with now, to a much greater degree probably. Anyway, we'd separated the charges. This was, and still is, a technique used to avoid contaminating one defence with another. We got him off, and afterwards he came over to me. He even knew my name.

'Thanks very much, Mr Ryan.' He was a little guy. 'I'd just like to tell you one thing. It was the worst ride I've ever had.'

I nearly fainted. I can't remember who said it but I think it must have been one of the other solicitors: 'You little bastard, you little shit.'

That night, I remember sitting at dinner with my father and mother, and just blurting it out: 'This guy we got off today *raped* an old woman – and *we* got him off.'

It had a substantial effect on me. I thought, Well, this is not a particularly savoury business. This, of course, was utter naïvety on my part, because the balance of justice requires you to do painful things. You can't just pick the nice, polite, politically correct issues to defend. I realized then that if I became a lawyer many of the people I came into contact with would be guilty. So how are you going to live your life, day in day out, trying to convince somebody that somebody else didn't commit rape when they had? That somebody didn't batter somebody else half to death when they had? That somebody didn't break into another man's home and take something from them that didn't belong to them? Always I got to the point when I was listening to the evidence and went to myself, *This fucker did this.* But we were stuck with him. He protested his innocence and we maintained the balance of justice. He had the right to be defended and he was innocent until proven guilty.

Today on *The Gerry Ryan Show* we ran a poll asking people did they think internment would be an appropriate way to deal with feuding criminal gangs in South Hill and Moyross in Limerick. Ninety-five per cent of those polled said, yes, internment would be an appropriate way to deal with the problem. People have become intolerant of our sacred duty to defend every man equally. I sympathize with the attitude but I know bloody well that internment was a solution to nothing. The Nazis dreamed up internment in 1938 to deal with homosexuals, Communists, dissidents and Jews, and it became a shortcut to genocide. There's a huge price to pay for the internment idea and that's why I believe that, despite the painful experiences I had working as an apprentice criminal lawyer, we have to maintain, utterly uncontaminated, the normal legal processes. It's better that fifty bad guys get off than one innocent man goes down. That's a very difficult thing to sell to people nowadays. I mean if I said today, 'OK, come on, let's be honest about it, these guys need to be put in ovens and gassed,' I think we'd probably have got a 95 per cent result on that too, which is pretty shocking.

And that doesn't mean I'm not intolerant of the crime levels we're having to live with now, and accept as normal. And these are pretty horrible people when you meet them. They live in a fog of lies. They are professional takers. They take, take, take, from everybody, their nearest and dearest, society, the old woman stumbling across their path with her handbag open. But the day you decide that you can with impunity declare them guilty without trial is the day on which we, as a society, will have fallen apart.

I'LL SAW YOUR FUCKIN' HEAD OFF

Every solicitor's apprentice gets a lot of donkey jobs to do – serving witness summonses, for example. As a young, middle-class boy, I'd never even heard of Fatima Mansions. This was at the height of the drug problem in inner-city Dublin, and there were some very aggressive, very nasty people down there, along with a whole host of others whose lives were falling apart. Really, it was upriver of the Do Lung Bridge; it was the outer limits. When you went to Fatima Mansions, there were heroin addicts all over the place, people waiting to meet dealers, children running wild because their parents were out of it on smack. And another set of people was just trying to survive, trying to get on with it. This was the first generation, the grandparents now, and they were completely mesmerized. Many of them didn't have jobs and they were trying to cope with unemployment and living on welfare. They were watching their children become heroin addicts, their grandchildren become uncontrollable. Fatima Mansions basically presented you with a foretaste of the Apocalypse.

My first few excursions taught me that nobody was really that interested in receiving these witness summonses. This is still an issue for authorities dealing with ghettoized communities. It's quite easy to knock on someone's door in Clontarf or Dalkey or Montenotte and give them a summons. They'll take it, they'll shit themselves, they'll ring the family solicitor, they'll respond to it immediately. In Fatima Mansions, the door would frequently be opened by a woman who was by herself because her husband was in jail or had gone out on the tear or was down getting his methadone, so the despair that greeted me was phenomenal.

Inevitably, I was asking someone to accept a summons for something they hadn't the faintest idea about. Or, sometimes, the guy who'd open the door would be a big rogue in a vest with a can of Heineken in his hand who'd tell me he was going to beat the fuckin' livin' daylights out of me if I didn't get out. Eventually, I just decided that I didn't give a shit whether the summonses were served or not, because the threat was too substantial to make it worthwhile.

I got to know some of the kids up there, and they'd say, 'Here, give us all the summonses. We'll hand them out.' And they did. 'Because, Mr Ryan, they're only going to beat the fuck out of you down there. The Murphys are sick of you knocking on the door.'

So I hated that part of it. I'm a complete coward when it comes to the whole social-deprivation issue. These people were in such a state of complete degradation. They were no-hopers. The drugs were having such a mangalating effect on their lives and the lives of their families. It was hard to see any family structure in some of these places. There was no dominant male, there was no dominant female; the grandparents were the only people who seemed together, and they were in short supply.

The Children's Court was something else that was always handed out to apprentices. I don't know why, perhaps because there wasn't a huge amount of legal science involved in dealing with young people. Back then, places like Daingean and St Pat's still existed, so it was possible for custodial sentences to be handed down, but mostly the kids tended to get probation.

I'd be defending somebody who was charged at eleven years of age with something like stealing a pallet of teacups from a standing carriage in Connolly Station. I'd meet him three minutes before we'd stand up in front of the judge, and the judge would listen and establish whether the child was guilty or not. A lot of the time, the kids didn't really understand the process. There was always screaming and shouting going on. More often than not, I wouldn't even be listening to the proceedings, particularly if the child had pleaded guilty. You just got up and said something ridiculous like, 'M'lord, my client is going to be an apprentice lagger.'

I remember saying this on a regular basis, that he'd been promised a job by John Joe Mahogany Gaspipes and Co. Ltd as an apprentice lagger, and as such he was going to start bringing in money for his family, and he would mend his evil ways and he'd go back to school while he was at it. I didn't even know what an apprentice lagger was, but all you had to do was come up with any kind of excuse – literally any kind of excuse – and the judge would apply the Probation Act. There were one or two occasions when this didn't happen. I remember one case when a custodial sentence was applied to a young boy for his own good. He'd been on the streets for about a year selling drugs, and his parents had no control over him. His mother had seven or eight other children and she was at the end of her tether. It was suggested that this boy be put into some sort of protective custody and I remember him roaring as he was being taken away: 'You fuckin' cunt, Ryan! When I get out, I'll fuckin' come and get you and saw your fuckin' head off!'

That episode taught me it was better to succeed for a client than not.

THE FRONT OF THE PLANE

I go first class with Aer Lingus to JFK. There's a big seat, everybody's attentive and nice. I have a few drinks, and when I'm with my family, I see them enjoying the fruits of my labour. They're so completely and utterly unfazed by the privilege, but still delight in it. Then we get to New York and there's a limousine waiting to take us into Manhattan. We check into Fitzpatrick's and go upstairs to one of the suites or, as we did last year, to the penthouse, and look out over the Manhattan skyline, and know there's a nice restaurant, like Tao, booked for the evening. And the path is always greased. Maybe U2 are playing in Giants stadium, and the backstage passes will be waiting for us in the Rockefeller. Or maybe it's down to the Ritz to meet Paul McGuinness for lunch, then jump on the U2 plane to head to Philadelphia.

I defy anybody to say that that's not a good way to travel.

There's nothing like boarding a plane, going through an airport, checking in at a hotel to distract you from the mundanity of everyday life. I've been blessed and very lucky to travel to some quite extraordinary places in my life, mostly through work. My holidays have tended to be fairly predictable because, as a family, we've always chosen the tried and tested route. It was mostly Walt Disney World, or somewhere else in the United States. My children are all quasi-American in their minds. But with the programme, I've travelled from Ethiopia to Somalia to South Africa, up and down the east coast of the United States, throughout Europe. I've always loved those trips. I've really enjoyed the five-star hotels, the first-class flights, sitting at the front of the plane, having a good whiskey, knowing there's going be a good movie to watch . . . that I'm going somewhere that's interesting and different where there'll be great accommodation, a big fuss made of me and whoever I'm with. That, my friends, is better than the 44A.

GIVE HIM THE HUNDRED BUCKS OR HE'LL SHOOT YOU

I've been in the back end of nowhere as well. I was in Somalia shortly before the *Black Hawk Down* incident in Mogadishu. It was low-level flying all the way in from Kenya, then a spiralling, high-altitude dive into the remnants of Mogadishu airport. The first person we met in the terminal building was this little guy with a Kalashnikov standing behind a green-baize card table with his wife, also carrying a semi-automatic weapon. He was selling visas for entry into Mogadishu for a hundred dollars. I remember thinking, This is fucking ridiculous. There is no government here. What the fuck is this guy doing?

And the guy from the Red Cross said, 'Well, he'll just shoot us if you don't give him the hundred bucks.'

So he stamped everybody's passport, then folded up his card table and walked off into the sunset with about two thousand dollars in his pocket.

I was there with an RTÉ film crew to make a documentary about the famine that was going full tilt at the time. It was an incredibly emotional experience. The country was in meltdown, politically and socially. It had more or less ceased to function. And I was fascinated by it. It was like being in a movie. There was death, destruction, annihilation and yet excitement everywhere you looked. You bumped into a selection of peculiar people from the different intelligence agencies everywhere you went. There was a range of non-governmental organizations trying to insinuate themselves into the country. All of these agencies and organizations were battling for primacy in the middle of this terrible tragedy.

I remember getting up very early one morning to go on the death-collection round with the International Red Cross. When someone died, their family would leave their body outside in a sort of rice sack, for collection before the sun came up. We saw relics of the Soviet occupation: people sleeping in MiG fighter cockpits with pigs running around the outside of the plane. It was like hell. We got very ill when we were there, and we also managed to erase a lot of the film we had shot; we had to reshoot it in short order.

BUNDIES AND OVERPRICED BANANAS

The year I left school, I went around Europe on the classic InterRail. It cost around forty quid. I and my then girlfriend visited a huge number of countries, some of which I'd been to before on a more exalted level with my parents. I remember trying to buy a banana from a street vendor in Lucerne, and not having enough money. The day's cash ration didn't cover the cost of a banana. I remember saying to myself, 'Fuck this. I'm gonna come back here one day and stay in a five-star. I'm never doing this again without funds.'

But it'd be wrong to say I didn't enjoy it because I got to see a lot of stuff. We would aim for places based on the sound of the name more than anything else. And the train journeys were fascinating. I remember going to see King Ludwig's castle in Neuschwanstein and hearing the Tyrolean cowbells at sunset, and the sound of trumpets in the Alps, and meeting Australians, Israelis and Americans who were travelling by themselves. We were fascinated by these people, by the range of different cultures we encountered, by the incredible places and amazing things. But the destitution was hard. I remember constantly eating processed ham, and Bundies without butter. Let no one tell you there's anything good about that. Diarrhoea was a major feature of the whole thing, and lack of sleep, and dehydration.

The one bit of first class I recall was on the Orient Express. My girlfriend and I bought couchettes on it, which was quite an extravagant thing to do, and slept the whole way from somewhere in Germany to Paris. And when we got to Paris, we stayed at the Hôtel Henri IV. I remember bargaining with the woman who let us have the room. There was a porcelain hand-washing basin, on a steel stand. It was like something from *Moulin Rouge*. The room was terribly poky, but it was still a hotel room in Paris and you could just see the Seine through the window. It was incredible for an eighteen-year-old to be in Paris at a time when most people were finding it difficult to get to Bundoran. Going down to the Left Bank with your seventeen-year-old girlfriend was so exciting, and so romantic.

Paris was probably the most exciting place on the trip because you could eat reasonably well for almost nothing on the Left Bank. I can remember ordering crêpes at a street vendor's crêperie for the first time, and the guy saying, 'Well, what do you want on it?'

'It's a pancake,' I said. 'I'll have lemon and sugar.'

'*Mais non!*' he said. 'You can have all these other things . . .'

I remember going down to the Marais, to the Jewish quarter, eating well and drinking well, and meeting some extraordinary people. But I knew at this point we were on our way home, because from Paris, we'd get the bus to Le Havre, then the boat to Rosslare. In Paris, the dream was coming to an end. I remember being very conscious of that. And I'd fallen in love with the idea of being on the road.

Another time myself and a few friends took four or five days to get down to Athens on what was known as the Magic Bus. You went through a selection of countries. It was an unpleasant trip, eating beans out of tins, not washing, fellas either farting or smoking dope on the bus, people getting left behind in public lavatories. Exciting? No. Different? Absolutely. I was with James Dolan, a very dear friend of mine who's now dead, and when we got to Athens I met his girlfriend for the first time. It was one of the great moments of jealousy in my life. Anna Power, who would become his wife, was this statuesque supermodel girl, and she was wearing these very tight little shorts. I had just finished in a relationship, and we arrived into Constitution Square in Athens, and I remember seeing this girl, and thinking that, Well . . . The bastard.

PLUS D'OXYGEN S'IL VOUS PLAIT

These days, Paris for me is staying at the Hôtel Meurice up at the Jardins des Tuileries. You can't even get in there unless you've got a grand in your sock, so it's quite a different experience. But maybe not so different. The French bottle romance extremely well, and that romance is intoxicating no matter how much you have in your pocket. But Hôtel Meurice is exceptional. It was the headquarters of the *Wehrmacht* during the German occupation, and was recently restored to its original pristine condition. It has an absolutely superb restaurant, and a great bar. I was there once with Willie O'Reilly. We were going through a phase when we were ingesting recreational oxygen. Going into dinner, I asked the barman if he would keep our oxygen tank behind the bar.

And he said, 'Yes, of course, sir.'

When we arrived back, he brought back out the oxygen tank with the mask, as if it was just a favourite bottle of whiskey or something.

Two really pathetic things happened to me in Paris as a result of not fully understanding the language. My wife and I were out buying clothes, and I insisted on buying her this coat, which, as it turned out, did not cost £120 but £1,200. This was at a time when I wasn't even earning £120 a week. There was a huge amount of to-ing and fro-ing with the American Express representative over the telephone. I was outraged at someone querying my ability to pay £120. On another occasion I was looking through the wine list before dinner – I was a bit pissed because I'd already been in the bar – and I ordered what I thought was a €200 bottle of wine. Same mistake. It was a €2,000 Pétrus. I should've twigged that something funny was going on when three people arrived with the bottle, the sommelier and two assistants. One guy had a sort of mechanical device that cantilevered the wine into the correct pouring position. Another had a selection of things, including a lighted taper and a fan. I should have twigged but didn't. I drank it. Then I ordered another bottle.

And, of course, checking out a few days later, I couldn't figure out why the bill was so high.

'How can it be this much?' I said. 'This is ridiculous. This is a mistake.'

And the guy said simply, '*Le vin.*'

And I looked at it and went, 'Oh, yeah. Right. The wine.'

And I knew in a nanosecond that I'd fucked up, that it hadn't cost €200. Thankfully, this happened at a point in my career when I could afford it, but the shock was no less.

INDIANA JONES AND THE ISLAND FOR RICH PEOPLE

I was always contemptuous of American culture when I was growing up, which is hysterical considering that a lot of what I really adored, whether it was Robert De Niro in *Taxi Driver* or Elvis Presley in *Jailhouse Rock*, actually came from America. I'd more or less determined that I wasn't ever going to go there. So it wasn't until I went to work in RTÉ and we forged an alliance with the Walt Disney World Corporation, when they were looking for European media partners, that I had an opportunity to go. So over we went. I remember sitting on the plane – a Delta flight to Atlanta – and being seduced by business class. There was a gay black steward – that was interesting and exotic, something you didn't see in Ireland. And then we arrived in this extraordinary place.

For several years going back and forth, I thought that America was Walt Disney World. Staying at the Contemporary or Wilderness Lodge with all the phantasmagoria of the Disney experience, a place that has its own power stations, that has its own rail system, that has its own transport system, even its own printed money. It's on such a hyper-sensory scale that you can't really compute it. It's narcotic. You couldn't but be impressed by it. It certainly worked very well for the show, and when my family came over, they fell in love with the place instantly.

After that, we would go down to Sanibel Island in the Gulf of Mexico to an entirely different experience. Though it's an extremely wealthy area, most of it looks like Brittas Bay, except with wonderful weather, no caravans, and turtles nesting on the beach. So we would go from the five-star, almost hallucinogenic experience of Disney to a much simpler, laid-back existence on Sanibel. Some of the happiest times I've ever spent were with my family there, walking along those beaches and going to those eateries, watching the sun set across the ocean, seeing the turtles hatching and making their way to the sea under the moon.

I remember one year sitting there, and my dad was dying in Dublin. I was constantly waiting for a phone call to say, 'Come home.' One evening I went out and sat on the beach, and I looked around and there were all these really wonderful, special people from all different walks of life and from all different parts of the world. Inevitably they were people with money because it's a very expensive place, but everybody looked like they were on a break from reality. I remember sitting there on the beach thinking about the fact that my father was going to die very soon. And I remember thinking how much he would've loved this place. I had a Chivas Regal, loads of ice in the glass, and the sun was sinking. The few yachts that were still out were heading back to harbour and I thought how much he would've loved to be there. Don't wait until it's too late to bring them to the places you've found. I have a deep regret that I didn't bring my parents to the United States. That evening as I watched the sun go down, I'd have loved my dad to be with me.

This guy came walking by, and he said, 'How're you doing?'

'I'm fine.'

'What an evening,' he said. 'Take a picture, if only with your mind.'

He'd gone before I realized it was Harrison Ford.

The next day John Clarke rang me from 2FM to tell me that the audience ratings had reached the highest they'd ever been. It was such a bittersweet mixture of all sorts of incredible things: being with the people I loved, knowing my father was dying, the figures going up. It was one of the most significant and memorable times of my life.

GOD AND VAT

When I got married, we had very little money. My first home was a rented flat behind the Meath hospital. But I've always had a reckless way with money. I managed, through fraudulence, to get a mortgage. I imagine everyone did it: you lied about your salary and your earning potential. And when we did get it and bought a little house in Marino, I don't think I ever managed to meet the payments. We were constantly getting reminders and even notices of foreclosure. My lifestyle wouldn't have indicated that, though. I always had a nice car. They were inevitably second-hand Italian sports cars that had been resprayed. My first was a Lancia Beta Coupé with a two-litre engine and front-wheel drive. It was an absolute rocket. After that, there was a Fiat 124 Sports Coupé. These were hugely sexy cars worth about a tenth of their original price. I went on good foreign holidays to Spain, I'd a good social life, I was never short for clothes, I ate out all the time. Basically I did everything a guy on ten times my salary was doing, so there was a constant knocking at the door in terms of debt and overspending.

It's always during times of fear that you deliver yourself into the hands of God. One of the most fervent prayers I ever uttered was at this time, when I discovered, to my horror, like my father before me, that I'd fucked up my tax. I'd failed to charge RTÉ VAT, but I was obliged to meet the VAT liability nonetheless. The bill was about the value of the house we were living in. I remember calling into the church on the way home. I remember kneeling down and saying, 'Please, God, I'll try to be a better person. I'll help people if you get me out of this tax problem.'

None of this changed my attitude to money. I still have a reckless lack of interest in the accumulation of wealth. I believe that money is there to feed people, to get you out of a jam, to take care of people, to educate. It's there to house you, it's there to make you smile, it's there to bring you from one side of the world to another, it's there to help you sit at the front of a plane instead of the back. I've no interest in counting the money, I'm only interested in what it can do. And my lifestyle isn't that fabulous. I restored a BMW 840ci sports car, pouring thousands upon thousands of euros into it. It's fantastically politically incorrect. I mean, it does about ten miles to the gallon with a 4.5-litre engine and has, basically, the carbon footprint of a small town. It's huge but you can barely fit yourself and one other person, with maybe two midgets in the back, into it. That's one of the few luxuries I've indulged in.

13

GIRLS, BEER, FUN, AND NOT DOING ANY WORK

Trinity was extraordinary. It was a world that I had suspected existed but had only seen in films and read about in books. The first time I walked through the place, I quivered with excitement. I had a sense of belonging almost instantly. I just adored it – I *absolutely* adored it. I adored the look of the place, the sound of it, the antiquity. The architecture dripped promise. I just knew that this was going to be a good place to be. In the year before I formally began my studies, I had already begun to use the library and had inveigled my way into eating in Commons in the evening. I loved the atmosphere there. I loved the names of all the different areas: the Buttery Bar, Botany Bay . . . I loved the look of the students, especially the non-professional ones, which was most of them. There were very few who, like me, had to combine study with an apprenticeship. These people looked so carefree, hanging out in the bars, visiting the tennis courts, lounging in the summer breeze on the cricket pitches, ambling down to the Pavilion Bar. There were girls everywhere, which was nice.

It had this feeling of antique time, a place apart from the rest of the city, a place that had hardly changed in two hundred years. Just as you come away from the cricket pitches and you're heading towards the front of college, when you come round by the museum building, there's a quiet, secluded spot where I used to sit often and watch the sun flickering through the trees – there seemed to be a stillness there that you couldn't find in the rest of the city. And there was always the promise of girls, beer, fun and not doing any work.

My first year was also the first year that more women were doing legal science than men. A lot of them went on to practise in other disciplines than law. This was a gregarious, exotic bunch of women. They were intelligent, highly opinionated, very glamorous and fantastic fun to be with. There was also quite an exotic collection of guys, who were unlike any of the people I had gone to school with. There was Douglas Heather and Peter Lennon. Kadar Asmal, who recently retired as a parliamentarian in South Africa, was one of our lecturers and a human-rights specialist *par excellence*. He taught international law. We all came from very different backgrounds. Count Ferdinand von Prondzynski, now the president of Dublin City University, came from a high-church German family. There was Alex Schuster, now a legal lecturer. This was a group of people who were as interested in rock 'n' roll as they were in legal science.

What did we do? The boring truth is that there was a huge amount of studying. I was a swot. I didn't cram as much as some of the others did because I got most of my work done when it was supposed to be done. I enjoyed it so it wasn't a trial for me, plus I was hanging around with a group of people who were very dedicated to their discipline. We would debate endlessly the difference between a breach of a fundamental term in a contract and a fundamental breach of a contract. I remember myself and Hayes Dockrell arguing for several hours, to the point at which we brought our argument back to our lecturer, believing we'd just rendered two-hundred-odd years of legal argument obsolete through our combined legal brilliance. They were tremendously indulgent of that kind of thing in Trinity.

So it was a mixture of some academic activity, a huge amount of studying and a huge amount of drinking. I had a lot of friends who had rooms in college, so you could usually find someone who'd put you up for the night. I lived at home officially, but I ended up being a bit of a vagrant. My brother had a girlfriend who had rooms on Front Square. He seemed to spend most of his time in a dressing-gown, paying for other people's lecture notes. Mano came to life for rugby practice and drinking only, a fact I deeply respected. He had a very, very attractive girlfriend, Vanessa. She was quite Anglo, very well spoken; the perfect girl-friend to have in Trinity, really. She was great fun, and always wore jumpers that were way too big for her – I suspected they came from some second-row or prop forward.

So we were constantly chasing girls, constantly chasing drink, constantly trying to come up with some plan to avoid anything that involved physical work.

I didn't take jobs to support myself in college. I worked in Temple Street Children's Hospital as a porter during part of my vacation, but I spent the money either while I was doing it or by going on holidays immediately afterwards, so I never supported myself. It was beneath me to support myself. The only reason I ever took a job while I was a student was to piss it up the wall. All around me there were students working in cafés, super-markets, pubs, doing all sorts of really appalling jobs. I, however, was made for better things.

ANAL CRACK

I had a band in Trinity – in fact I had two bands, both of which were very short-lived. One of them was Anal Crack & the Vomettes. The other I formed with my friend James Dolan. As I've said, he's dead now. James looked a lot like David Bowie. He and I were obsessed with Bowie, Peter Gabriel, Bryan Ferry and all the art-school rock that was around at the time. We formed a band called the Wires, which we said was punk, though really we spent most of our time trying to learn 'Panic In Detroit' from David Bowie's *Aladdin Sane*. Also, we had two or three different blues guitarists, which was pretty weird for a punk band. The final concert we played was in the Dalkey Island Hotel.

I now think that all that stuff about Iggy Pop diving on glass is really not true because when I did it I injured myself badly. I had blood all over my arms, so I started covering James with it and, of course, the audience was appalled. We were dragged off the stage. It was very rock 'n' roll. I had to be taken to Casualty, but then we went to a house party somewhere and I got to show off my injuries. 'I was performing tonight on the stage with my band . . .'

I still have the scars.

DON'T GO IN THERE, THEY'RE SCUM!

The first time I met Joe Duffy in college I was wearing a morning suit and top hat, and I was on my way to the Elizabethan Garden Party. Joe was outside the Elizabethan Garden Party protesting against it or something.

'Don't go in there!' he shouted. 'They're scum!'

'Oh, no,' I said, 'they're lovely. You should come in too – but you'll need to get a tie.'

I don't remember any student politics in Trinity, although

apparently the place had a history of aggressive left-wing agitation and anarchy. I missed it. Either it hid from me in the corridors or it happened before I got there because I didn't notice it.

ROCKING IN THE DOCK

I joined the Dublin University Law Society and became their public-relations officer. I felt that this was a really staid, cobweb-ridden organization and decided it was time to rock the thing up. Once I took over, we brought in a lot more entertainment – we started having picnics, dinners and lunches, and to invite slightly more unusual speakers alongside the usual high-court judges. Every year the society staged the Mock Trial, which they took very, very seriously. In years gone by, fellas would make great efforts to emulate Daniel O'Connell or Robert Emmet . . . so I decided to turn it into a musical. We called it *The Rock Trial*. Bullshit, when I think about it now, but at the time it was cool. We were all nearly sent down because we destroyed the coping or something in the common room.

Becoming PRO was probably the most significant thing that happened to me in college, because it was in fulfilling this role and speaking in public for the first time that I developed a taste for holding forth, for oration and speechifying. Prior to this, all the way through secondary school, I was shy, retiring and extremely reticent about opening my mouth in public.

PROMISCUITY ON CAMPUS

One particular girl I knew had a very sophisticated apartment, not that far from Liberty Hall. She also had a Triumph Spitfire sports car. This apartment was like something from *Austin Powers*; a spectacular thing to have in those days. There were a couple of very wealthy students who came from African states and were paying fifty or sixty grand a year to be there, and a few rich kids from the North of Ireland. But there were also a couple of mystery people who came from the south. This particular girl was one of them. We became friendly, in a purely platonic way. She had this sports car, this wonderful flat, she was always dressed in designer clothes. I remember going to the Shelbourne for dinner with her. I always assumed she had a rich dad, but she eventually confided the truth. She was a call girl. Today, she's a successful barrister.

There was no sex when I was in college. I think for those in stable relationships, or unstable relationships, there must have been some, but promiscuity on campus? I saw none of that. I certainly sat up for hours on end with male colleagues trying to persuade girls to take their clothes off, but I don't recall us being successful. The positive side of that was that we got to know these women really well. In all honesty, I'd come from a generation of misogynists, not all that different from our fathers, so this was an important experience for us all. These were really intelligent women, a lot of them quite different in ambition and attitude from our mothers, certainly our grandmothers, and so while your immediate response to them as a young Turk was inevitably sexual, you were very quickly put in your place. Many of the relationships that started in secondary school, those mini-marriages, they either continued or were replaced with something similar when we went to college.

Don't forget, this was a time when contraception wasn't freely available. And when it did become available, you had to prove it was for legitimate family-planning purposes. Many doctors wouldn't give it to somebody unless they were married, and the idea of going to a family-planning clinic to score some contraceptives was, well, pretty weird. I remember there was one on Synge Street, but of course everybody was terrified of going there. Couples used to formulate these mad stories about how they were living together and married for years! I mean, they looked twelve years old. Nobody was going to believe them.

So, before you could persuade someone to have sex with you, you had to get condoms, and condoms were hard to come by. The number of girls who were on the pill was minuscule, and there were no other prophylactics, no pessaries, sponges, douches, any of the things that the Trinity College handbook cited as indispensable to your sex life. I mean there was a huge amount of stuff in the union handbook about having sex of all descriptions, even homosexual sex. I remember thinking, Good Christ! I can't even get heterosexual sex, much less the other sort.

There was an awful lot of talking about it. I mean, guys are always going to be up for it, they're always going to be keen on it, but that doesn't mean they're always going to be able to get it. As I say, this was a new generation of women. Very bright, very sophisticated, but essentially middle-class conservative women who just didn't drop their drawers. They had been given, and followed, the advice that their grandmothers had given to their mothers. Keep your hand on your ha'penny. Don't let him shag you until you've got a promise. Sexual encounters through the early years in college, I'm sorry to admit, were little different from the adolescent fumblings that went on when we were in school.

DEVELOPING THE CRAVAT LIFESTYLE

Trinity provided me with one of those incredible moments when you feel you've found your skin. I wanted to stay there for ever. There was a short period when I contemplated academic life. I thought, This looks great: Talking About Important Things, bit of a lecture here and there, and then . . . Wine! It really was like Brideshead. I've looked at the *Brideshead Revisited* DVD recently and the buildings are identical. The affected students and their nonsensical dress were remarkably familiar to me.

When I'd started my apprenticeship, it didn't take me long to become immersed in constitutional law, jurisprudence and the workings of the courts. It paid nothing, but it opened my eyes to contemporary Irish history, to the situation in the North and how legal science was engaging with politics. But at this point, I was beginning to look around and go, 'Hmm, there doesn't seem to be much money here.' I was continually meeting brilliant barristers who seemed to be alcoholic and penniless, and that worried me a bit. The law that made you money was not, it turned out, the interesting stuff. No one was talking about jurisprudence or constitutional law when they came out of college, they were talking about conveyancing and insurance and company law. I found all that stuff coma-inducing.

So here I was with my money obsession, my obsession with material things, my obsession with showing off financial and economic success, and here I was simultaneously taking a left turn instead of a right turn. It was a sticky wicket, and probably explains why, during that time, I hid away in Trinity, where you could act out Lord Sebastian Flyte on tuppence a day. It was a difficult time, because if I wasn't going to become a rock-star lawyer, what was going to happen? I remember one day sitting in the library in Trinity and thinking, Fuck. I'm not going to make any money out of the stuff I'm interested in – and I seemed to have become pathologically incapable of studying and being successfully examined in the stuff that actually mattered.

More than ever I wanted the good things in life, and I wanted to get them in such a way that I did not have to exert myself too much. There was a Dining Society in Trinity. The idea of it was to train young professionals how to behave at a dinner party or a business lunch, how to navigate the cutlery and how to order wine, how to deal with the bill and the correct way to engage with People Who Might Be Useful To You. All it did for me was increase my knowledge and love of claret, which led, once again, to the cash register.

There was a set of people around Trinity at the time, professional chancers who were developing what I called the Cravat Lifestyle. This was a group of guys who were never going to work but would instead insinuate themselves into either rich marriages or trophy positions in their fathers' firms. Once entrenched, they would do fuck-all and get the things I wanted. No such position was available to me. The one thing you cannot do if you're a lawyer is take people's teeth out.

After my six years of penury at college and during my apprenticeship, my father was beginning to wonder, Oh, Christ, is he ever going to leave Trinity? He never actually said it, but I'm sure it was in his mind. In any case, I was becoming less and less interested in studying and the rest of it, and Trinity was becoming less an academic experience and more a home away from home.

HOW TO RUN THE COUNTRY: 2

I'm a great fan of property developers because I really believe they turned the country around. They gave gainful employment to thousands of people, not just the Irish but those arriving from beyond our shores. These guys are really our merchant princes. I think there's been a lot of pointless tut-tutting in relation to the amount of money they've made. The likes of Sean Dunne, Harry Crosbie and Johnny Ronan pulled Ireland up by its bootlaces and propelled it into the future. Because I've celebrated the merchant-prince class, I get asked to officiate at the launch of new developments, something I'm more than happy to do . . . if the price is right.

These guys rejoice in profit. And I'm not ashamed to say that I do too. It's Woody Allen's thing. If only for financial reasons, money is preferable to poverty. And I have yet to meet anybody who thought that a free and thriving economy was less desirable than a stagnant one. When I sat in the classroom of St Paul's

College in Raheny, every family I knew had somebody leaving for the United Kingdom or the United States to create a better life for themselves. And it was crap. It was awful because unless you were able to get into the bank or become a professional or join the army or the guards, there was little hope for you. We weren't an entrepreneurial society. And now we are. And it's been largely down to the guys who brought the cranes that I can see outside my window.

I find myself most comfortable among those people. I also find myself the least wealthy man in the room.

I was interviewing a guy one day on a totally unrelated issue and I mentioned somebody I knew who had a lot of money. And the guy I was interviewing said, 'You know what? You get the horn when you're standing beside money.'

And I said, 'Fucking right I do, and so should we all.' No money is crap. More money is better.

We should celebrate what we've done in this country. We have a terrible problem with not recognizing achievement in Ireland. I mean, I've heard it said so many times before. In the United States, they see the guy in the big house up on the hill and they say, 'Some day that's gonna be me.' Here it's 'How did he get that? What chicanery did he get up to? What skulduggery was involved?' It's a bad attitude. We should take much greater pride in what we've done and in what our princes have achieved.

PRICKING AROUND WITH BERTIE

The Ryan Show's always worked on some pretty basic principles. If you're going to meet a president, meet President Clinton. If you're going to support a prime minister, support Bertie. We always aimed for the lead singer. *The Gerry Ryan Show* is the official radio programme of U2, not Dervish. We always aim for the winner. Bertie was the leader. He was the man. He was the guy who rocked it up. He turned up the volume, and we should celebrate that.

Bertie Ahern is, without doubt, more than any other politician in the history of the Republic, substantially responsible for the success of this country, and he has been pushed, shoved, prodded and pricked around beyond all toleration. For what? The delight some of my colleagues have taken in his difficulties is incomprehensible. How much was it? Two grand? Five grand? Did they have a better plan? Have they got a better guy? Was there somebody we didn't interview for the job who would have been better than him? No. We're a begrudging bunch of fuckers, basically, and we're playing a very dangerous game, because you know what? We may just make it utterly implausible for our brightest and best even to consider entering politics.

We are setting ourselves up to be represented in the next generation by a cabinet full of clean duffers. I mean, I saw John Gormley yesterday in the paper. In his sandals. That's not gonna work. He's not gonna crack any eggshells.

And if we're not careful, we're gonna ring the bell on the whole Ireland Inc. thing. Worse still, we're going to create a generation of young people who look upon politics as a kind of quagmire, a place you Do Not Go, because if you fart, you'll end up in court.

I believe very strongly that politics should be a career option. I believe your personal life should be utterly irrelevant. I believe you should be paid incredibly well to do it. I think the country should be run like a company with a constitution. Soviet Russia didn't fail for no reason. It failed because it tried to tell the doctor that he was no more important than the bin-man. But he *is* more important than the bin-man. And that's not easy to say, but it's true. And those who run the country well should be rewarded – and fucked out when they're not doing it right.

Why does corruption happen? Corruption only happens when you are not being appropriately rewarded. Corruption will not be a problem if we've given this guy or this woman everything they require to live well. Why can we not organize things like that? Good governance is the key to everything. Good governance and performance. Those who perform the best get rewarded the best. Is that so difficult? Could somebody please tell me why that would be impossible to achieve? Did Christ come down to tell us that if we ran the country like that it wouldn't work?

GERRY RYAN, TD

Mary Harney asked me if I was interested in standing as a PD.

I said I'd think about it.

TDs are among the most hard-working individuals in the country. It's very easy to be cynical about the workload, and to imagine that all they do is get up occasionally and mouth platitudes. Really, the average day for a TD is incredibly busy and mind-numbingly boring. At the clinics, you're expected to be a mixture between a social worker and a handyman. There's an intense level of scrutiny on your personal life, with constant attacks from the media, and on top of that you have to represent your constituency *and* form part of the legislative fabric of Parliament. I mean, you're just not that well paid for it. Now, I do think we're ill-served by many of our representatives. I worry about the calibre of person who rocks up to politics, these days.

But, to be honest, being a mere TD would not be enough for me. I'd like to be the president. I would also like executive powers and control of the army. I would integrate the radio programme into the governing agenda, and we'd come live from the Áras. And the kitchen cabinet will be the *Ryan Show* women. We would have a daily State of the Union debate, not address. God, it'd be great. Wouldn't it? Think of the parties!

DRIFTING ON TO THE AIR

I came from a household, a family and an extended family in which presentation, articulation and performance were a huge part of what they did. In my grandmother Bourke's house on a Sunday in Gaeltacht Park, our reading test would be to stand on a stool and read Robert Emmet's speech from the dock. My grandmother gave prizes for those who did it best, who put the most passion into it.

But I was never going to be the poet in the garret, satisfied with a sixpenny gas-meter system. I remember watching *Withnail and I* and thinking that the main character reminded me enormously of how I could have ended up. You start with huge pretension and ambition, but miss the boat and end up drinking Brasso. I was desperately concerned I wouldn't be able to indulge in foreign travel, desperately concerned I wouldn't be able to have a nice house, desperately concerned I wouldn't have nice clothes, that I wouldn't have a nice car. All of these seemed to come to everyone else way in advance of them coming to me, so it meant that the pressure on me to come up with a scheme to earn money, having rejected all of the conventional routes, was pretty fucking huge. At that time, to be perfectly honest, if I'd met the Great Train Robbers and they'd told me they needed an extra guy to do a bit of talking, I'd have done it.

THE RADIO REVOLUTION AND ME

I've talked about pirate radio in dozens of interviews over the last quarter of a century, and my analysis has been that we were part of the Radio Revolution, that we were Pushing Back the Boundaries. We weren't. The truth is that I was only in it for the free records. I could go up to EMI and spend the whole afternoon in the library taking every single album I wanted. Can you imagine what that was like if you were a student? I recently interviewed Tony Blackburn, and he described life at Radio Caroline, which broadcast from an old lighthouse ship anchored in international waters three miles out from the British mainland. It sounded absolutely appalling, this bunch of guys locked up together twenty-four hours a day. No women, poxy food, warm beer . . . I mean, they were real pirates. We weren't. We were broadcasting from semi-derelict Georgian houses in the middle of Dublin. There was no pain. If there was going to be a raid, you'd always be tipped off so there was plenty of time to get the transmission equipment and the record collection out of harm's way.

I got into pirate radio because I was living with and hanging out with a guy called Mark Storey, who was a radio nut. When Mark came out of the closet, I was flabbergasted, which entertained him highly.

He said, 'How could you have lived with me and not known I was gay?'

The vanity of the heterosexual man: 'Well, you didn't try to fuck me so . . .'

Getting on to pirate radio wasn't exactly difficult. I mean, there was no such thing as an audition. The fact that you had some records and could talk and knew how to switch the thing on was sufficient qualification. I could certainly talk so I did a selection of programmes for Alternative Radio Dublin, or ARD, and afterwards for Big D. ARD was in Belvedere Place and Big D had its premises, when I worked with them, on St Stephen's Green in a beautiful Georgian house. Mark had several roles in ARD, because he knew a lot about the technology of radio, especially transmitters. Some of the other guys who were into transmitters were a bit weird, smoked a lot of dope and didn't mind getting electrocuted on a regular basis. And Mark was absolutely obsessed with radio. He adored radio, he loved the whole ethos of the pirate-radio scene, he loved music radio, he loved and celebrated all the jocks who had grown up through Caroline and Radio London. I learned most of what I knew about radio from him.

James Dillon, who ran both ARD and Big D, was, for my money, the quintessential pirate-radio businessman. Some of the other guys involved might have been good at what they did, but essentially they were deluded because, God help them, they really believed they were going to get the licence. They believed that because they had efficient, well-run businesses that earned a lot of money and had huge audiences, because they even paid VAT and deducted income tax from their employees, the government would smile on them and they would become legitimate commercial stations. The guys I was working for had a much more bald-headed approach. James Dillon knew instinctively that the pirates were going to be dumped in the shit, that none of the main guys who'd led the revolution in broadcasting in this country was ever going to end up earning anything out of it. He understood that there was a limited time-frame for pirate radio. He wanted to get into it, milk it for as much as possible and get out again.

Big D was a very successful station with large audiences, but there were very few regular business protocols. Along with broad-casting, you were actually expected to get out there and sell advertising. The fact that this was beneath my dignity was another worrying factor. How was I going to earn any money if I wasn't willing to go out and sell anything?

I remember James Dillon bringing me out and buying me a drink and saying, 'You know, Gerry, you really are going to have to get your hands dirty doing something . . .'

I just couldn't accept that. I lived in this little make-believe world. My wife, who was my girlfriend at the time, used to help me do the programme. She would help me put the music together and carry the stuff. I paid her three quid out of the fifteen I got. There was any amount of money to be had at the time just by going to the local shop, getting the advertising, giving a bit to James and keeping the rest yourself. I couldn't fucking do it.

GLEN CAMPBELL AND RATATOUILLE SANDWICHES

When Radio 2, as it was in the beginning, started up, Mark got a job as a producer.

One night I was on my way to a party at an old girlfriend's house – Ann O'Neill, whose father, Paddy, was head of com-munity radio in RTÉ. I was with Morah, and Mark said, 'They're auditioning guys to present the radio programmes, and they're mostly crap.' I can say this because most of them don't work there any more. 'You'd stand as good a chance as anybody.'

I was wearing a tuxedo when I arrived in – with absolutely nothing prepared. Billy Wall, who was to become the controller of Radio 2, was doing the auditions himself. You had to do a fifteen-minute slot, topping and tailing a few pieces of music, interviewing Billy, and reading a script you'd written. I had no script. When he said on the talkback, 'OK, do your script now,'

I thought, Fuck, what am I going to do? But there was a Glen Campbell album on the desk so I picked it up and read out the liner notes. When it was over, he came back on the talkback and said, 'That was very well delivered. Did you write it yourself?'

I said, 'Oh, yeah.'

He was sufficiently impressed to bring me back for another audition, then another and another. Then they called to tell me I'd have to leave pirate radio if I was going to get a job in RTÉ, so I said, 'Wow, have I got a job? Have I?'

No, I had no job. They just wanted me to give up the job *in order to apply* to RTÉ. This, of course, was my introduction to the arrogance of RTÉ, something I would learn a lot more about as the years went by.

So I said, 'Yeah, yeah, I'll do that, OK.'

But I didn't because I was getting the odd tenner here and there, along with the free albums.

Eventually, after an inordinately lengthy process, I was told I would be presenting two shows. *Here Comes the Weekend* on a Friday night, and *Saturday Scene* on a Saturday morning. At first, I was a bit pissed off because I thought it didn't sound very high profile, but then I was told how much I was going to get – seventy-eight pounds a week! Seventy-eight pounds for doing something on a Friday evening for an hour, and for three hours, from nine to twelve, on a Saturday morning!

This, I suppose, was the story of my life: on a sleigh ride to bankruptcy and perdition one minute, having more money than anyone else the next. And it was FANTASTIC! It was absolutely fantastic. All this money, all this free time . . . That was when I began to believe I was different from my father. He'd had to work really, really hard to earn his living, he had principles he stood by, protocols he observed. I began to think, Well, that's bullshit, really, because I've just proved you can do something you haven't been trained to do, that you've never had any ambition to do, that you haven't anticipated, that turned up by a complete accident, and end up getting seventy-eight quid a week.

OK, I had only a three-month contract, and at that time, RTÉ personnel people were always very happy to remind you that you were only temporary, but I was absolutely convinced I was in there for the long haul. I'll infiltrate it, I thought. I'll end up owning it, and I'll get loads of money out of that. And I'll get free records.

My father was reading the newspaper when I told him about the job. He put the paper down and he said, 'Can you earn money out of that?' I'd been in college for about five years at this stage.

I said, 'Yeah, seventy-eight quid a week, actually.'

He went, 'Oh, right,' and went back to reading the paper.

I drifted almost imperceptibly from Trinity into broadcasting. I spent less and less time attending to my studies, less and less time attending lectures. I had almost completely given up going into the legal firm I was apprenticed to. They were probably as happy for me to move on as I was. They needed somebody who was going to come in and, you know, work on a nine-to-five basis. I had all these exalted ideas about what the legal profession meant to me, none of which included the dull grind of everyday work.

RTÉ was very much like a university. There was a campus atmosphere; the place even looked quite like a place of learning. The people there were unusual, certainly compared to the rest of the community. Even though it was a fairly conservative organization, there was no real dress code or formality. To me, there was little that seemed much different from college life – except, of course, for one very salient fact. You got paid.

There was a confused culture in RTÉ at the time. It didn't really know if it was an organ of the state or one of popular reflection or possibly even change. It was very driven by its public-service remit. I thought, Surely the thing is to have as many people as is humanly possible listening to or looking at what you do. Time and again I was reminded that it wasn't about that, and to prove it to me, they would tell me that I didn't get seventy-eight pounds because there were seventy-eight people listening to me, that I would still get the seventy-eight pounds if there was one person listening to me. I should remember that, and I shouldn't concern myself with how many people were listening to me. From the word go, I thought, This is horseshit. I knew we were entering a world of commercial competition, and that if you didn't have ratings, it didn't matter how many speeches were made about public service, it didn't matter how many accolades or awards you were given about the fabulous thing you did that only one and a half people listened to or looked at, that at the end of the day, when the survey came out and the advertising and sales people got their hands on it, the only thing that bloody well mattered was how many people listened to you. I was proved right time and time again.

We were the first generation of broadcasters to come in and not do the Irish-language test, and the last generation to do the pronunciation course (It's Port-lee-sha, not Port-leesh). To me, the whole thing seemed like a *Monty Python* sketch. There seemed to be hundreds of guys, with foppish hairstyles, wandering around with tapes under their arms, who didn't seem to do anything else. You had the same people doing the PR for the orchestra and Radio 2: 'Comin'atcha!' They brought in a couple of guys like Shay Healy, who were meant to be more rock 'n' roll, and, in fairness, Shay did try to sex it up a bit.

I was there from day one, from the launch. I had come from quite a sophisticated background – I was well educated and articulate, I'd quite a broad knowledge of music, I wasn't without a certain wit – yet I was introduced in the press release as some- body who was interested in ratatouille sandwiches. This was meant to be Hilarious and Wildly Rebellious and Crazy and Who Knows What He's Going To Do Next? 'Zany' was a word that was bandied about an awful lot in the early days.

Don't forget RTÉ didn't come up with the idea of putting Radio 2 on the air. It was the cabinet came up with that one because the law was being flouted. Everyone had a pirate radio station. You could set one up in your bathroom if you wanted, and some people did. RTÉ's attitude was: It's Nothing To Do With Us. Radio 2 was more or less foisted on them. They saw it as unhealthy. Toxic, even. Best stand well downwind of it and not go contaminating the pure Aryan strain of RTÉ. But the government decided that the only way to counter the rise of the pirates was by producing a hip, cool, rocking, groovy pop-music station. RTÉ was more or less forced into it. I remember Vincent Hanley saying to me once, 'Just remember one thing. They hate you.'

Of course, now I've become they.

The organization was deeply offended that huge resources were being given over to these loudmouth pop-music people, who, when they left the studio on the weekend, got into bigger cars than anyone else, drove to Killarney or Sligo or Mullingar and appeared in front of a crowd of two thousand people screaming and shouting about Bryan Adams and came home with a thousand pounds . . .

MONEY HELPED ME OVERCOME THE SHAME

I earned an absolute fortune travelling around as an incompetent celebrity DJ. For some reason I'd tend to be booked by fellas whose nightclubs were failing. If you were on Achill Island and you had a nightclub, the best thing to do if it wasn't going well was to get Gerry Ryan down. Did it work? Hardly. Worked for me, though. In a month I could earn my entire annual salary by going around and signing a few autographs. It was unbelievable. People like Jim O'Neil, Jimmy Greally and Vincent Hanley pioneered this stuff. They were real jocks. Smooth, professional, at the top of their game. I didn't even have the proper records. I absolutely adored music, I was obsessed with it, but my tastes were pretty eclectic. I simultaneously had *Led Zeppelin III* and Abba's *Arrival* in my record collection. So I'd be playing

Genesis and they'd all be looking up at me going, Huh? Eventually I decided the best thing to do was bring somebody else with me who actually did know how to do the jock thing, someone who had the right music. They played the records and I'd hop around the place and shake hands and kiss girls, collect five hundred quid and go home. It was mind-boggling, and also sort of shameful for a guy who'd spent so much of his life studying so hard for such an exalted career to end up earning so much money out of bullshit.

The money, however, helped me overcome the shame.

There's a great line in a Peter Sellers sketch where he's playing a fictitious version of Elvis Presley's manager, Colonel Tom Parker. He's being interviewed by a journalist who asks, 'How sane are these young pop stars that you represent?'

'Oh,' he says, 'they're as sane as any ex-plasterer's mate who's suddenly earning forty thousand pounds.' That was me.

And I loved it. Loved it. I loved working there, though I would get kind of melancholic about the legal thing. Distance began to open up between me and the people I'd been to college with. They'd all gone off and bought suits and got proper haircuts and proper jobs while I was indulging in a prolonged delinquency. I was wearing a leather bomber jacket, I'd grown my hair into the full mullet. T-shirts and jeans were the dress code for work.

I began to spend all my time in RTÉ, even though I was only doing two programmes. There were two reasons for that. One, I had nowhere else to go. In the very early days Morah was still in college so she was off doing her thing. But being in RTÉ all the time also meant I got to know people very well. I slowly began to understand how the politics of the organization worked, and even within the first two years, it had become abundantly clear to me that surviving within RTÉ was 90 per cent politics and 10 per cent broadcasting. I made it my business to get to know those who were in positions of influence, to get to know those who could tell me what was going on behind the closed doors. I did, for a time, become a bit obsessed with the management structure. I was fascinated by those who had my life in their hands.

The odd thing was I became convinced at a very early stage that there was no point in toeing the line. There was no end of people willing to tell you that, you know, you'd better keep your bib clean, keep your head down, work hard, don't rock the boat. There was a whole kind of celebration of good behaviour on-air. No foul language. Everybody seemed to have this special personality they adopted when they went on-air. I just thought, Well, this isn't going to produce anything unique or special. And the thing was, no matter how conservative the management were at RTÉ, they were still in the business of directing talent. They were looking for different things. So I reckoned there was a balancing act involved. If you were going to stick your head above the parapet, two things could happen: one, it might get shot off, but two, you might get noticed.

IT'S OVER, YOU'RE FUCKED

It wasn't long before I got pretty fed up with playing records. I mean, I wasn't really all that interested in doing music programmes, and even in the early days of *Lights Out*, the night-time show I presented in the mid eighties, I was more interested in talking to people. Maggie Stapleton was the producer. She developed something unique for a radio programme: a database of people we would use to review music and talk about movies and whatever else. I always conducted these interactions in a very conversational way. Maggie made this possible with that database. You got the impression, listening in, that there were always different people calling in to chat but in fact it was at most a hundred, carefully rotated over the weeks. Maggie would give each of them star ratings and we'd always try and bring back the most entertaining. We were slowly developing a style of research, production and presentation late at night that was essentially the embryonic *Gerry Ryan Show*.

We didn't have it all our own way. Louis Hogan, who was the deputy controller of Radio 2, called me in one day and said, 'I don't want you to talk any more. I want you to stop the reviews on the radio programme at night.'

I was absolutely devastated. I wasn't much good as a disc jockey. I didn't have the mid-Atlantic patter and my musical tastes were, on the whole, fairly odd compared to those of most music-radio presenters. I'd never thought there'd be much demand for my talents as a disc jockey, so if I couldn't talk, what was I going to do? I thought this was the end of the world.

Because I got so upset about it, he said, 'Look, I'm going to listen in tonight, I'm going to listen to what you're doing.'

And I remember thinking, Right, I'll make it the best ever.

But that night it just fell apart. None of the people we wanted to talk to were there and we ended up with lousy callers instead of good ones, while I sounded nervous and stilted.

The next morning he said, 'I listened last night. It was terrible. I don't want to hear any more of it.'

But because he hadn't written it down, I ignored him.

Soon afterwards, Willie O'Reilly became producer of the night-time show. The first thing he said was 'OK, this is going to be all about personality.'

We'd interface more with Mark Cagney, who was doing a sort of grown-up album programme, and Dave Fanning who was doing *The Rock Show*. We started doing outside broadcasts and bringing the three shows on tour around the country. We dressed as if we were in a band and behaved as if we were in a band, which, to be honest, just meant drinking a lot and staying out late. That began to give an identity to the programme. Dave was doing a huge amount of talking anyway. Cagney was impossible to control from the talking point of view. And then you had me. So there were three big-mouths on at night-time. And it worked extremely well. We were very good friends, the three of us. Dave was a hyperactive, south-side rock guru. Mark was this obsessive, meticulous Corkman who would annotate every single milli-second of what he played on-air. We were surrounded by a selection of highly talented people. You had Willie O'Reilly and you had Ian Wilson, who was producing *The Rock Show*. Siobhan Hough and Pat Dunne came on board, two people who would be pivotal to *The Gerry Ryan Show*.

In between times, there was an early-evening show called *Rocksteady* that I presented on a week-on-week-off with Barry Lang. There was plenty of interaction with the audience on that. But it was very juvenile, almost childish. I was quite concerned at that point because I was now getting into my late twenties and I was presenting a music programme that, to me, seemed to be aimed at fifteen-year-olds. I felt a bit silly. But between that and the night-time show and starting to appear on television, I had become reasonably well known. It was around now that it began to dawn on me how embarrassing it would be if I was dropped by RTÉ. What would it be like to be a famous nonentity? That really did disturb me. It disturbed me an awful lot.

Coming up to the announcement of a new schedule, I would be distraught. This was a terrible time not just for me but for everyone around me because I couldn't focus. Broadcasters still suffer with this. Instead of ambition and instead of a game plan, I had paranoia about being dropped. And RTÉ would be very, very careful not to let you get your hopes up that your contract was going to be renewed. The power that gives the people who are holding the purse strings is absolutely enormous. They can dangle your livelihood in front of you. Some producers were very direct and would tell you, 'It's over, you're fucked, you're not gonna get your contract renewed.' And you might hear this halfway through your season so you'd have to come in and go on-air every night or every day in the certain knowledge that the game was up. It was a kind of mad, honourable, self-immolation thing that some people had to go through.

In particular I remember Declan Meehan, who was a night-time DJ. He was one of the first big names whose contract was not renewed in 2FM. He was a great DJ and, to this day, I can't figure out what he did wrong. He didn't bloody anybody's nose, he didn't poo on the carpet. I got to know him quite well the last few months of his time with RTÉ. And I watched this absolutely wonderful man, this gentleman, go through so much agony. I remember thinking, Jesus, if this happened to me, I'd never be able to survive it. I mean, I never would have been able to go on-air like he did and not say, 'Well, why don't you all just go fuck yourselves? I'm having sex with a donkey tonight.'

I sometimes wonder whether he was a sacrificial lamb of sorts, chosen to remind us that no one was indispensable. There was the constant utterance, 'I could go down to the Historical and Philosophical Society tomorrow and get twenty Gay Byrnes.'

I used to hear this stuff and go, 'Where are the twenty frigging Gay Byrnes? Why aren't they in here? Why don't we have twenty Gay Byrnes on the air? If they did exist, they'd be in here right now, on about a tenth of the money.'

I remember when I was coming towards the end of presenting *Here Comes the Weekend* and *Saturday Scene*, Billy Wall, who was now head of the station, came down to see me. Because I was in there so much, I'd found a desk for myself.

'Oh, by the way,' he said, 'we're dropping *Here Comes the Weekend*.'

I almost vomited.

I don't think he meant to be unpleasant, but it certainly had an unpleasant effect on me.

A short while later he called me up to his office and said, 'Oh, and we're getting rid of *Saturday Scene* as well.' Or, actually, it was more like 'We're finishing off the current series.' I don't think they ever say 'getting rid of'. They're always 'resting' programmes or 'moving on' from something or other. I got back to the desk and sat down. I felt so light-headed I thought I was going to faint.

I rang up my girlfriend and I said, 'I think I've just been sacked.'

And she said, 'What do you mean, you think you've just been sacked? Either you've been sacked or you haven't.'

But RTÉ always worked on this nod-and-wink basis. No one ever said, 'Take your things and leave.' And also, of course, hope sprang eternal that they were about to give me *The Gay Byrne Show*.

It was a couple of hours later. I'd stayed, I remember, because I was doing something that evening.

Billy came in and he said, 'Oh, I forgot to tell you that we have this new Monday to Friday programme. It's at seven, it's a music slot, and we think you should do it.'

So, first thing, I'm hugely relieved to have the job, second thing, I'm hugely elated to have been chosen for it. But I also felt kind of . . . humiliated. I'd spent several hours almost vomiting. I'd truly believed that I'd lost my programmes and was officially on the broadcasting scrapheap. I mean, I don't think Billy was being malicious; I think he was just too busy doing other things at the time. But there were others who used to relish telling presenters that a series was over, finished. And what fascinated me about some of these guys was that they had come into RTÉ with leftist or at least liberal backgrounds. Yet they became more vicious than concentration-camp commandants and seemed to totally enjoy telling a presenter, 'You? We won't need you next Monday. Thanks, good luck.'

So, it's a cruel system, but is there any other way of doing it? I'm not so sure that there is.

CHASING COCKROACHES DOWN THE HALL

So, someone decided it would be a good idea to treat the three evening programmes like a heavy rock band, like Cream or Led Zeppelin. We were three very different characters, Cagney, me and Fanning, but we took to the idea straight away. We dressed like we were in a band. We felt like we were in a band. We certainly got recognized as much as any band in Ireland when we'd go out in the street. The difference was that we didn't play the music. The drugs and the groupies weren't really there either. But certainly we attempted to construct what we thought was a rock-'n'-roll-on-the-road lifestyle. This amounted to booking into awful hotels so that you could spend your per diem on drink and staying out too late in dodgy nightclubs. Then we started putting on these live shows, some of which were huge. You could have twenty thousand people at them. Effectively they were gigantic open-air discos. But we engineered a kind of theatricality around it. We'd all been to see big rock shows, we knew what was involved, which amounted to, I suppose, a lot of shouting at the audience. We had a huge sound rig with a rock-'n'-roll lighting system, plenty of dry ice, and a lot of jumping and leaping around the place.

Jim Lockhart, who had been keyboard player with Horslips, joined RTÉ and became a producer of one programme. There was a selection of different producers who used to wander in and out of the three programmes. It was unclear, to be honest, who was producing what at any given time. Jim, the only actual musician among us, sometimes ended up on stage. We'd also bring on these very early synthesizers: the music would be going, Frankie Goes to Hollywood or something, and over the top, we'd have these incredible synthesized sound effects – particularly bass-pedal riffs. Now it all sounds very twee and very naïve, but it was actually fairly groundbreaking in terms of what was essentially a record hop. And with the lights, the stereo sound rig and the extra effects thrown in, we became pretty convinced that we were whoever was playing on the CD at the time. The audience bought into it and went completely frigging mad.

We started affecting the trappings of the rock-'n'-roll performance. We had the guys with the torches bringing us to the stage, and the arrows made from gaffer tape to point the way in the dark. And there was a pecking order. We'd treat younger DJs or local guys very badly because we were the main act. And it worked. Stupid and self-conscious as it may sound now, it did actually work. Huge crowds showed up and they all loved it. Don't forget, this was Ireland when very few rock-'n'-roll bands visited the country. There was a heck of a lot of people jostling for attention wherever you went. And that made it feel like you were the centre of attention. As a young man that kind of thing is very seductive, but utterly, utterly transient. I mean, it's will-o'-the-wisp territory. I had the mullet and the leather jacket, but I had never written a song, never lifted a guitar. We were affecting the image of Jimi Hendrix, but none of the content. There was really nothing glamorous about it.

A lot of my life has been spent talking up what I do and, in those days, you were talking it up to the heights of Kilimanjaro. In reality, it was getting dressed in a toilet in the back of the Grand Parade Hotel in Cork. One place we stayed I remember chasing cockroaches up and down the hall with Cagney and Fanning. When I look back on it now, it's mostly with embarrassment. A little bit of affection, but mostly embarrassment. A guy with a mullet and a leather jacket jumping around on stage to music he'd had nothing to do with? That may explain why we weren't really fending off thousands of groupies. But thousands of people turned up at the events. They all went home again, though.

HOW DO YOU SOLVE A PROBLEM LIKE GERRY?

RTÉ were never quite sure what to do with me. They'd have me on at weekends, on weekday evenings, they'd have me on doing junior versions of Dave Fanning's *Rock Show*. I was going nowhere financially, but I was still earning a decent living, I had a proper house, I'd a car, I'd a family I was able to support. But what was I? A failed lawyer who was now doing discos. There was the odd foray into television, but that seemed even more unstable. And I couldn't believe how easily you could end up being hated when you went on television. Even if the audience numbers were good, the critics decided from day one that, in television terms, I was donkey shite.

This didn't really tie in with my impression of myself as a world leader. I had kept in touch with the people I'd gone to college with and now I began to feel they had more *legitimate* lives than I had. Slowly but surely they got bigger cars, bigger houses, bigger wives . . . That mullet hairdo time, when Dave Fanning, Mark Cagney and I were popular night-time DJs, that was a period when I was really worried about where it was all going because I felt quite disposable. These, for me, were the lost years.

MAKING STUFF UP

Extract from the record of Dáil Éireann, 9 June 1987

Mr Tony Gregory asked the Minister for Justice if, in view of the many complaints from members of the public, the gardaí are investigating, with a view of taking criminal proceedings, the matter of the killing of a newborn lamb as part of a survival course sponsored by RTÉ's 'Gay Byrne Hour'; and if he will make a statement on the matter.

Minister for Justice (Mr Gerard Collins): I am informed by the Garda authorities that the matter referred to has been investigated by them and that they are satisfied that the animal was not killed in the manner alleged and that there was no cruelty involved in the killing of this animal.

Lambo was so long ago that it's difficult to work up a huge amount of enthusiasm about it. To be honest, I've kind of grown tired of trying to give it a context, but at the same time, there's no doubt that the episode was hugely significant in my career.

At the time I was presenting late-night radio programmes on 2FM. Gay was still at the height of his powers at Radio 1, and anything attached to Gay got noticed. Philip Kampf, who has since become a very successful television entrepreneur and producer-director, was working as a researcher on *The Gay Byrne Hour*.

Philip was one of those hyper-dedicated researchers, incredibly creative and smart. He came up with the idea of sending a selection of people out into the wilds armed with nothing more than the *SAS Handbook*. Gay would talk to them every day, Philip would direct the operation in the field, and this, it was hoped, would make for entertaining summer listening. They chose a selection of people; there was a sound operator from the West of Ireland, there was a housewife, someone from An Oige, there was an outdoor activities expert – and me. I gave him one extra person: my cousin and pal, Ciaran Bourke.

'This guy will be perfect,' I said. 'He'd be good at acting out stories . . .' Because I thought that that was what it was going to be about. Sure, there would be sleeping under the stars and washing your knickers in the stream, but really, at the end of the day, you'd need some good stories to make the thing work.

I'd already arrived at the conclusion that most broadcasting was smoke and mirrors, that there were no real rules unless you were doing a documentary or a news report. I believed what we were doing was essentially light entertainment with a current-affairs flavour. If reality wasn't delivering anything interesting, well, then, you could just kind of . . . make stuff up. As it turned out, this could not have been further from the truth. I didn't understand that incredibly strict rules applied. I had no idea that telling a lie on the radio would generate not just confusion, upset and trauma within RTÉ but that it would exercise the imagination of the nation to such an extent that I would be interviewed by the guards and the incident would be brought up in the Dáil.

As far as I was concerned I had been brought into this thing because of my descriptive skills. Philip had said so himself. 'You'll be great because you can tell a story.' Tell the story, to me, meant make up the story half the time.

So, anyway, we trained for it, there was a great deal of talk about it. We appeared on *The Late Late Show*, and then it was off into the wilds with Philip.

At the start, we tried to live by the book. We attempted to catch fish with our hands – tickling fish, it's called. Well, I can tell you now, if I had to feed myself by catching fish with my hands, I'd be dead. I'd love to meet anybody who can do it. Sleeping under the stars was uncomfortable, smelly and not even slightly romantic. We were living on very, very, very meagre rations and marching across the wilds of Connemara with all our equipment . . . And you know what? The odd thing now is, apart from Philip and Ciaran, I can't remember the name of anyone who was involved in it, which is probably due to the fact that I blocked out the whole incident for years and years and years.

I was also doing my own late-night radio programme from the west. I'd arrive into the studio and Jim Lockhart, the producer, would be there with a chicken sandwich and a cup of tea. I was supposed to be sticking rigidly to this survivalist ethos and not eating anything other than freshly tickled fish. I thought it was ridiculous. What was this mad moral obsession all about?

But, anyway, we were about halfway through it, halfway through a lot of farting in tents, marching up hills, being soaked by the rain . . . And it was rubbish in broadcasting terms. One afternoon or one morning, whatever it was, Philip said to me, 'This isn't going anywhere. We need something really exciting to happen.'

'Like what?' I asked him.

'Well, you know,' he said, 'imagine if you killed something.'

Because there was stuff in the handbook about killing and skinning things like monkeys and rabbits. But we couldn't catch rabbits. We weren't able to do anything that involved cooking anything, much less catching it. And in the book there was this ridiculous description of killing bears by putting a rock in your sock and clubbing them to death.

So we were camped out near this famine village not far from Maam Cross, which was very, very beautiful, extraordinarily quiet and very surreal. And there, in this tranquil place, we spent a full day running around after sheep – fully grown sheep – with a rock in a sock, trying to club them to death.

Now, everybody thinks that sheep don't go that fast. Well, they do. Everybody also thinks that sheep are stupid. Well, they're not. They know when you're trying to kill them. And even when we did get close to clubbing one, it didn't have any effect whatsoever. I mean, I hit one or two, all right, but it had absolutely no effect. The rock just bounced off.

We had already hiked over a mountain range to get to this valley, so by the end of a day of sheep-chasing, we were completely exhausted, and still had no pivot for the week's broadcasting. I was getting sick of it. It had also occurred to me that if you were really in the SAS, you'd just take your rifle and shoot a lamb, or you'd go to the local village, hold somebody hostage and take their food.

WOULD IT BE AGAINST THE RULES?

We met this woman – Werner Meis was her name – out on the hillside in her Land Rover, and she brought us back to her and her husband's farmhouse. She'd been tuning in to the whole sorry adventure on the radio all week, and seemed much more excited about listening to it than I was about participating in it. All I could think was, maybe when we got to the house I could steal some food. Anyway, we arrived up to this very sophisticated, very cool house and she said, 'Look, would it be against the rules if you had something to eat?'

At first the others were, 'Oh, yeah, yeah, we couldn't do that.'

'Well,' I said, 'you can make me something.'

And so she made something for all of us. I can't remember whether or not everyone ate it.

Her husband materialized. He was this very sophisticated sheep farmer. He had a silk shirt on, I always remember that. I told him we'd been running around after bloody sheep all day.

'They were my sheep,' he said. 'I've been watching you . . . You know, you guys will never catch a sheep, and even if you did, you wouldn't be able to kill it. You're not strong enough and you don't know how to do it.'

He asked us what we needed it for, why it was so important.

'We need to be able to tell Gay this story tomorrow on the air. We need something really, really dramatic,' I told him.

He thought this was absolutely hysterical but he was also still keen to help out. 'I'll give you a lamb,' he said, 'and you can say you killed it.'

I remember thinking, That's no good, that's not a story. 'A dead lamb?' I said. 'Have you got a dead one out the back?'

'No,' he said. 'I'll go out and kill one now.'

'Well,' I said, 'I think at least I should see you do it.'

So he got his shotgun, brought us out the back of the farmhouse and selected a small spring lamb. And he blew its head off. Just like that.

You just don't anticipate what something like that is going to be like. I remember the lamb just stood there for a second with no head, and so much blood gushing out of it. So much blood for such a tiny creature. I can't remember who else was there, but I remember the crack of the shotgun, which was much louder than I'd thought it would be. I can still see the lamb's face; there one minute, gone the next. And blood everywhere.

When I came to tell the story live on-air the next day, whatever I said was always going to be imbued with the shock of having witnessed an extraordinarily traumatic death at such close quarters.

I can't recall whether we skinned the lamb there or whether we waited until we got it down to our campsite that evening, but I do remember myself and Ciaran making our way down the country lane with the headless lamb dangling by its legs from a pole. Hunters returning from a hard day's rocking and socking in the hills.

Philip met us at the campsite, by which time we'd gone into heavy-duty method acting. 'Well?' he said. 'What's this?' And I could see him thinking, Thank Christ, they've done something that's going to be interesting – because his head was on the block. The lamb's was gone and his was on the block.

'It's a lamb,' I said. 'Look. We killed it.'

'You killed it yourselves?'

'Yeah.'

No one else was quite as comfortable with the lie as I was, but I believed there was a job to be done, and the job required us to have a bloody good story to tell. We didn't have it so we had to make it up.

Philip said, 'What happened?'

'Well, you know,' I said, 'we chased it, we caught it, we killed it with a rock in a sock.'

Philip smiled. 'Gay's gonna love this tomorrow.'

We didn't tell him the truth. He didn't know what really happened. I don't know whether he ever suspected what really happened. I mean, there's no reason to believe that he did, but certainly afterwards, he became extremely distressed by the whole thing, and didn't speak to me for several years as a result. Today, I'm happy to report, he's a good friend and a colleague and works very closely with me on *Operation Transformation*.

Anyway, the next day on the radio was a turning point in my career. Gay was clearly delighted that at long last we'd come up with something other than failed fish tickling. I told him in very grave, hushed tones about this terrible deed we had done – how, driven wild by hunger, we had bludgeoned a baby lamb to death. There was an almost biblical character to the story, and Gay relished it. Were we OK? Were our emotions in tatters after committing this heinous deed?

The night after the broadcast we cut the lamb up and tried to cook it, but it was so tiny we got almost nothing from it. And with all the smoke it was horrible. Cooking food over an outdoor fire is not as glamorous as people think.

But, unbeknownst to us, we had started a chain reaction. The piece was repeated on *The Gay Byrne Hour* the next day, and that evening it was on the news. People got extremely excited about it.

THE LAMB AND THE ROCK AND THE SOCK

In the meantime, we had moved on from it and were engaged in what we considered to be far more serious events. I nearly died from exposure at one point, crossing over to an island. We were canoeing in extremely cold wet weather into gale-force winds and very, very high Atlantic waves. I had to be dragged out of the boat, stripped and wrapped in foil and towels because I was in shock. The bonding effect of going through those things was massive. We forgot about the lamb and the rock and the sock. By then it was almost a joke to us.

The whole thing finished up on *The Late Late Show* when we were paraded in our filth and our dirt and our smell.

And then the ball really started rolling. There were people who were quite offended by these middle-class twits running around the hills of Connemara bludgeoning innocent, defenceless lambs. In the Dáil, Tony Gregory wanted to know whether or not we were going to be prosecuted for what we were supposed to have done. I was amazed. But it got worse. Next thing the guards rang up and invited me down to the station in Irishtown for a chat. There were all these people milling about in the interview room so I said to the inspector, 'Can I speak to you by yourself?'

He cleared the room, and I said, 'Look, this is complete bollocks. We didn't kill any lamb.'

He roared laughing. Maybe I should have stuck to the story, maybe I should have gambled on it, but I was sick of carrying on the charade, sick of living as one of the Survivors. We were making public appearances as the Survivors, with people asking, 'Why aren't you in your survivor outfit?' So I thought, This is the way out. Just come clean, tell him the truth. I thought that would be the end of it.

It wasn't.

Garda stations are basically sieves. Within an hour the press had found out. It was the summer and nothing was happening so the papers became obsessed with the fact that someone had lied on the radio.

I just could not take this seriously. What were they talking about, lying on the radio? I mean, as far as I was concerned, this was *The War of the Worlds*, Orson Welles's famous radio-drama hoax, albeit on a smaller, sort of organic-farming scale. As far as I was concerned, we'd done our job. We had created a very exciting piece of radio, most of which was true, and during a dull moment we did what any professional would have done. We made it up. I genuinely did not realize that this broke some sort of sacred law. Within RTÉ, it was as if we had burst into the cathedral and shat on the floor. They initiated an investigation, an incredibly aggressive investigation, run by a senior producer, John Caden.

Even then it took me one or two taped (taped!) interviews to grasp that somebody's head was on the block, that they were looking, as it were, for a sacrificial lamb. So I just said, 'Right, I'm not going down.' Every single thing I'd learned about obfuscation, fudging and confusing people came into its own. I just refused to admit that we didn't kill the lamb.

I said, 'Yeah, well, you have to say that to the police, you know?'

Charlotte, my eldest daughter, was three years old at the time. I used to bring her to the interviews. I used to say, 'If you want to interview me at this particular time, I'll be looking after Charlotte. She'll have to come too.'

So I encouraged Lottie to run riot in the room while they were doing the interview, and consequently it was very, very difficult for John Caden to get anything out of me. Halfway through a sentence I'd say, 'Oh, John, I'm sorry – she's knocked that over.'

It must have been an absolute nightmare for him.

Today, the reason I have great respect for John Caden is that when it was all over and done with his relationship with me developed in a very positive way. He wasn't and isn't one of those people who felt oh-goddamn-that-bastard-Ryan-he's-after-causing-me-a-lot-of-anxiety-more-heart-tablets-please-Patsy. For him, this investigation was just another moment in his day. Now, at that moment you were staring down a very smart man with great powers of inquiry, someone with a very serious agenda – to get to the bottom of the matter and find a solution. RTÉ needed somebody they could hold up not just to themselves but to the nation. They needed to be able to say, 'Here, this is the problem. That thing there, this cancer: Gerry Ryan. He caused it.'

Adavin O'Driscoll, one of the senior heads of the radio division, was freaked out about it as well. She brought me in and said, 'You do understand the implications of this?'

'Yeah,' I said, 'but I didn't do anything wrong.'

And she'd say, 'Well, what did you do?'

'I did exactly what I said on the radio to Gay, that's what I did.'

And I stuck with that religiously. I don't know whether they thought that the United Nations were going to come and close them down, but they certainly were extremely agitated – I mean *extremely* agitated – by what I had done. I was like the delinquent child who doesn't understand why his parents are so freaked out about the fact that he's thrown a petrol bomb into the neighbours' garden. When I think back on it I realize I was being incredibly, perhaps deliberately, naïve about it. I used to ring up Adavin O'Driscoll on an almost daily basis to thank her for all the behind-the-scenes work she was doing on my behalf. Of course she wasn't. This was pure malevolence on my part. I think a lot of people were hoping I would either commit suicide or be sacked as quickly as possible.

This did not happen because of one man. The director of radio at the time was a deeply Christian man and a great broadcaster. His name was Michael Carroll. What people didn't know was that Michael Carroll rated G. Ryan and reckoned that G. Ryan had a future. Michael Carroll brought me in at the end of the summer – remember, this went on for an entire summer and it was utterly nerve-racking: I remember getting sedatives from the family doctor. I was convinced that my career was over. The glare of publicity was phenomenal. I couldn't go anywhere but they were talking about it. Kevin O'Connor, a colleague in the television news department, doorstepped me outside RTÉ, as if I'd just come from a tribunal.

At the end of it all Michael Carroll called me into his office. 'You know,' he said, 'a lot of people would like to see the back of you over this, but I'm not going to let that happen. I'm sending you a letter. I don't want you to get too upset by it because it's quite strongly worded.'

'So I'm not going to be sacked?'

'No,' he said. 'In fact, I think you're going to go on and do a lot of good stuff . . . But the next time you make something up, make sure there's a few more people involved . . .'

When he left that job, years later, he gave me the file. A big thick file, with all the tapes from those interviews. It had been years in the vaults.

I owe my career to Michael Carroll.

JAYSUS, LOOK AT THE FAT ARSE ON THAT BITCH

I was asked if I'd like to present a three-hour daytime programme, featuring music, callers and chat. I did not jump at the
opportunity.

For a start, things were going very nicely at night-time. Dave,
Mark and I were pretty much left to our own devices and we
had a certain cult status among the audience. Plus we also affected
a kind of disdain for daytime radio. Plus it had been years since
I'd had to get up in the morning. Set against the comfy little
niche I had carved out for myself, the idea of indulging in an
experiment that involved going up against Gay Byrne did not
strike me as particularly attractive. It was the head of 2FM, Bill
O'Donovan, who convinced me to do it. I thought, OK, sure,
we'll give it a go. I remember, as the starting date loomed, I asked
Bill, 'Well, like, what's going to be on the flipping programme?'

And he said, 'You.'

He was putting it up to me. He was basically saying, 'You have
this great opinion of yourself, you think you're the source of all
knowledge, you think you have the popular touch, you think
you understand women. Well, go on. Off you go. Let's hear it.'

Originally the idea was that no single item or call would be
longer than a pop song, the ridiculous notion being that the attention span of the average 2FM listener ran to only three minutes
and ten seconds. Siobhan Hough and Joan Torsney were the
first broadcasting assistants. Pat Dunne produced. It was March,
twenty years ago, and, in fairness, the conditions could hardly
have been more perfect. The pirates had gone, Century Radio
hadn't started. The only competition was Gay Byrne, and he was
away on holidays.

Despite that, it was terrifying. Back then, the amount of prep-
aration that went into each show was very, very scant, while the
amount of time I was on-air was huge. From day one there was
a massive reliance on me pontificating. There were one or two

difficult weeks when I was convinced that the whole thing was just going to go down the tubes. I worried that if the programme relied too heavily on my personality, a bad mood or fatigue would completely derail things. What I hadn't anticipated was the willingness of the audience to roll with those punches, to go along with me, whether I was tired or sick, happy, joyful or afraid. Where I went, they would follow.

I looked back recently at some of the old running orders and they're incredibly sparse. We might have something like 'Dublin City Marathon: 9.00–10.00.' You go, 'Are we meant to get a whole hour of this?' One thing I realized quite quickly was that the audience were very interested in sex. Up to this point, sex had not been talked about on Irish radio, except in a dry, academic sort of way. I decided very early on that if we were going to talk about orgasms, we were going to talk about how to get them and how to give them. We were not going to examine whether or not it was morally correct to pursue this particular ambition. But how to kick the whole thing off? This was in the days before texts or emails. We had a single phone line, and that provided a lot of interest, but mail was still the preferred means of contacting the show.

I would always suggest, 'Well, why don't we just make up a letter?'

Initially the reaction was, 'You can't do that – you can't make up letters.'

And I said, 'Why can't we make up letters? I mean, does anybody check it?'

And everyone would say, 'That's not the point, it's just not appropriate.'

Even the people who eventually became the most audacious *Ryan Show* researchers and producers wouldn't take what I considered to be absolutely the most logical and sensible shortcut to getting material for the programme.

And so one day I came on, and I remember looking out through the control-room window at the people I was working with, and I said to myself, 'Right, I'm not gonna read out this frigging thing they've given me to read out.'

Instead I made up a letter on the spot.

'Dear Gerry,' I began, 'I've had a terribly disturbing experience. I am an attractive, voluptuous woman and I think I have a nice personality . . .' I was trying to paint a picture of an average female listener. 'I went out to the pub one night last week, and I was talking to a group of men who I felt found me attractive. We were all getting along very well until I got up to go to the bathroom. Gerry, I was wearing quite a tight outfit and I have put on one or two extra pounds recently, but at the same time, I still thought I was looking quite well. But as I walked towards the door of the toilet, I distinctly heard one of them say, "Jaysus, look at the fat arse on that bitch . . ."'

Bingo. The phones lit up. Everybody was full of opinion. Nobody working on the show had enough time to go, 'Hold on a second, we'll have to write a report on this . . .' Suddenly they had callers, more callers than they could handle, all of whom were outraged. I remember saying, 'Have you got anybody out there who thinks she should have stayed home if she had a fat arse?' So we put up a couple of nasty people who absolutely infuriated those who had sympathy for the poor imaginary woman. So then I thought, Well, let's have this thing out. We put nice and nasty on-air together and they started shouting and screaming at one another. That was probably the first real *Gerry Ryan Show*.

After that, we didn't have to make up material. That one made-up letter became an invitation and the floodgates opened. The biggest thrill for me was when we could get three or four people together shouting and roaring at one another. I would stand back and let it go on sometimes for fifteen or twenty minutes. Too long, probably, but this was us establishing an identity. This was phase one of *The Gerry Ryan Show*. It was an extraordinarily exciting time, because the whole machine shook. I mean, you could really feel it. It was like the space-shuttle engines starting up. What's gonna happen? Is it gonna blow up? Will it get airborne? Those early years, it was touch and go from various points of view. We didn't know, and I still don't, what the Suits Upstairs made of it.

From day one, Bill O'Donovan was a kind of a self-appointed guardian in the sense that we never, ever heard what senior management thought about us. He used to lie and say they thought it was fantastic. 'Oh, they love it. They think it's just great.'

And he'd make up these complimentary things that they'd apparently said at corporate editorial board meetings. 'Groundbreaking', 'Revolutionary', 'Keep up the good work'. None of these things, it turns out, was actually said. But if we didn't know what was really being said upstairs, there was no mistaking what was being said elsewhere. In the beginning we attracted a massive amount of complaints. What was worse, people in the press and information offices were equally ill-disposed towards us. They were saying to callers, 'Yes, we know, it's terrible, isn't it?'

We were very lucky to have a chairman of the RTÉ Authority in the early years, John Sorohan, who rated the programme. He thought, This is the future. When the chairman of the Authority thinks that, it makes an incredible difference. It didn't stop the people with 'down with this sort of thing' placards, but it did prevent us being shoved over the cliff.

MELTDOWN AT SELLAFIELD

We decided we would create a scenario whereby there had been a catastrophic accident in Sellafield and the winds were right for the radioactive material to be carried across the Irish Sea. I had bought a copy of Orson Welles's *The War of the Worlds*. This was a 1938 broadcast by the Mercury Players in New York of a radio dramatization of H. G. Wells's novel. It was performed as a live newscast, as if Martians were actually landing in the city, and it completely terrified people. I remember listening to it thinking, This is absolutely phenomenal. It's almost still believable – there was just so much urgency in the performance.

In the early days of *The Gerry Ryan Show*, when the content was a lot more surreal than it is now, I really wanted to try something like *The War of the Worlds*, so we started investigating what sort of precautions the Irish authorities had in place, what the Civil Defence might do. For about a year we planned a broadcast that would start at night and run all the way through to my show. We would take over the breakfast programme and keep the thing going until twelve o'clock, when we would reveal it as a hoax. It was meticulously planned. We were going to give out dramatized instructions about what to do in the event of exposure to radiation, how to deal with dead members of your family, looting, urban chaos, social breakdown. By the time we were ready to go with it, I suspect that the *Ryan Show* nuclear meltdown plan was better thought-out than anything the government might have planned.

Bill O'Donovan was another huge fan of *The War of the Worlds*. He privately thought this was an excellent idea. To this day I don't know why he wouldn't let us go ahead with it, but I suspect he might have mentioned at one of the corporate editorial board meetings what we were planning. In any case, he said maybe we should put it on ice for a while. Subsequently we forgot about it, but that was an indication of the kind of radio I was interested in.

I still have a romantic hankering for that sort of broadcasting, but one thing I've discovered is that when you're dealing with mass audiences, there's a moment when you have to decide whether you want to be the Mercury Players or the most rockin' show of all time.

In the end, we decided to be the most rockin' show of all time.

17

THE GERRY RYAN SHOW

I've always liked being in the public eye.

I've got opinions that, while they're not that well worked out, they're strong and passionately held, and I masquerade them as truths, or at least as pillars of conviction.

There's no point in having these passionately held opinions and a desire to disseminate them without an audience. The audience can be your immediate family, but that gets a bit tiresome after a while. There's a certain type of man out there who spends his entire life treating his family to his intellect and opinions and, to be honest, I can't think of anything worse. It's absolute purgatory to live through something like that. In fairness, my own family lived through some of it, but there was always a safety valve: I had this enormous other family I could speak to and who were always supportive of my right to speak on anything, from the fall of the Third Reich to vaginal secretions to Lavinia Kerwick's rape. The variety of things that are spoken about, the churches that are visited, the different platforms upon which we base debate on *The Gerry Ryan Show* are phenomenal. There is nowhere that we do not go. If, like me, you have a compulsion to communicate, debate, argue and speechify, there's no better place in the world.

I am the first person to say that if there aren't people listening, there's no point in broadcasting, so I try to mix the surreal, the prurient, the pornographic, the vile, the headless chicken running around in a circle with serious debate. I think that brings a lot of people to the party who mightn't otherwise be there. You hope that it will entertain people, that it will give them food for thought and force them into a debate about something that matters.

Do you know what? Maybe that doesn't happen.

You have to put food on the table, you have to get by, whether you're Randolph Hearst or G. Ryan. That's a given. After that, it's really about leaving something behind that people will re-member, or that has at least been a positive experience. I've been hugely blessed that I've been given a chance to say things, that I've been given a platform on which to stand. There's huge potential for both good and bad in that. I can go as low as the lowest common denominator or I can go as high as the best public servant. Which direction I take is entirely up to me. I can find myself drifting into mediocrity, successfully entertaining people but doing nothing of any value. So now I've arrived at a mixture of trying to tell the truth about things as I see them and acting the maggot to get the cheap laugh. The thing is, everybody remembers the cheap laugh. That's quite worrying.

I say, 'What about that thing I did on female genital muti-lation?'

'What? What's female genital mutilation?'

'Well, I was only talking about it for a week . . .'

Then I did 'Can You Fart the National Anthem?'

Everyone remembers that.

In broadcasting, ambition is about reinvention. Really that's the biggest challenge, to continue to be relevant. It means reassessing your position, looking at the format, not being afraid to dump dimensions of your delivery or personality that are no longer working. You've got to reinvent constantly to speak to fourteen-year-olds and seventy-year-olds equally. That's a huge challenge. You're never going to see your ambition fulfilled because your audience is dying and is being born and it's going through mid-life crises. There are so many different dimensions to the *Ryan Show* audience, and everything is happening simultaneously, in terms of demographics, in terms of the age groups, in terms of the gender breakdown.

At the end of the day I think I'm a politician. I'm utterly driven to convince people of my way. I'm driven to convince people that my opinion is the correct opinion, that I can save them, that I can make their lives better, that my analysis of something is the right analysis, and that I will make you smile and I'll make you laugh, and I'll tell you what's right and what's wrong. That, I think, is the vanity of the politician and I have it in spades.

THEY COULD HAVE JUST SHIT ON IT

You can't just say 'cunt', 'fuck', 'shite', 'Down with the pope' and think you've got a show. That doesn't work. It didn't take us long to realize that the first thing you must have is chutzpah. You must have the willingness not to be affected by the organization's expectations of how you're going to behave. From day one on the radio show we had no interest in anything other than the law. All we had was the Broadcasting Act and our ambition.

We decided we were going to form a band, get a good manager, go on tour and sing the songs we wanted to sing. G. Ryan would speak extempore, he would be allowed to give his opinion. We wouldn't use the normal protocols for balancing out a discussion, we would be provocative; we would take a stance on issues. We would campaign.

These were all anathema to RTÉ.

We were going to be opinionated; we were going to be prurient. Adolescent sexual curiosity would be expressed on a daily basis, and hopefully we were going to change opinions, whether they were religious ideas, moral principles or political affiliations. Those were our ambitions. We've met some of them, we haven't met others but, contrary to what some people think, we were given great latitude and support by RTÉ. Not by everybody in RTÉ, but by enough people to keep the thing on-air because the simple truth is that the *Ryan Show* could not have been kept on-air if RTÉ hadn't wanted it. I mean, if RTÉ had wanted to stop *The Gerry Ryan Show*, it would have just shit on it. It would have been there on a Friday and gone on Monday.

Bill O'Donovan was head of Radio 2, as it was called, at the time. He used to say he was presiding over a Golden Era in Broadcasting. I remember thinking, I wonder what he means. Is he talking about us? And he was talking about us. He had a great nose for radio, a great nose for talent. He wanted to get the *Ryan Show* on-air. He didn't understand completely what it was any more than I did, but he was convinced it would fly. He wanted to go down in history as the man who made it happen, and there was an awful lot involved in making it happen. It's one thing to be the director, the producer, the researcher, the presenter. It's an entirely different thing to be the guy who goes to corporate editorial board meetings every week and tries to convince a collection of guys from completely different backgrounds that his vision of widescreen radio is going to fly.

RTÉ, not unlike the BBC, is all about innovation. When the commercial guys look at digital, they go, 'Ah, it's too expensive.'

RTÉ is developing it. We do things other people are afraid to do. I know at the time I thought even our supporters in management were fuddy-duddy grey suits, but when I look back at some of them, guys like John Sorohan, Vincent Finn . . . They were conservative people who were absolutely determined that if there was anything to this new-fangled *Ryan Show* thing, it would get the full support of the organization. They were very capable civil servants who would ensure that you were protected until you had spread your wings . . . or not. There is a popular delusion among media commentators that there were a couple of wildly liberal left-of-field guys, a minority of people in RTÉ who supported the *Gerry Ryan* project. There weren't. Our real supporters were the conservative leaders of the organization who had decided to buy into it because they believed that if anybody was going to be doing this new thing it should be RTÉ.

I AM THE MINISTER FOR EVERYTHING

Lavinia Kerwick was raped, and when the guy who was convicted of the rape was given a suspended sentence, she and her family were extremely upset. Under normal circumstances the affair would have remained deep within the middle pages of the broadsheets. It mightn't even have made it into the tabloids. Lavinia might have appealed it, she might have fled the country; she might just have returned home to Kilkenny and tried to get on with things. Instead she decided to ring *The Gerry Ryan Show* and tell me.

We were in a different studio from the one we're in now. In Studio CC1 there was another, separate studio between me and the control room. It made for a very unsatisfactory and ineffectual work environment because I had to look through another room to see the people I was working with. But on this day, despite that acreage of space between me and those who were producing and directing the programme, we were connected by Threads of Gold.

Lavinia came on and told her story. For the first time it occurred to me that maybe the story was more important than the question. Keep quiet, just listen, let her speak. It was an absolutely sensational experience. She wasn't ringing a news programme, she hadn't written to the editor of a newspaper, she wasn't telling a counsellor or a lawyer. She was telling Gerry Ryan, and telling Gerry Ryan was significant for her. Why? She trusted me, she believed that was the right thing to do, that people would hear about her story and maybe something might come of her telling me. I know, too, from talking to her afterwards that she found it therapeutic to unburden herself. But in public? How could that be therapeutic? How could it be psychologically good for you to unburden yourself in public? I don't know.

Within that tiny space between the microphone and the telephone, there was nobody except me and the other person, and a whole country listening in.

People were stopped in their tracks. The laughter earlier in the show was forgotten instantly. You couldn't but be compelled by Lavinia's pain, and subliminally the message was, *She's telling Gerry*. It was like some sort of rite of passage for the programme. It made people think, Well, it's a great laugh, it's a bit of fun, he talks about his family, he has a lot of opinions, he's a bit of an eejit, he's a bit narcissistic, but do you know what? When we've got something important to say, he's the man. We're going to tell him.

Lavinia opened the floodgates. At that moment, everything changed. At that moment, I gained a credibility that the schoolboy Gerry Ryan didn't have. Now, all of a sudden, I had a signpost pointing to me, and people in similar circumstances all over the country were calling to tell me their stories. Suddenly hundreds were unburdening themselves on the airwaves.

I can't actually tell you to this day how powerful an effect Lavinia Kerwick's call had on me, on the show and the people working on it. It was the moment when I felt I'd been elected.

I am the Minister for Everything.

Now, there's a bad dimension to that as well. I'm not elected. I have no psychological training. I'm a failed lawyer. Articulate, maybe, but in that moment, I became absolutely convinced that I was a significant figure.

The reaction was absolutely huge. That was where the symbiosis between the print media and the radio programme began. The print guys were on to the story in a flash and it ran for months afterwards.

Lavinia became a friend of one of the producers on the programme, Joan Torsney. I remember the time she came up to Dublin to meet us. By now she had developed anorexia as a result of her ordeal. Joan arranged to meet her in Furama, a Chinese restaurant. That suited me fine because it was quite a good restaurant. I remember when Lavinia had gone to the bathroom, I said to Joan, 'What's she gonna eat?'

Joan hadn't thought about this. 'Oh, Christ,' she said, 'I can't believe I've done this.'

'It's fine,' I said, 'it's cool.'

I suppose it told you all you needed to know about the *Ryan Show* that we'd bring an anorexic to a Chinese restaurant. When Lavinia came back, I said, 'Well, I suppose you won't be eating much . . .'

But it was fine, in a bizarre way. Lavinia Kerwick was happy that day, sitting with me as I stuffed my face. I had this fantastic shredded chicken they do in Furama. She ate nothing because she was an anorexic. She had nothing à la King.

We used to call her Slim, which she was totally cool about.

THE LIFEBLOOD OF THE PROGRAMME

The Gerry Ryan Show is run very much like a newspaper. First of all, Murphy's Law dictates that if you don't have a full agenda, a complete running order, the whole thing is going to fall apart. Every day we could do a full programme between callers from the previous day who didn't get on, organized guests, celebrity book reviews, pieces that have been prepared months in advance. You could do an entire programme with the sheet, and if you don't have that, you're fucked. Nothing happens. But if you're well prepared, you can throw it in the bin and do whatever comes up.

More often that not, the audience decides the agenda for the day. As we've got older and the audience has got bigger, we've had to get more sophisticated. The music must be varied, the items must be varied. We have to be on our game in terms of political analysis. The amount of information that's required to stoke the boilers of the show is absolutely gigantic. That means I start the morning by listening to *Morning Ireland*, BBC Radio 4, Terry Wogan. Colm and Jim-Jim, my compatriots on before me, are my light relief. They're my parachute when I become irritated by the news, so I often end up cramming like mad before I go on.

One of the joys of working with people who've been with you for a long time is the telepathy that develops between you. Sometimes it's difficult to figure out who came up with an idea. The best feeling of all is when nobody gives a shit who it was; the only thing that matters is that it got on-air, and that we were either there first or we did it better than the next guy.

Our two broadcasting assistants, Helen and Lorraine, have been there from day one. They filter the calls, texts and emails. Their instinct is second to none. They know exactly what the producer is going to want and, more importantly, they know what's going to work with me. The hit on calls, emails and texts now is phenomenal; the workload has increased threefold since we started. Twenty years ago, we didn't have texts or emails. You might get one fax per programme from a government minister to contradict something you'd said. The broadcasting assistants have a very tough job, very tough indeed if you're talking about something significant like child abuse or rape. Recently, one of our researchers took a phone call from a guy actually in the process of committing suicide. She got in touch with the local guards, who found him sitting in his car with a hose running from the exhaust in through the window. The only thing I wanted to know was why she didn't put him on-air.

There are thousands of texts and emails. The phone calls are the most primitive part of it but also the most important because they're the voice of the show. At the end of the day, it's the person who calls in with a hugely powerful or strong opinion or who has something very special to tell us who really gets the thing going. They're the lifeblood of the programme.

Recently a woman rang in about her teenage daughter who was suicidal. She was at the end of her tether dealing with the girl's depression, and was getting no help whatsoever from the HSE. This is the kind of story that Joe often features on *Liveline*. We got in touch with the HSE, and our intervention secured a level of support for that family that they just were not getting on their own. This kind of thing is pretty much the staple diet of *Liveline*. Sometimes we start something on the programme and it blooms later in the day or the week on *Liveline*. And sometimes it happens in reverse. Joe's programme will kick something off and the story will mature on the *Ryan Show*.

Then there are those who come on because they're members, basically, of the *Ryan Show* community, and they're there to answer a question, like where you can buy a certain face cream. Or explain a particular piece of terminology. These people are quite happy to make a very brief appearance on the programme, and in so doing, they feel part of the family. Then there are others who like to shock and entertain, and they're part of the family too. And there are the Takers, the people who are constantly angling for free stuff. LOADS of greed in the *Ryan Show* audience.

SOMETIMES I GET IT WRONG

We had a perfect example of a *Ryan Show* caller today. Somebody rang about hyperhidrosis. That's excessive sweating from your feet, the palms of your hands, or even your groin. This, of course, has LOTS of *Gerry Ryan* dimensions to it. First of all, it's a

Real Medical Condition. And, judging from the very substantial reaction, loads of people suffer from hyperhidrosis. And besides it being a Real Medical Condition, it's also . . . kind of weird. You imagine people with sweat flooding from their armpits and their groins and their feet, and being just so covered with it that their shoe leather disintegrates within a day. Then there was the surgery dimension. The *Ryan Show* community LOVES surgery. The more graphic the descriptions the better. The idea that somebody got so compromised by hyperhidrosis that he *succumbed* to surgery to have *glands* taken out! Even the word *Glands*.

Sometimes I get it wrong.

We were talking recently about blood transfusions and Jehovah's Witnesses, the fact that their religion forbids it. There was a case at the time about a mother carrying twins. They had a condition, a type of anaemia that would require blood transfusions to keep them alive. Anyway, a caller came on, God love her. She said that members of her family were Jehovah's Witnesses and they were lovely people. She said she totally respected her sister-in-law's wishes when it came to blood transfusion.

So I said, 'If your sister-in-law wanted to refuse her child a blood transfusion, in the certain knowledge that the child was going to die without it, what would you think of that?'

'I'd accept it,' she said. 'I'd abide by their wishes.'

And I got so angry I just utterly lost it. I didn't mince my words in letting her know exactly how wrong-headed she was, and told her that, frankly, to deny an infant a life-saving procedure was outrageous.

She got very upset.

This woman was a *Ryan Show* fan. The last thing on God's earth she expected was for Gerry Ryan to light into her. Now, on that occasion, I was very lucky. That day I touched a nerve in relation to the way the public felt about the issue, and even though I didn't think it out, I got it completely right. Most of the audience felt exactly as I did. And some of the people who came on afterwards and backed up what I'd said were even more forceful and aggressive in their language. But I should not have lost my temper. You can't rush in shouting and screaming and roaring about everything. That gets very old very quickly. Look at Jerry Springer. Everyone else might be screaming and shouting on his show, but he's always very relaxed. He knows that losing his temper is something he has to be very, very careful about. You'll find quite ordinary people who don't have strong opinions about Gerry Ryan will develop extremely strong negative opinions very quickly if they think I'm being arrogant or attacking somebody for fun.

I think on every talk show, particularly a radical talk show, you always fear that somebody is going slander someone else, or say something awful about you. And the thing is, it doesn't really matter whether it's true or not. Imagine somebody getting on-air and making something up.

'You raped my sister in 1978. I'll never forgive you.'

How do you come back from that? 'Well, of course,' you say, 'that's completely ridiculous, and I'm suing the guy.'

But all that's left in the public mind is the comment. This fear puts a brake on everything, because if you can see yourself in that compromised position, you'll see the potential for everyone else to be in that position too.

WOMEN 101

We had a great female listenership right from the beginning. There was no genius in that. It was just that I talked about things that no one else did. I understand gynaecology. I understand childbirth. I understand childcare. I understand about makeup. I understand about female hygiene. I understand about erectile dysfunction. I understand that women want to have orgasms. Women don't want episiotomies. They do want epidurals. They want to figure out how you can have an epidural and not end up tearing . . .

I wasn't afraid to discuss this.

They wanted to discuss vaginoplasty. Are their vaginas as attractive as when they were young women? Maybe the labia major have fallen, and they need to be taken back a bit. Who else was gonna discuss this? Nobody else was gonna discuss this. For better or worse I knew about this stuff and I was willing to talk about it, and I was surrounded by women who were willing to back it up and pursue it. And I was married to a woman who wasn't embarrassed that I was talking about it on the radio.

Women were hearing about these issues for the very first time.

I'm fascinated by women. I love women's company, and I relate well to women. When you have that kind of experience with women, there is a temptation to believe that you understand them. Earlier in my life, I thought I understood women. I thought I'd done enough homework in terms of the feminist movement to understand the politics of it. I thought I understood the biochemistry. But in actual fact, I don't understand anything whatsoever about women. I'm no more enlightened than any other man about women, and I believe there are very few men, if any, who actually genuinely understand what women are about.

I appeal to women because I know how to speak to them.

That's a male thing. It's not the feminine coming out. It is a strategic analysis of the other sex, undertaken consciously or unconsciously. Probably unconsciously. I understand from a strategic point of view what makes them tick, the things they like to hear. That doesn't mean I understand intellectually or emotionally. I'm just scratching the surface. I will say this in my defence: I think I have a much better ability than a lot of other men when it comes to having a conversation with a woman, or anticipating what her reaction is going to be. I understand a selection of things that upset, annoy or excite women. That is a completely different thing from understanding the heartbeat of a woman.

It took me a huge part of my life, for instance, to understand how women can be utterly transfixed by something like fidelity in a man. In essence, women celebrate the truth to a much greater degree than men do. Men are strategic about how they use truth. They will use it to get out of a corner, to inveigle themselves into something, to extract themselves from something, to tantalize, to excite, to obfuscate, to blank. Women, even though they may do all of those things, celebrate truth to a much greater extent.

That's not to say that I think women are intrinsically better. In fact, I think if the truth be known, the simplicity of men makes me feel, at this late stage in my life, that maybe men are a safer bet. I've often wondered what would it be like to be gay. One gay friend of mine says it's great. You can have sex, and then you can go out for a pint with a guy who knows what you're talking about, who understands you, who isn't going to try and second-guess you. Then you can come home and watch *Band of Brothers* and have more sex.

It sounds very attractive.

WOMEN, KNOW YOUR LIMITS

I don't think I've been emotionally reliable and dependable to the women in my life. And it's that very capacity, that you disappoint them, that continually makes women want to offer you the opportunity to step up to the plate. This is their tragedy: I Can Change Him. It's a challenge that men too frequently accept without understanding the consequences.

My father's generation worked on the premise that women were basically slaves to the male ideology. My mother was extremely unhappy to have to give up her job and Dad was really quite conservative; he certainly didn't believe that his wife should be out working. He wanted somebody to stay at home, make the dinner, look after the children and, most importantly, agree with him. It didn't make him a bad man. That was the template from which he was drawn. My father's generation was the last to believe that men were in control. We had witnessed our fathers trying to keep women at home, trying to make them sexually compliant. There's that great Harry Enfield sketch 'Women, Know Your Limits', which beautifully describes the fear when women begin to disagree with the status quo.

Then my generation came along and there was all this new thinking about how women were to be treated. But, really, the only experience we'd had was watching our fathers, and our fathers were still coming home and expecting their dinners to be on the table. They were the ones driving the cars. My father took three minutes to drive his Jaguar XJ6 from home to his place of work, whereas my mother went to the shops to get the groceries on a bicycle. A *bicycle*. That's what I was watching. So it didn't matter how much Richard Neville I read or how much Andrea Dworkin seeped into my psyche. At the end of the day, the only experience I had was of men telling women what to do. So when we ended up in the midst of the cultural mélange that the seventies produced in Ireland, we were incredibly confused. We had to pretend we were liberal and celebrate a new generation of independent women when all we really wanted were compliant women who would cook the dinner.

VIVE LA DIFFÉRENCE!

I do believe that men and women are very different. We all have the same ambitions. We want to be happy. We want to be healthy. Men and women want to be celebrated and cherished and loved and taken care of, but we're utterly different.

Utterly and completely different.

I didn't believe that for my entire life. There was a lot of negative stuff around men through the sixties, people like Valerie Solanas from the Society for Cutting Up Men, and the widely accepted truth that a man will do anything to get to a friendly fanny. The original feminist movement had to be very aggressive. Some of my best friends when I was in university were girls in feminist societies like Bell Jar, but if I'm honest, when I look back at it, I was probably more intrigued by the challenge they presented rather than the solutions they offered.

Despite the fact that we may not be as bright as women, despite the fact that we may not be able to multi-task, despite the fact that we may not be as sophisticated in our emotional responses, guys have one component that continues to facilitate success. Single-mindedness. Whether it's hunting or trying to close the deal, men tend to be single-minded in the way we pursue our ambitions. Women are not single-minded. A guy will never be able to resist the opportunity to take advancement in his job. Women are capable of turning down advancement in favour of less stress, raising a family, or just expanding their horizons and doing something completely different. Women do not allow themselves to be described by their job. You ask a guy what he is, and he will say that he's a pilot, or a dustman. A woman will have a much more complex description of herself.

It's the complexity versus the single-mindedness that causes the problems. The ability of women not just to multi-task but also to think on several planes at once makes them difficult to access, difficult to understand and highly mystical creatures in the eyes of men, because there's a multiple-personality dimension to most women. Men find it very difficult to figure out exactly who they're talking to. There's the nurturer. There's the creator. There's the fighter. There's the lover. There are so many different characteristics that a woman can present, and those characteristics can be amplified and accentuated by the menstrual cycle, by the way she's dealt with and responded to. I think women can be absolutely terrifying. I think they can be hugely challenging. I think they can be amazingly destructive. The power of the feminine is absolutely grotesque when it gets out of control.

Men, on the other side, are slovenly and lazy from an emotional point of view. I think that the best thing we can do is stand back, pause, relax and begin to teach ourselves and our children that maybe celebration of the difference between ourselves and women would be better than trying to force each other into a mould that just doesn't fit.

Some guys can fake the feminine quite well. They're usually men who have been around women a lot, or who've had a strong relationship with their mother. These are the guys who understand the menstrual cycle, the moon, the twenty-eight days, the different shapes and sizes of moods. They're the guys who can celebrate that, who can see the different things that can happen in the space even of a few hours with a woman. If you give off some sense that you understand that, and that you're capable of buying into it, that you're not shocked by it, I think women become very excited. The problem is can you go to second base? Can you say, 'Well, I'm willing to live with this. I'm willing to accept this as a regular feature of my day'?

You will inevitably seek refuge in the Premiership, the war film, the company of men, the pint of stout, the Led Zeppelin album, and you will pray to be delivered from the menstrual cycle.

Ultimately, propagation of the species is at the heart of everything. At the end of the day, the premise is Shag Girl – Make Her Pregnant.

You can pour as much intellect on that as you wish, but the premise remains undiminished. Once you accept that, and you've a sense of humour about it, you can begin to understand the forces that are driving and compromising you. Really, I think, a lot of the time even the brightest of us would be better off just going with instinct. And if you stick with a few basics – don't be cruel to anybody, don't be vicious, be supportive, be courageous – you'll be fine. It's only when you over-intellectualize the whole thing, or when it turns into a sort of cultural battle royal that you get into trouble. Or when somebody's got a frigging point to make. That's the worst ever.

You must have respect, understanding and a sense of humour. Those three things will get you through what has turned into an incredibly sophisticated dance.

TOXIC EAU-DE-VIE

In the last few years, we've witnessed the emergence of a highly sexually predatory young woman who's out there to get fucked, who's out there to humiliate and make fun of the man she comes into contact with. She's drinking a lot. She's taking a lot of drugs.

She's rocking and rolling. She's dressing in a very provocative way and she's having a good time. And when men complain about this, women say, 'Well, fuck you. We've had to deal with this for centuries.'

But the truth is that women have had to deal with something much more Goliath than that. They've had to deal with an entire society that was designed socially, legally and culturally to keep them out of the frame. Up until relatively recently, they couldn't constitute the government. They couldn't constitute a jury. They were effectively barred from business, from banking, from all of the different institutions that defined and described where society went. Those doors have been opened. The invitation is there for women to do what they want.

But the biggest noise has been made socially. These young women have distilled hedonistic behaviour into a very toxic eau-de-vie. This is shocking for young men in particular. They really don't know what to do with it, and I think that that's a dangerous place for us to be. I'm not quite sure what the scrum is going to create. Is it going to be better for our daughters, for our sons? I look at my eldest son. He's a very strong-willed young man, but I think his generation will probably distance themselves quite a bit further from women than my generation did. Their antennae are up. Their self-preservation instincts are telling them to keep back.

I think they'll seek the company of men more. I think they'll be much more conservative about how they get involved in relationships. I think they'll be less likely to commit themselves emotionally. And I think they'll be much more suspicious of the ambitions of their female peers.

Is that good? Where does that bring us? I don't know.

WHAT THE WORLD ROTATES ON

My instinct is that sex is pretty much at the very heart of everything people do. I believe it's probably the most significant component in everybody's life, if not through its presence then its absence. For better or worse, it drives people to an enormous degree, so how could you avoid having it in the mix? It comes naturally. It's not something we had to work on – people are transfixed by sex.

Marian Finucane was the first person to talk about the female orgasm on *Liveline*. She broke the hymen of the whole thing. Gay Byrne had talked about sex on *The Late Late Show* but those discussions and debates were very clinical and very mature. I was determined that when we spoke about sex, if it required a gentle, understanding, empathetic hand, that was what I'd give it. I have a certain amount of knowledge about the subject. I was quite willing to expose my own sexuality, my own doubts, joys and fears. I would allow people to ask me questions about myself – and I found that an incredibly liberating experience. It was also very liberating for the audience because they thought, Well, I'm in the same boat as Gerry. But on other occasions, there's only one way to talk about sex, and that's in a boyish, adolescent way. That works equally well *when the time is right*. And that's when you can have a lot of fun with it. We often do.

On-air, I had no qualms about using the word 'vagina' or 'pussy'. These were simply descriptions of the very essence of women, these were topics that they had not had a chance to discuss before. They had never before talked in public about the über-magnet of the world: PUSSY. This is what the whole frigging thing *rotates* on. I acknowledged that there was this huge power in women, that there were huge conflicts in relation to the way that this power was expressed, the issues and problems associated with being a woman – because being a woman is much more physically complex than being a man. And I think that when we unleashed that on the airwaves, women became emboldened and excited by it. I think they became sexually aroused by it, and still to this day I feel that women are sexually aroused by being able to stand up and talk about their vaginas, or that their husband never touched their breasts properly, or whatever it is. They know that Gerry isn't gonna be shocked. He will understand.

How did all of this vaginal on-air banter go over at home? I never really talked about it. I think my daughters were probably quite squeamish about it. My wife never mentioned it. That was as much support as I needed. My mother and my mother-in-law have been huge parallel influences in my life over the last twenty years. I think both women, Noreen and Maureen, were hugely proud that I was on the radio and that I had achieved such a high profile, and both were very defensive if anybody criticized me. And I think they probably just put their fingers in their ears and whistled 'Supercalifragilisticexpialidocious' when vaginal secretions were mentioned.

We, meanwhile, believed that we were broadcasting the *Kama Sutra*. The audience were having sex with us, and men were dipping in and out of it, kind of skirting it, flitting round it like sperms round the egg. I think that a lot more men listened to the programme than people actually realized.

We reached the plateau that we'd always been subconsciously aiming for one morning when we'd been talking about the lack of sex in a relationship, and the problems it can create. This woman, a well-spoken upper-middle-class woman, came on the air, and she talked about how sex was a huge dimension to her life, and that there wasn't enough in it, and that she'd been masturbating.

'Have you masturbated already today?' I asked her.

And she said, in an even voice, 'Yes, I've masturbated. I've just come, just before I've spoken to you.'

And it was absolutely electrifying. She didn't say it in a salacious way. She was calm, measured, understated, but she wanted to expose herself. She wanted to talk about her sex, about the essence of her. She wanted to say it to everybody, and she knew that there was only one place she could do that. It was incredibly empowering for us, because there was no other point, or rationale, or rhyme or reason to what had happened. This woman had come on the air and said, 'I've just masturbated. I've just come.'

This was a woman who was having a crisis in her sex life. She wanted to tell the world: I Am Alive. My Sexual Heartbeat Is Strong. And that was all there was to it. There was no need to go into any more detail. But it was amazing to hear somebody in a moderate tone say that she had just done this thing and she'd done it because she had to. It was a cry for recognition. It was showing off. It was lust. It was a whole host of things. Most especially, it was the kind of thing that you normally don't hear on the radio.

Of course, the shock threshold has changed completely since we started delving into all this stuff. People are no longer frightened or shocked by the language of the show, at least not to the extent they once were. There's probably less use of expletives now because you don't really need it, but I think the sexual dimension to the programme is intact. That, I think, will never change. People are as demanding, as shy and as confused about their sexuality as they ever were. The discussion has broadened now to include things like reproduction, infertility and sexual plastic surgery. Which is not to say we've matured: there's always room to go back and be adolescent and be bold when it comes to sex, but we do get a chance to talk about it in more serious tones, particularly where we're dealing with sexual dysfunction. And we can talk about it with authority now because we're past the whole fanny thing.

We've certainly seen a lot of change in people's general attitudes to sex too. Right through the population, right through the age and gender divide, and I think we've been responsible for pushing some of that. Certainly, talking about sex in the early days, and talking about it in a humorous way, opened up the debate. The number of times that people have come on the air and quietly asked a question about sex. Was such and such normal? What did I think? What did the audience think about something that happened? The lack of sex in a marriage, or too much, or I don't like sex and I'm ashamed that I don't, and how do I deal with that? Is it me? Or is it my partner? Am I gay because I don't like heterosexual sex? Or have I just not met the right person?

There's an endless list of questions that are usually only asked introspectively. If you're lucky, you can ask a friend or a lover. But if those options aren't open to you, for whatever reason, people feel that they can come and ask us. Many people do, and I know from the tone of their voice that they aren't doing it for the crack. They're not doing it to show off. These are people with what may be deep phobias, or self-doubt. And sometimes they're just very celebratory, and they want to come out and just shout to the rooftops that they are alive and well and proud of their sexuality.

I think we've helped to drive that.

FIFTY-TWO VULVAS AND ONE PENIS

Eventually I arrived at a point when I went, 'Right, fifty-two vulvas, it's time for a penis.' It was time to start injecting war films, the Premiership, some unstintingly unreliable male qualities into the mix.

I went, 'Yeah. That's fantastic. That's very interesting about vaginal secretions, but last night I watched three episodes of *Band of Brothers*, and here's why I really enjoyed it.'

I think it must've been quite interesting for women, and I'd love to have been in their heads when I explained why I was fascinated by aviation and military things, why I was obsessed with sport and gadgetry. This came spontaneously from me. It didn't come from the female researchers or producers on the programme. While the template was still there, while there was still lots for women to relate to, I began over the years to inject more and more male things, more sperm, into the mix because why not? Why not let them get a sense of the male? Why not help the female listenership towards an understanding of why a man is willing to watch a war film? Why the opening sequence in *Saving Private Ryan* can bring a man to tears.

I hope that women were generous enough to listen to this, in the same way that men had had to put up with listening to G. Ryan talk about the vulva for so long. I hope that women listened, if only to try and figure out why their husband needed fifteen minutes to himself when he came home from work, why he wasn't capable of listening to a story about the children going berserk, or why he wasn't able to address the problem of the broken cooker immediately, why he needed a quarter of an hour to go into his cave and scratch his balls and come back out again.

ICE PACKS ON MY BALLS

I can't ask people to discuss their most intimate issues without revealing at least something of myself. Obviously there are things that I will never reveal because there must be a private person. If there is no private person, there is no person.

I decided to get a vasectomy for very personal reasons. I don't believe that a woman should have to undergo a major operation like a tubal ligation if the man in the relationship can do something that's much safer and more straightforward. Of course, in my case, the irony is that it turned out not so straightforward as everyone said it would be. It went badly wrong, much to the amusement of the women in my life.

I woke up in Tallaght Hospital, groggy and very, very sore. I remember thinking, Hang on, nobody mentioned pain, nobody – as they surrounded my balls with ice packs – mentioned anything about sheer, unadulterated agony. So I went home, and the wound became infected, which was incredibly not nice. Subsequently, I had to go back and have further treatment. Eventually everything worked out fine.

It wasn't until about a year after the whole thing was done and dusted that I realized, That's it, my baby-making days are over. One day in the office we were talking about fertility issues and I came away from the conversation thinking, I'm never going to make anybody pregnant ever again.

It wasn't quite the menopause, it was just a moment: *This is a bummer.*

I remembered the fantastic celebration that had been involved in making all five of my children. And what that moment gave me was an insight into what it must be like when a woman comes to the menopause, when she is no longer capable of creating children. And at least I have five. And I should say that I found it quite sad *on the day.*

It didn't last for too long.

IS IT POSSIBLE TO BE FRIENDS WITH A WOMAN?

If you can get over the sexual chemistry between men and women and park it, you can create very powerful alliances and friendships that are much more powerful than male friendships. This, however, rarely happens because men are cretins and usually succumb to the chemical imperative. Driven by the chemicals, they will pursue the woman and compromise the relationship.

When it comes to working with women, there should always be some sort of frisson because that's what men and women are about. I mean, I always calibrate the whole male–female thing in an adolescent way. When you're on the bus and you're fourteen, every single girl who goes by, you're going, *Yes, no, yes, no, yes, yes, no.*

Every guy does that. *Yes, no, yes, yes, yes, no* . . . Then something else comes along – you're distracted by bright lights or the

Granby's Pork Sausages ad but, basically, the constant backdrop to the male vista is, *Yes, no, yes, no.*

So now you're working. You're an adult. You're not fourteen. But the *yes, no* thing's still there. You just have to get through it and park it.

WELL, AH, HOW'S THAT OTHER SITUATION?

I just love the insincerity of men. Our incomprehension, our inconsistency and our lack of understanding. If only the anal-penetration thing wasn't such a no for me, the gay thing has a lot going for it.

Shagging and pints sounds good to me. But, unfortunately, the anal-penetration thing, no thanks.

Since the break-up of my marriage, some of the best moments I've had have been with my male pals watching a movie, usually about the Third Reich or something like that. Then, at the end, they go, 'Well, ah, how's that other situation?'

And you go, 'Oh, not too bad.'

And they go, 'Oh, right. Excellent. OK.'

It's amazing the total lack of articulation you find in incredibly articulate and eloquent men. I had a wonderful conversation recently with a new friend, John Banville, who was introduced to me by Harry Crosbie. We were having lunch together and I think, I'm not entirely sure, but I think we were talking about my current situation, and it was very much nod, nod, nudge, nudge. Here is one of our foremost writers, a genius of description and eloquence, but in that pursing of the lips, bowing of the head, touching of the elbow, he said more than a whole gospel.

THE PERFECT WOMAN

I watched the remake of *Stepford Wives* with my two sons. Those glamorous, utterly controllable robots: you have sex on demand, no backchat, no guff, constant praise for the menfolk . . .

The three of us looked at one another and kind of went, 'Well, what's so bad about that?'

And even though, you know, this is utterly the wrong thing to say, and we must never suggest such a thing in front of our sisters, our mum or, in fact, anybody else in the community, I think when men watch that film, a large proportion of them is thinking, What the fuck's wrong with that? Looks pretty good to me.

But, of course, the world wouldn't be as Exciting, Rich and Vibrant if that were the case. (Sigh.)

THE PERFECT MAN

There's no such thing as a perfect man either.

Women love consistency. Honesty is something they treasure. Men realize this too late in their middle-aged adolescence. I believe that women, no matter who they are, want to be protected. They don't want to be overwhelmed, they don't want to be cosseted or suffocated, but they do want to be protected. They want to be entertained. They adore humour. But they also want a patient man. Even if you don't fully comprehend what's happening in front of you, you should be able to give a woman space so that she can work the issue out in all her glorious complexity. And then, maybe at the end, you'll be invited to the party and you'll find out what on earth all that was about . . .

THE ROMANCE OF THE IRISH MALE

Irish men have become much more sophisticated than their fore-fathers were. In John B. Keane's Ireland, the fact that you could put bread, butter and tea on the table, and a roof overhead, was romance. The fact that you had a donkey and cart was romance. These days, of course, bread and butter, tea, accommodation and donkeys are more easily available so more subtle factors come into play. Even the most successful, the most powerful, the most dogmatic, the most ambitious women harbour a desire to be wooed, to be taken care of, to be wined and dined, to be treated like princesses. That's not to say they want to be subjugated or controlled or led. Romance really is to gaze upon somebody, to adore them, to be fascinated by them. And if that means champagne, dinner, going to a play that you're hopelessly incapable of understanding, if it means sitting by your partner's side, nodding and smiling blindly at her delight over Maeve Binchy's *Circle of Friends*, then so be it. It's indulging, really. That's what romance is. It's indulging her.

ARSE WAXING AND THE BIRMINGHAM SIX

Young people have always wanted a uniform. When I was seventeen, it was loon jeans and T-shirts, Wranglers and long hair. When I look back at pictures of myself at that age, we all seemed to look like members of the Birmingham Six. But that was the uniform. It was a style of sorts.

My eighteen-year-old boy is going to his graduation dance in a fortnight, and he's talking about getting himself a dark Italian lounge suit. When I was eighteen, I didn't own a suit. I rented tuxedos on occasion or borrowed them, more likely, from Bourke's Costumiers, my mother's family business. I was quite stylish, or at least I had an affected style, which was kind of a mixture between Bryan Ferry, David Bowie and John Lennon.

But I look at my kids' generation, and they've taken it to a whole new level. Rex is incredibly well groomed. He's very conscious of the names – Hugo Boss, Calvin Klein, Roberto Cavalli. He wants to go to Louis Copeland to get the suit. He has some ideas about the cut. He can tell the difference between a Charvet shirt and Dunnes best. OK, maybe at the end of the day there isn't that much difference, but he understands there should be. He knows how to mix and match colours and styles, and what's appropriate for one occasion and not for another.

And I don't think he's that desperately unusual. He does come from a kind of high-profile family; maybe he's been exposed to fashion a little more than the average young fella, but I see a lot of his friends with similar ambitions.

They don't always get it right. I'm quite dismayed to see the mullet making a comeback among that generation. Kind of hard to figure that one out. It just shows you that the sins of the fathers can be often repeated, particularly when it comes to style or fashion. But I do think that Irish men are better groomed than they were when I was a young man. Hygiene is much improved. So is hair styling. Men's use of vanity products has increased 1,000 per cent. Men are no longer afraid to consider things like waxing and personal spa treatments. If you suggested when I was nineteen or twenty that you were going off to get your back or your arse waxed, you'd have been committed.

IT'S SORT OF A ROCK-STAR-CUM-DERMOT-GAVIN THING

I think anybody who's in the business of interviewing is a flirt. You have to be. And that's not gender-specific, either: you flirt with everybody. You tempt and tease people to tell you things. And, of course, I've been interviewing people now for a quarter of a century, so in one way or another, that's become part of how I relate to the world.

I'm quite conscious that I have a lazy, flirtatious personality when I'm at a social gathering. I use it so that I don't have to engage too strongly because there's this expectation that I'm going to be hyper-animated and completely transfixed by whatever issue is being discussed at any given time . . . whereas if the truth be known, I'm usually pretty talked out by the time I get to a social event. And I do have this kind of defensive flirting technique, which makes people feel they're getting the best side of me, but in fact it's more a sort of charm pill than anything else. It's a kind of posturing and smiling and a tone of voice. I think my voice has quite a powerful effect – on men and women. It carries with it the resonance of 'Oh, I'm speaking to your man.' It's a sort of a Rock-Star-cum-Dermot-Gavin thing.

THE RSGS

We're like a rock band. The girls on the show, they know that their every move is observed when they're in my company. They never do anything stupid. If they're going to let their hair down, it's got to be behind closed doors. Nobody's going to know anything about it.

We had one wonderful young producer who's since gone to Radio 1. She was heading to her first *Gerry Ryan Show* Christmas party – and they're good Christmas parties. They involve fine dining in private dining rooms, a good reception beforehand and a handbag disco officiated over by my good friend and colleague David Blake Knox. She was sitting at the pre-dinner drinks reception in the suite at the Four Seasons, and Pat Dunne, one of the longest-serving guitar players in the band, was there.

She said, 'I can't believe I'm here,' and explained that when she was studying on her media course in college, one of the things they often talked about was the *Gerry Ryan Show* Christmas party and what might or might not go on at it.

I said, 'What did you think was going to happen?'

'I don't know,' she said. 'I was too afraid to think.'

Pat and I just cracked up.

THE CIRCLE OF TRUST

I've had to deal with disloyalty on one occasion, it seems. We had one person who worked for us who, during a very difficult time in my life, during moments of personal pain, I suspect went to the newspapers and told them things.

Maybe that person will recognize themselves in print, maybe they won't. Suffice to say that it caused absolute chaos and mayhem in my private life. It caused chaos and mayhem in my office. And it reminded me in stark terms that you really do need to be very careful about who you let into – in the words of Robert De Niro in *Meet the Fockers* – the Circle of Trust. But in the main every single person I have worked with on *The Gerry Ryan Show* has been obsessively loyal.

They're all very different people, and they're inevitably women. They know that they're at the top of their game. They've had a cocktail named after them by the Four Seasons. How many people can say that? It's called the RSG – the Ryan Show Girl. It was created by Simon, the sommelier.

I was having lunch with Adrian Moynes, the managing director of radio, in the Four Seasons. We were in the early stages of negotiating my current contract. Simon came over and asked did we want two RSGs. Maybe cocktails are not the best way to start a meeting with the boss – and Adrian is very much The Boss. A good boss, a benign boss – a father figure in a way – but very much The Boss. And on this occasion, I wanted to be more the well-behaved son than the character I'm usually painted as: the reprobate, errant, partially psychotic guitarist. So Simon brings over the two RSGs, and Adrian just looks at me and says, 'What is that?'

And I said, 'Well . . .'

Simon jumped in. 'They're cocktails. They're the Ryan Show Girl cocktails!'

And I smiled, and said to the director, 'This cocktail was created at the Four Seasons Hotel, named after and to celebrate the girls who work on *The Gerry Ryan Show*.'

He just looked at me. 'Is this a good thing?'

'It is, Director,' I said. 'It is absolutely a good thing.'

These are the no-shit girls: Siobhan Hough, Deirdre McGee, Louise Ní Chríodán, Therese Kelly, Joan Torsney, Lorraine Dunne, Eileen Heron, Helen Howard, Fiona Murray, Sara Walsh, Mairead Sweeney, Deirdre Ryan, Brenda Donohue, Barbara Jordan, Lisa Crowley, Jackie Corcoran, Evelyn O'Rourke, Maggie Stapleton. They don't really care about anything except me and the broadcast. They produce great work. They are fiercely loyal. They're afraid of fuck-all. If you can find that anywhere else, bottle it and sell it.

The fact that it's usually all women on the show has something to do with the fact that women crowd the media now, particularly from a production and research point of view. In RTÉ, women have insinuated themselves into positions of influence that were previously male-dominated. And the female ability to think about several things at once is a huge asset in putting together a radio production. I always think of a *Ryan Show* girl as somebody who's drinking a vodka martini, ironing, holding a child in the other hand and dictating a brief for the next day over the phone.

Guys can't do that.

THE LONGEST AUDITION IN HISTORY

Kevin Lenihan, who produced one of my first big TV shows, *Secrets*, was very good at managing people. He was very good at convincing me to go on stage. This was not always easy. Sometimes I'd be sitting in the dressing room having a drink beforehand with the producer or the director. You're not meant to drink before you do a television programme. Kevin would come in and say, 'You know, you guys shouldn't really be doing this. You'll go blotchy.'

I used to think, Well, if that's our only problem, we'll be OK.

He had a very paternalistic approach to dealing with me. I remember, at the time, my telephone might get cut off because I hadn't paid the bill and somebody at home would be ringing the office saying, 'The phone's been cut off.' Kevin would pay the bill just to get me on stage. He was a real old-fashioned impresario, prepared to do whatever was necessary to get me to work.

Pat Cowap was a hugely talented director and a massive personality. Pat and I brought RTÉ television production backstage as close to being on a Led Zeppelin tour as you could bring it. A lot of people were afraid of us. They used to call us the Belushi Brothers. We always lived close to the edge. Pat would sometimes throw fits and walk out of the control box while the show was being filmed, and I loved that. I *loved* the drama. See, nobody could complain about us. We were the best people they had.

I don't know what that says about the rest of the country.

We used to drink an awful lot, something which few people in RTÉ did. I've heard stories about certain personalities being on TV, sitting behind their desk with their suit jacket on and no trousers, allegedly pissed out of their minds, but I don't believe most of that stuff. Maybe back in the old days there were guys on intravenous whiskey drips, or maybe not, but we really did go for it. I remember going out recording television programmes and being fairly out of it, wondering, Wow, am I going to slur? Am I going to fall over? Will I be able to follow the floor manager's instructions?

But at the end of the day we were a pretty good team. Which is beside the point. RTÉ had paid their fucking money. If they wanted me, this was how they got me, and they had to put up with it. Don't forget, while *Secrets* wasn't exactly critically acclaimed, it was hugely successful in audience terms. I often think, though, that if the critics had seen what was going on backstage rather than what was going on in front of the cameras, they might have had a better take on the whole thing . . .

GUILTY SECRETS

The accepted structure of television programmes always bored me to tears.

You came out.

You said, 'Good evening.'

You gave a menu of what was going to be on.

You had your star turn.

You had a house band.

You had a competition.

You had a commercial break.

From the word go I thought it was boring. OF COURSE, however, the reason you had all of those things is so everyone else knew what you were doing in order that you could actually *film* it. I didn't get that. I thought we were doing *Easy Rider* or *Monty Python*, or something even more surreal. That misconception made me very difficult to work with.

I mean, I was beginning to get quite a good idea of floor strategy, of how you worked in a TV studio, but I was still overwhelming everybody and everything. I was still far too much in your face: too loud, too aggressive and, crucially, too much in charge. I was absolutely convinced that I could be in all places at all times. I never trusted anybody who worked with me. I tried to direct against the director in the box, I tried to floor manage against the floor manager, I tried to orientate the cameras against the head cameraman. Despite all this, *Secrets* became very successful, for the same reasons, I think, that Noel Edmonds's *House Party* and Chris Evans's *Don't Forget Your Toothbrush* became successful. It had the same frenetic energy. They, however, had what I didn't, which was a very strong format that they stuck to religiously. Though it looked crazy, the format was sacrosanct.

In hindsight, I think we would have been much better off simply copying one of those programmes.

A BUCKET OF MAGGOTS

I was completely obsessed with shocking people and doing peculiar things. Frequently I came up with ideas that I thought were cutting edge. Such as, for example, throwing a bucket of maggots over the studio audience.

This idea led to several weeks of discussion before we ever got anywhere near doing anything even vaguely related to a bucket of maggots. Consequently, because this discussion about throwing a bucket of maggots at the audience or not throwing a bucket of maggots at the audience went on for so long, it took on planetary significance. The director at the time thought the bucket of maggots was a good idea, though, now I think back on it, that was probably because he was fed up with the rest of it, while the producer wasn't too sure that the maggots were the way to go. I, meanwhile, was absolutely certain that flinging a bucket of live maggots across an RTÉ studio audience would produce fantastic images, and I still believe that to be the case. People would be talking about it for months afterwards – *Jaysus! did you see Gerry Ryan last night? He fucked a bucket of maggots at the audience!* I had visions of maggots going down the front of the blouses, wriggling into underpants . . .

Eventually . . . eventually we arrived at this ridiculous compromise, which actually summed up everything I hated about RTÉ. We took a shot of the bucket with the live maggots in it and showed it to the audience to give them the impression that there was a load of live maggots in a bucket nearby. Then we threw an empty bucket at them.

What was the point of all the BLOODY discussion? Everybody, right down to the guy who made the tea, knew that if you threw a bucket of maggots at an audience, there would be a gigantic reaction, a reaction that would be worth seeing – but, of course, we ended up with this ridiculous RTÉ compromise that only the production team *got* because only they knew that we had *talked* about throwing a bucket of maggots at the audience and *wouldn't that have been a scream*? And can you *imagine* what that would have been like? Except we didn't fucking well throw a bucket of fucking maggots at fucking anyone. We didn't do anything, and that really pissed me off and only confirmed in the minds of everyone I was working with that I was delinquent and obsessed with the wrong production values. Probably they were right, BUT I STILL BELIEVE to this day that if Pat Kenny had got a bucket of maggots and fucked them at *The Late Late Show* audience, he would have got a reaction.

I SHOT HIM IN THE HOLE

At the same time I was doing *The School Around the Corner*. This was a programme that had originally been made famous by its creator, Paddy Crosbie, who was himself a teacher. Paddy's interviews with children were among the most memorable and iconic pieces of Irish television history. John McColgan of *Riverdance* fame, whom I'd got to know quite well over the years, thought we could resurrect this format. He did a huge amount of research into the psychology of talking to children and looked very closely at what Paddy Crosbie had done. While his approach was hugely entertaining, Paddy had used the children more as props than truly engaging with them. No disrespect to Paddy, that was the television of its time, but he would constantly egg the child towards the joke.

'Where did you shoot the horse?'

'I shot him in the hole.'

And Paddy would look to the audience to milk the gag. So we looked at it and said, 'That's disempowering the children. Let's try and find another way.' We went to St Pat's teacher-training college and talked there to classroom trainers about the psychology of dealing with children. There, we learned a couple of basic rules.

Number one, never ask them anything they can answer with yes or no; always get them to tell stories, to describe things.

Number two, never look away from them; always try to engage them as much as possible.

With those two rules in mind, we revamped and reinvigorated *The School Around the Corner*, and I believe what we came up with was a charming snapshot of Ireland at the time. I've met kids, now grown adults, who were interviewed on the show and who remember it as a very positive experience.

There were, however, one or two negative ones.

One child we had on obviously came from a much wealthier background than everyone else. He talked about his dad's Jag and the house in Dalkey . . . and I took the piss out of him.

He was more articulate than most of the kids on the programme, and we allowed him very eloquently to describe a world of great privilege. Because *The School Around the Corner* had a fairly working-to-lower-middle-class ethos, this boy stood out like a sore thumb, and he was humiliated. It was very wrong of me to do it, and it was very wrong of us as a production team to broadcast it. His mother wrote me a letter afterwards, in which she described giving birth to the child. She talked about how she worried about this little boy, and how he'd battled a number of different challenges through his life and how he'd come out the other end fighting fit. This was a little boy who was tremendously proud of his dad. He hadn't been boasting. He was simply proud of his father and we'd made him look like a grasping, greedy little Philistine.

I was deeply ashamed.

This was one of the first times that I realized television not only provided a huge opportunity to entertain and educate and inform – and, of course, to make you a living and turn you into a household name – there was also a huge opportunity to debase yourself and those around you.

I felt this happened to me a lot more on television than on radio, and it was something the critics were delighted to discover. On television, you've much less control. Radio is measured, it's much more literate. Television is dangerous because there are so many other things going on that can conspire to give an impression wildly at odds with what was originally intended.

Thus began another relationship in my life. Me And The Critics, who began to castigate me on a daily basis. This was tremendously good fun for everybody except me and the people I worked with.

YOU'RE A BIG BOY, YOU CAN TAKE IT

David Blake Knox, who was deputy head of television at the time, brought me into his office. He said, 'More people watched you last weekend than have ever watched anybody over a weekend on Irish television.' This was on *Secrets* and *The School Around the Corner*.

'Yeah,' I said, 'but did you read the Sunday papers yesterday? They say I'm a gobshite, they say I'm a virus . . .' Over a very short period of time, the language had become incredibly overblown and hysterical. Gene Kerrigan described me as if I was some sort of threat to Irish culture, as if I was bludgeoning Ireland on a grand scale with the RTÉ mast.

Very stupidly, I used to ring the critics.

I rang the guy at the *Sunday World* and said to him, 'Why do you keep writing all this negative shit about me every single week?'

'Because,' he said, 'people like to read stuff about you and it's good fun to take the piss out of you. And you know what? You're a big boy. You're earning a lot of money. You can take it.'

I was deeply, deeply hurt by some of it. I mean, anybody who says they wouldn't be affected by it is a liar. When people say you're useless or accuse you of being a fraud or when they say you're lazy or disingenuous or tantamount to excrement on the shoe of society, I defy anybody not to be affected by it.

I remember Shane Hegarty, at the *Irish Times*, when the second series of *Ryan Confidential* had just got under way, wrote that I had returned to television screens like a fly you thought you had chased from the room. I remember thinking, He wouldn't write that about anybody else, so why has he decided to write it about me? And it made me absolutely hate him. I despised him for it because I thought he was weak. I thought it was hysterical. I thought it was absolutely and utterly unnecessary. I wrote the editor of the *Irish Times*, Geraldine Kennedy, a very long, personal letter. I said it was completely beneath contempt that the paper of record would stoop to such a tabloid way of analysing somebody's work. She wrote back and said, 'You're a big boy, you should be able to take it.'

She was completely right. I was taking it far too seriously. And, of course, nobody paid it the slightest bit of attention but me.

So, while the radio programme was becoming more and more successful, I was doing television that was reviled and rejected by the critics. I began to get very down about the criticism. Performers are human beings with bigger and more fragile egos than anyone else, and they will be affected by negative comment. It's bollocks to say there's no such thing as negative publicity. There is. My wife used to cut out parts out of the Sunday papers before I got to them. She threw out the *Sunday Independent* on a regular basis. I was friendly with Tony and Gavin O'Reilly growing up, and I found it hard to resist saying to them, 'Can you guys not stop this? It's doing my head in.'

The kids were never badly burned by it because they were too young. My wife may have felt compromised by it. She's incredibly loyal and never once betrayed embarrassment. I know she defended me when I wasn't there, I know she worried about what it did to me, but she was always amazingly supportive. When I decided to go with a decision on television, she was there at my side.

There is a downside to that. You feel, well, if she's there I must be right. But without her I think I would have gone mad.

I know some of my friends used to be kind of mesmerized by the strength of the negative opinion levelled at me. When I would suggest meeting in a pub or restaurant or any public place, they'd go, 'Ah, sure no no no, we'll meet in your place . . .'

There were a substantial number of people in RTÉ who really thought that what I was doing on television was an anathema to everything RTÉ stood for, to the obligations we had as a public-service organization. I remember there was one guy whose job it was to move cardboard boxes from one place to another. I mean, he had no editorial role. He actually stopped me one day and told me he was ashamed to work for RTÉ because of *Secrets*. I mean, they never stopped anybody else and said that to them. They never stopped Pat Kenny or Aonghus McAnally. Why had they decided that it was OK to say that to Gerry Ryan? It took me a long time to figure out that I was giving off a kind of no-holds-barred, derring-do vibe.

But I wanted everyone to say I was great. I wanted *points for trying*. I thought people would go, 'Sure he's trying to do something different, he'll get it right in a while . . .'

I remember a *Secrets* production meeting when we discussed whether or not we were going to pay any attention to the critics. I used to fabricate this kind of Fuck Them attitude, although of course, deep down, I was deeply hurt and amazingly confused.

I mean, the terrible thing was, the guys who were writing about me were substantial. You can't go, 'Gene Kerrigan's a halfwit.' So I open up the *Sunday Independent* and there, alongside Gene's copy, is a picture of my head on a turkey's body. It's a full fucking page! In the broadsheet *Independent*! How could I have merited that? I mean, you want a full page, you want to be written about, but a whole fucking thing about you being a turkey? I want people to love me! I want people to clap because I tried – but, of course, that's bullshit. It doesn't work like that.

I'm still shocked when people say, 'That's rubbish, he's being disingenuous,' and conversely, I still get overly excited when Gerry McCarthy in the *Sunday Times* writes something positive about the radio programme. I'm going to people, 'Whey-hey! Did you see that?'

And the guys in the *G. Ryan Show* office are all going, 'Whey-hey! Did you see it?'

But nobody else has read it, or no one else cares.

Anyway, the general argument around the table was 'Fuck the critics, this programme is hugely successful. Keep the spangly jacket, keep shouting, keep dancing, keep letting snakes loose in the studio.' I remember Anita Nataro, the director, saying, 'No, hang on, we're doing something wrong. What we should be doing is getting what Gerry's doing on the radio and putting that on the television. All that's happening is that we're throwing a hand grenade into a fireworks factory every week. Sure there's a huge explosion, but what else is there besides that?'

Things began to change. I got bored with what we were doing, and the producer was taken off to do something else. John McColgan got the job of trying to put a format on the show. He probably had more success than anyone else with it by turning it into a large-scale variety show, with a house band and karaoke competitions and a series of repeated segments. It was now more dependable, I was a bit more controlled, the jackets were a bit less spangly – but at the end of the day all it was was a big old-fashioned *Sunday Night at the London Palladium* kind of show.

John McColgan, I believe now, saved me: if we had just stopped *Secrets* when it was at its most chaotic, that would have been the last memory anyone would have had of me on television, so even though the show with John really wasn't the show either he or I wanted to do, it acted as a decompression chamber between the hysteria of the original *Secrets* and whatever I did next.

But! To this day, I still believe, if we had had proper foresight, proper vision and proper lead-in time, and if we'd done the kinds of things they were doing in the UK, we could have made a success of that show. At that point, however, it had gone on too long. I was now the tallest leper in the valley. And my radio team, though they were shy about saying it, were becoming increasingly concerned about the onslaught of criticism. There was a legitimate concern that what looked like my dismally short TV career would seriously damage my radio career.

Secrets was dropped.

The School Around the Corner was dropped.

I was asked to do *The Rose of Tralee*. I'd kept away from variety television for a couple of months and I remember thinking, Do I want to present *The Rose of Tralee*? Absolutely fucking not. I'd taken off the spangly jacket. I'd put it in the cupboard with the firm conviction that it would never again see the light of day. But when I refused, those in authority in RTÉ who'd asked me were apoplectic – and more than a little surprised. I was told that if I didn't do it, I could forget about doing anything else.

A day or two earlier I'd signed a five-year contract for radio and television, and after the *Secrets* experience, I was more than happy not to step in front of a TV camera ever again. Suddenly I had the extraordinary release of opening the papers on a Sunday and not having to read that I was fucking useless. The radio people drew breath, and very quietly muttered that this was probably a good thing and maybe I might keep away from television for ever. I thought, Well, look, I'm after signing a huge contract, the telly just isn't working . . . and I'm getting paid all this money for doing just the radio programme.

But that wasn't to be. There still were some people in television who thought well, you know, you can't have an elephant and not have it do tricks in both rings in the circus.

WE REALLY CRACKED IT THIS WEEK

Ryantown was the worst television experience I've ever had in my entire life, even though I worked on it with some of the best people I've ever worked with. Fiona Looney wrote the theme music, which she still claims she was never paid for. A former producer of *The Gay Byrne Hour*, Julie Parsons, was given the job of producing *Ryantown*, which was kind of like *Secrets* but with *less* format. There was going to be a sort of town or village or something that I lived in. Now, Julie's original idea was brilliant.

She wanted to do a programme called *The Bearpit*, which would be me in a pit, surrounded by a seeded audience, and we would argue about things, with me acting as ringmaster. But RTÉ, because of their addiction to shite formatting when it came to Gerry Ryan, decided no, no, that *Bearpit* thing, which looks really good, we're not going to do that, we're going to do the *Secrets* thing again.

The main input I had into *Ryantown* was to persuade them to let me have a dog on set with me. Murphy was the best thing on *Ryantown*. Even though he was a highly trained performing dog, he wouldn't take any instruction whatsoever. Murphy did whatever he wanted. And it was he who was responsible for the entire series' one iconic moment. Niamh Kavanagh, who won the Millstreet Eurovision, came on to sing the winning song, and Murphy, despite having been asked at least fifty times to sit down beside me while Niamh performed, went up and kept his snout in her crotch throughout her entire performance.

Ryantown nearly gave Julie a nervous breakdown. She was a charming, gentle woman – now a successful author – and she used to be in tears. Here was one more person with impeccable broadcasting credentials who got involved with me and suddenly found themselves swimming in shit. RTÉ, meanwhile, were extremely unhelpful. Suggestions would arrive at our production meetings: *Maybe Gerry should wear a hat. Maybe Gerry should sit down. Maybe Gerry should run around a bit more.*

I remember when I realized, Right. This is it. I'm absolutely fucked.

I was in the K Club for the weekend. *The K Club.* I mean, here I was still earning substantial money from all this shit. Anyway, I was getting ready to go down for dinner, and I was really looking forward to it. Fine dining in opulent surroundings, a beautiful woman on my arm, Didier the sommelier picking the wines . . . This was all I wanted to do, just eat really good food and drink really good wine and go to the K Club and Dromoland and fly helicopters. Would it not be better if I was just really fucking rich? Why did I have to do any of this broadcasting stuff?

I said to my wife, 'Look, it's still early, we'll watch *Ryantown* before we go down.'

It was the only time I ever remember her saying, 'Do we really need to do that?'

'Yeah, yeah,' I said. 'I really think we cracked it this week.'

And I remember the two of us there in the hotel room. I was in a fabulous Cavalli suit, she was as beautiful as ever. We sat and watched the television in silence. I was almost in tears. She was almost in tears. When it was over, I switched it off and I said, 'Well, that wasn't too bad, sure it wasn't.'

She didn't say anything.

We went down to dinner and I got absolutely fucking hammered. I had a row with Didier over the wine, and I remember coming back up that night thinking, I'm never going to get this right.

Not only that but we were only halfway through the series. I went back to RTÉ and I said, 'Look, could we just stop it?'

And RTÉ said, 'Nobody's ever asked for anything like that before.'

'I really think we should stop it,' I said. 'It's shit.'

And they did. They cut it halfway through.

Fiona Looney sometimes brings it up. She'll go, 'Remember *Ryantown*?'

And I'll go, 'Fuck off. Don't bring that up.'

THIS IS IT NOW. I'M COMPLETELY FUCKED

David Blake Knox and Liam Miller decided to concoct something with a format and my radio personality in mind, and *Gerry Ryan Tonight* was born. At the time, the industry in both the US and the UK had decided that soaps and chat shows could quite legitimately go out several times a week. Wogan – much to his detriment, I believe – had been on three nights a week, as had *EastEnders, Coronation Street* and *Fair City*. Charlie McCarthy, a very talented producer, was brought in to design *Gerry Ryan Tonight*. It would go out, as these other shows had done, three times a week.

This had disaster written all over it from the word go. Not from Charlie's point of view – eventually from Charlie's point of view – but from my point of view, because this was somebody else's baby. This was Charlie's dream. He was going to create a virtual world that I inhabited. There would be a sophisticated set that had a conference room, that had a performance area, that had an interview room. Cameras would be able to move freely around it; the lighting would be state-of-the-art. There'd be actors and actresses playing my assistants and researchers, but we'd have real guests, a real band . . .

One of the problems was with the formatting. I'm an old-fashioned interviewer. I ask a selection of questions. I like a beginning, a middle and an end. Charlie's instructions were to join me a third of the way into the interview and leave maybe two-thirds of the way through. I found it deeply frustrating and unsatisfying. Ann Gildea, one of *The Nualas*, was playing my assistant. She's a very talented performer, but I'm pretty sure she hated having to do what she did because she was playing a character, and I wasn't playing a character. I was me. I didn't know whether I was meant to be me, a hyper version of me or a subdued version of me. She'd be acting away like mad in front of me and I'd be looking at her like she was cracked.

Very, very bad blood developed between myself and Charlie McCarthy.

I was used to controlling editorial meetings. I was used to controlling the schedule of production, whether it was radio or TV. Charlie wouldn't allow that. He openly said to me that he despised the cult of personality. He wasn't interested in stars. At one point it got so bad that we were put together in a room with

David Blake Knox. David said it was like trying to sort out a really serious marriage breakdown ... and he didn't manage to sort it. I was determined not to be beaten by Charlie, and Charlie was determined not to be beaten by me, and I ended up hating him and he ended up hating me. The programme collapsed and Ferdia Mac Anna was brought in to produce it. I ended up hating Ferdia as well because at that time I thought he was weak-willed, that he was afraid of facing down the authorities.

This, of course, was all just perceptual bullshit. Both of these guys were very talented and only had my best interests at heart. I, however, wasn't willing or able to submit to their vision of how the programme would work. I'd grown up with Ferdia, I'd been in his house dozens of times, his sister went out with my best friend, so it should have been a marriage made in heaven. Instead it was an absolute disaster and nearly destroyed our friend-ship. He held the format, but was also insistent on invoking his rule as producer and allowed me little input into what went on. So here again was a great idea with some hugely talented people that absolutely fell on its arse.

I remember that when *Gerry Ryan Tonight* collapsed I thought, Well, this is it, now I'm completely fucked. I'm never going to be on the television again.

PATHS TO FREEDOM

Paths to Freedom was a fantastic breath of fresh air. This wonderful mockumentary was about two guys getting out of jail — one a gynaecologist going off the rails, the other a dim-witted northside skanger. I was really chuffed to be involved in it, playing myself, interviewing the gynaecologist live on-air. I asked them how they wanted me to act.

'We'd like you to kind of act yourself.'

'What do you mean, kind of act myself?'

'Well, you know, sort of, kind of, like you are, sort of thing.'

'What's that?'

'Well, you know, kind of, sort of an arrogant, foul-mouthed, aggressive cunt, basically.'

'OK.'

THEN FOR FUCK'S SAKE DO A TELEVISION PROGRAMME THAT INVOLVES TALKING TO PEOPLE

I literally auditioned for twenty years on the telly to find a programme that would suit me. It must be unprecedented that someone could have had so many critical failures – not audience failures, but critical failures – and still be given another chance. And another, and another, and another. I think it must be very confusing if you're a young critic or, even worse, an older one. You're looking at what you consider to be talent floating around all over the place, so why is Gerry Ryan constantly being brought back for another go? Who did he sleep with? Who did he pay? What voodoo doll has he got in his bedroom?

Bob Collins was the director general who had the most influence over me. When Bob was responsible for output, he was very paternal. I remember him sitting with me and, almost in exasperation, saying, 'Look, what do you do best?'

'What do you mean, what do I do best, DG?'

'What do you do best, Gerry? What's the one thing you do best, better than anything else?'

'Ah . . . Talking to people?'

'Then for fuck's sake do a television programme that involves talking to people.'

'So what do you think I should do, DG?'

'I'm the director general, Gerry. I don't normally have these conversations with presenters.'

'Oh.'

Bob was completely right, of course. He'd hit the nail on the head. That was the ghost in the machine. But fuck me, it had been in the machine for two decades and no one had spoken up.

I'm almost never written about in terms of television now, which is Fine By Me. The critics have given up. Either they respect what I do, which I hope, or they just feel that when it comes to Gerry Ryan, fuck it, there's no accounting for taste. I've lost no sleep over the absence of reviews, good or bad, for the last three series of *Ryan Confidential*. We've had pretty good audiences – in fact, most of the stuff I've done on television has been well received by audiences – and now, of course, we have very sophisticated research to tell us what an audience thinks about a programme. And *Operation Transformation*, with the 360-degree production bringing together the Internet, radio and TV, has been hugely successful. In making that happen, I teamed up with the guy who was responsible for bringing me to the public's attention in the first place. Philip Kampf was the man who led that fateful trip into the wilds of Connemara all those years ago.

I believe *Confidential* has presented a visual of G. Ryan and a level of authority that people are comfortable with. It's one of my favourite things to do.

I've now become obsessed with working with people I trust. This is something I learned from people like Bono. U2 always work on a family basis. I decided I'd make the production teams on the radio show and the television programme like a band. We'd all work together and trust each other and believe in the same thing. I orchestrated the contractual arrangement with RTÉ so that David Blake Knox would do most of my television programmes. He does career-development projects and stuff like that with me.

I love the fact that much of the team who started the radio show with me are still there. These people are genuinely obsessed with what we do. David is now part of that clan, along with Deirdre McGee and Siobhan Hough. I love working with them because they know me inside out. The approach I've evolved is hugely challenging to the broadcaster, because I've now said to RTÉ that I will not work with most people. I will only work with people who are in the band. This requires a huge amount of arrogance, and huge devotion from the people who work with me. We have created a world in which we're more or less independent, where we're seemingly uncooperative, where we don't submit to the same laws that everyone else has to. It has to be like that, because otherwise you're not going to get Gerry Ryan.

21

EUROVISION

Kevin Lenihan called while I was on-air. That alone should have alerted me to the fact that something was seriously wrong. He asked me if I'd come to his home for a meeting with himself and David Blake Knox.

Late in 1992, Kevin was taken off *Secrets* to work on the Millstreet Eurovision. Fionnuala Sweeney, one of the sexpots of Irish television at the time, and I had been asked to present it and we had already started rehearsing in a sound studio on Harcourt Street. Fionnuala was really easy to work with; she was very sharp, great fun, and the two of us had worked out a pretty good routine. I mean, I was fairly convinced I was doing it, and most people around me were convinced I was going to be doing it as well. It's impossible to say how difficult it was to be told that no, you're not actually going to be doing the Eurovision after all.

This was terribly difficult for Kevin, hugely difficult. We were good friends, he and I, and Kevin was fully committed to me as co-presenter. I believe the decision to have me taken off came from the top. So, Kevin, David and I went to Kevin's home. Despite the fact that both of them were agitated and uneasy, I had no notion of the bombshell they were about to drop. I mean, I was pretty used to being brought into meetings in RTÉ where there were people who were agitated and uneasy. By now I was a master at obfuscating, talking for ages and eventually just boring people into the ground with convoluted eloquence and retarded explanation. I thought this might be another of those occasions. I thought they were going to say that something I'd done or said would have to be explained to the minister or the RTÉ Authority.

David said, 'I think Kevin's got something to tell you.'

Kevin looked at David, wishing, I imagine, that David would tell me.

But it was Kevin who said it: 'You're not going to be doing the Eurovision.'

I was devastated. I was absolutely devastated, because I'd bought into it, I'd told people. It was partial knowledge within the industry that I was going to be doing it and even though it sounds ludicrous now – why does anybody care? Why don't you just have a drink and forget about it? – I cannot explain how devalued I became at that moment. This was the moment I realized you cannot beat the system.

I know, too, that this whole episode, and in particular my reaction to it, was very difficult for my wife and family. To see a father and husband become so devastated and so affected by his work . . . and maybe not as affected or as devastated by things that happened in his personal life. It must have raised questions in people's minds. Who are you close to? What exactly moves you? Was I more concerned about my work than about my family?

I decided I had to overcome it, I had to exorcize the ghost in some way, so when it came close to the show, I decided there had to be a *Ryan Show* presence. I remember one of the guys on the radio show saying, 'You know, you've been badly burned by this – we've all been badly burned by it. I don't think we should go near it.'

'No,' I said. 'We should go near it . . . We should be there.'

So we did *The Gerry Ryan Show* from right outside Green Glens Arena in Millstreet. We interviewed Fionnuala on the programme, which was a very weird experience. The interview took place in one of these transparent roadcaster studios, and behind her I could see the arena where the show was going to take place. It was the final day of rehearsals and here I was talking to my ex-stage wife. It was bizarre and weird and hugely emotional. So, to shake off that trauma, I made a big fuss about arriving: I got a suite in one of the hotels, and the party my wife and I organized was the most sought-after event during that production.

I now had no faith in RTÉ.

I thought, If this is the way it is, if they judge you on whether or not they like you, I'm fucked. The problem with me is I've always had a great sense of invincibility. I've always believed that even those who despise me will put up with me because I'm *Valuable*, I'm *worth* something. That turns out not to be the truth.

So I was determined to two-finger the situation as much as I could. We got first-class seats on the night of the Eurovision. It was a fantastic production, Fionnuala was great and now, when I think back on it, I believe she was probably better off doing it by herself.

THE *RIVERDANCE* EUROVISION

It was a great go-fuck-yourselves the following year.

I don't think Joe Barry, who was director general, was a great fan of the 1994 Eurovision, the *Riverdance* Eurovision. I don't think he was a huge fan of Michael Flatley. I believe he was extremely ambivalent about me presenting it. At one stage, there was an issue over the fact that I had been talking about my penis on the radio show. I'd referred to it, as I often do, as being particularly large, and Joe took offence. He came to visit us in the Point. Everyone thought he was coming to look at *Riverdance* or the set, or to listen to the music, but in fact he'd come down to talk to myself and Willie O'Reilly, the *chef de village*, and also the producer in charge of *The Gerry Ryan Show*. He basically said that if he heard any further mention of the G. Ryan Penis on-air, he'd sack us both – that's Willie and me, not my Penis and me. David Blake Knox, who was an executive producer on the *Riverdance* Eurovision, spent a lot of time throwing oil on troubled waters.

Anyway, Moya Doherty was given the job of producing the show, which in television terms was, I believe, one of the most significant things that ever happened in this country. Moya was a hugely talented television producer. I had absolute faith and trust in her judgement when it came to making television. She was the only person up to that point that I ever really believed. Everybody else had to go through hoops of fire to convince me that they knew what they were talking about, which is maybe more my problem than theirs.

Anyway, Moya went to RTÉ and said she wanted a double-headed presentation; dark and fair, male and female. Cynthia Ní Mhurchú was the first choice. Cynthia: a consummate professional, very glamorous, a statuesque beauty. Moya then said to RTÉ, 'I'm not doing it unless Gerry Ryan is presenting it.'

'Well,' she was told, 'there's a lot of mixed feeling about Gerry on television, much less as a presenter of the Eurovision.'

Now, the Millstreet experience or, at least, my Millstreet experience was one of those things that had been consigned to history in RTÉ. To dark, locked history. It was never talked about. Nobody ever explained to me what had happened and any time I tried to bring it up with anybody in authority in RTÉ, they tried to make me feel I'd imagined the whole thing.

That I hadn't been told I was doing it. That I hadn't been in rehearsal for weeks. I was very confused and shocked, but this, I've since discovered, is simply the way that large organizations work.

So when the production team approached me and said, 'We want you to co-present the Eurovision,' I was less than enthusiastic. 'It's not an audition,' they said, 'you're going to co-present it.'

'Well,' I said, 'I don't think I really want to do that.'

The reaction was a mixture of bemusement and amazement.

Moya was her judicious self. She said, 'Yeah, I know, I understand you've been through a lot of pain with this before . . .'

The Millstreet experience had caused huge anguish at home. My family had had to put up with me sulking for months after I didn't get it. I know this sounds stupid now, and I'm one of those people who had taken the piss out of the Eurovision for years, but the simple fact is that everybody thinks it's a load of shite until they're asked to do it. Then, suddenly, it becomes Significant. Important, even. So I went off and spoke with my wife about it, and she was pretty negative. Throughout my career, she'd always had a much better nose for these decisions than I'd had. She posed a question that nobody else did, a question only your wife can pose.

She said, 'How can you possibly allow these people to do this to you? They threw you on the scrapheap. You were strangled emotionally. Why are you going back to them now?'

Why? Because I had to. Despite the humiliation, the smirking, the people reminding you that you said never, never, never, never again, there you are, back in the room, signing up to do the thing you said you'd never do.

My wife was always the best person to analyse what I was doing on the radio, she was the best person to tell me whether I was living up to my expectations or not, whether I was being credible or not. I didn't always heed what she said because sometimes you can't — sometimes even when somebody has spotted that you're flawed or that it's disingenuous or you're lying to yourself about what you're doing, you just have to push through that to get to the place where you want to be, to that moment when the show sounds like it should, when it has the edge, the sharpness it needs.

Most of my inspiration and most of my guidance came from my wife.

There certainly have been others who were formative in my thinking. Harry Crosbie for one. I've known him for almost all my broadcasting career. He's been a very powerful influence. He's one of those iconic property moguls who's managed to become something of an Irish pharaoh. The Taoiseach makes speeches about Harry's vision and other developers drool at the thought of the deals he manages to do. When Harry tells you something's good, you know it's good, and if he tells you something's shit, you know it's shit. Michael Flatley is another. He's an immensely strong character and a very exciting person to be around. He was hugely responsible for reinvigorating my interest in performance and being at the centre of things. He's just so strong and he's a great sense of personal belief. He's quite like Bono in a lot of ways; he singles out people he thinks are the best at what they do.

Of course, the Irish, we've found a way to slag Bono and Michael Flatley. Nowhere else in the world do they slag Bono and Michael Flatley, but we do here.

YOU'RE NOT EISENHOWER

You get locked away for the best part of a year planning it. You end up in this kind of half-marriage with your co-presenter. The production team becomes your best friends and family, and you become obsessed with something that only takes up an hour or two of everyone else's life. Quite simply, it becomes everything to you. EVERYTHING. And so, once again, there was the radio team, heads in hands, going, 'Oh, No. Not The Fucking Eurovision Again.'

As it turned out, it wasn't such a bad thing for the radio show.

For the first time ever, here was a Eurovision presenter who was on the radio talking about what was happening. And then there was *Riverdance*. Every day, I watched Michael Flatley and Jean Butler put the thing together. I watched Michael stop the entire production, the crew, the orchestra, stop everything, as he choreographed the *Riverdance*.

I'm sitting at the side of the stage: 'Ladies and gentlemen . . . the *Riverdance*!' And once I've said that, I sit and watch this thing that has become of stellar significance to Irish culture build and grow before my eyes. I must have seen it rehearsed fifty or sixty times. Did I know how big it would become? Well, Willie O'Reilly and I were offered the opportunity to invest in it. We didn't. Twenty grand would have got me a stake in it. (Sigh.)

Cynthia had a kind of ice-queen way of presenting herself, which I really liked so I tried to dovetail into that. And we gave each other a lot. Cynthia wasn't particularly good on the geography of the stage. So, coming down on the gantry with all the fireworks and other pyrotechnics, we developed our own language. I'd squeeze her hand once for walking forward, twice for stopping, three times for turning left to the audience. Together, we were the least human of all Eurovision presenters. We intended it like that; cold, sharp, studied, Nordic almost. I think that fitted in perfectly with the design and the *Riverdance*.

On the night, Bono and his wife, Ali, sent me a nappy and a note that said, 'Good luck, you may need this.' I remember showing it to Cynthia in her dressing room. She and I had fantastically well-appointed dressing rooms, which Willie O'Reilly had insisted on. He said our dressing rooms should reflect our perceived status. *Perceived* status. Ha! So we had mini-bars and sofas and stuff like that. Cynthia had fresh flowers all the time. Anyway, I showed Cynthia the nappy and she laughed. 'That's good,' she said, 'that's funny.'

'What does it mean?' I asked her.

'It means,' she said, 'that you're going to be shitting yourself.'

I was so arrogant and self-obsessed that the idea of shitting myself was the furthest thing from my mind. I was the Practitioner *Extraordinaire* of the Golden Jacket.

As it turned out, I did shit myself at one point. In the very early stages of the counting, my earpiece went dead. I couldn't hear what the juries were saying. I remember there was this guy crawling behind me, trying to put fresh batteries into the earpiece receiver, and I was looking at Cynthia, going, 'Well, I think you can take it from here, Cynthia.'

She came back with, 'No, Ger, I think it's you . . .'

That was a pretty mind-boggling moment. I've looked back on it recently and, to be honest, I don't think you'd notice it. There was no dead air. Cynthia took up the slack until my earpiece started working again. The close-living scenario really paid off at that moment. She understood what was happening instinctively and was able to deal with it, and I did not fall over. I remember thinking, This is pretty cool, I've managed to do this. It was one of the golden moments of my life, that I was able to keep going at that moment, in front of that audience.

And to top it all off? A win. 'Rock 'n' Roll Kids', with Charlie McGettigan and Paul Harrington. That gave me faith that I might just have a television career. Might. The success of the night made it almost impossible for the critics to have a go at me. Subsequently, when the dust settled, some people did, and if you look back at it now, it is quite gauche, but in the context of 1994, it was huge.

Afterwards, I didn't really do anything except the radio show for a while. It was a bit like playing Oxegen and then going back on the dole. The peculiar thing about the whole experience was that I ended up with a completely overblown impression of what I'd done – to walk out in front of the audience in the Point and know that I was being watched by two hundred million people, to know that the President and the Taoiseach were there . . .

And in the run-up to the thing, Cynthia and I acted as sort of Eurovision ambassadors. We used to do tours for visiting dignitaries. You get these jobs and you begin to get a sense not just of importance but of over-importance. You have to keep reminding yourself that, really, you're a bit of a puppet. I wasn't dancing, I didn't sing 'Rock 'n' Roll Kids', I didn't write it, I didn't direct or produce the show, I didn't design the set and I didn't write the music for *Riverdance*. So, then, if you haven't done any of those things, what exactly have you done?

You've Stood Beside It.

And that is exactly what I've done with a lot of things. *The Gerry Ryan Show* has always been there at the beginning of every U2 tour. That's what I do. I stand beside things that are much bigger and better than I am. Sometimes the charisma, the spark rubs off. It also gives others the impression, at the very least, that I'm on the same trajectory, if not in the same league. People think, well, *The Gerry Ryan Show*, that's like the U2 radio show, isn't it? My colleagues and I have always worked very hard to cultivate and maintain those friendships and links.

I know that the *Riverdance* Eurovision was a very difficult time for my wife because I basically retreated into a world of Eurovision. Even as I say it, it sounds ridiculous, but there it is. I think it was a difficult time for colleagues, friends and family alike because I became very pompous and self-important. A production of that size is all-consuming. All of our families, I believe, got badly left behind. By the time of the performance, I'd probably seen more of Cynthia than I had of any other person in my life. You tend to think that this is it. You think you're Eisenhower and you're about to get the final weather report that decides whether the landings go ahead or not, but, of course, you're not Eisenhower, you're just introducing a couple of really bad pop songs.

Thankfully I didn't realize that until several hours after the whole thing was over.

There are loads of different ways of doing theatre, rock 'n' roll shows, light-entertainment shows, making movies, but let nobody be disavowed of the certainty that when you operate as a family, you always get a better result. There's a price to pay for that. You upset your real family, your pals and colleagues who are outside that immediate circle. You may lose their friendship, respect and support for ever. You may also turn into something monstrous. The fact remains, though, that you get a better result when you're obsessed and when you're working so closely together as to exclude all other interests. This is because you convince yourself that what you're doing is the most important thing in the world, that you're at the epicentre of the most fabulous thing ever conceived. When you believe that, you exude it. You convince the audience: We Are Gods. That's what it's all about. *Being* It.

In the end, I don't believe any lasting damage was done to my personal life – though you'd really have to ask my friends and family about that. My way of surviving is that I don't really notice the damage I cause to people when I become obsessed, when the entire compass is taken up with what I'm doing as opposed to what I should, privately and personally, be paying attention to. My talent is to imbue a project with much more significance and theatricality than it actually deserves. This gives a sort of incandescence to it that makes things that are not all that bright shine very brightly. I can bring that to the party. But, like it says in *Bladerunner*, the light that burns twice as brightly burns twice as fast.

How brightly I have shone.

22

I'M BEGINNING TO LIQUEFY

I'm reasonably healthy, considering I drink too much and I don't exercise enough. I did go through a period for several years where I was in the gym three to four times a week, but now I've become so busy I haven't been able to replace it with anything. My diet is much better than it used to be. I tend not to binge on food or drink as much as I used to. I'm also on medication now for cholesterol because I have high blood pressure.

I have a good doctor. I get myself tested regularly, so hopefully I can fend off the prostate and cholesterol problems. I'm lucky to have a full head of hair at fifty-two years of age. That's quite good.

But I could be much healthier.

I certainly eat nowhere near the amount of food I used to. I had several years of over-indulging myself. You can probably mark the years from when my salary really increased. I was hanging around with a bunch of wonderful guys who lunched an awful lot. They're great friends of mine. All of them had very successful businesses in the nineties in particular – at the beginning of the Celtic Tiger – and we'd be in the Polo Room having lunch two or three times a week. I'd always had a liking for fine dining. Then I got nerdy about whiskies, wines and cigars. I enjoyed knowing about them. I liked consuming them more. This was me sowing the seeds of my future downfall. Even though I'm certainly much fitter now than I was then, the damage is done. The liver's taken a hammering. The heart probably isn't the way it should be. I only eat one main meal a day now, and, I suppose, you could call it two snacks. If I have a proper meal at lunchtime I will not have a proper meal in the evening. I love my food. I absolutely adore food. I think it's one of the great sports of all time, eating. And I enjoy drinking liquor as well.

But I find, as I've got older, I've developed allergies that I never had before. I've always had a minor sinus problem. Now my minor sinus problem is a major sinus problem. If I drink a glass of red wine – and I love red wine – bang! Knocked over. Can hardly speak. Some of my favourite whiskies have the same effect on me. It hasn't stopped me drinking, but I've cut back a little bit. If I drink too late in the evening, I know I'm not going to be well when I get up the next morning.

These are all the little knock, knock, knocks on the door of mortality. They remind you that you aren't a robot, that you are not Iron Man, that you are slowly degenerating.

I've done a lot of degenerating. I'm beginning to liquefy.

I used to be very, very fit, and I seemed to burn up carbohydrates at a rate of knots. Then the bad moment arrived. Let nobody dispute this fact. This is as sure as death and taxes. You will arrive at a moment when suddenly you start melting. And that would be fine if you melted into a drain. But, unfortunately, what happens is that some of it seems to travel from one part of your body to another.

My back isn't as bad as it used to be. Losing weight helped me there. But I have arthritis in my hands. I'm finding myself taking

Udo's Oil tablets. I would have pissed myself laughing at people who did that a couple of years ago. But I've now found that Udo's Oil tablets do more for my arthritic hands than any of the over-the-counter medications you get at a pharmacy. So I've become a little bit more open-minded about alternative therapies and organic stuff than I would have been before.

But I'm still slacking. One night recently I found myself washing down my cholesterol medicine with a glass of whiskey.

I don't exercise enough. I still drink too much, and I still eat the wrong things. But you know what? That's just me, and I'm probably always going to be like that. I feel like a really good Ferrari that's been driven too hard and not serviced enough.

Still an attractive car, though.

THE BEST DRUG-TAKING EXPERIENCE EVER

Taking diet pills was one of the best drug-taking experiences I've ever had. They really worked.

I was just sick to death of being told to do this diet, that diet, the other diet. My doctor, who's also one of my best friends, has a good measure on my personality. He understands my difficulties around practising what I preach, so he suggested a pill called Reductil. I don't know how it works, but it really suppressed my appetite, and without any side effects. Well, one or two members of my family thought that my personality changed while I was taking it . . . but it really, really modified my eating patterns.

And, what was more, it modified my eating patterns long-term. Pre-Reductil – and I want money for saying this – I would go to Shanahan's, and I would get the entire T-bone steak into me. Now that doesn't happen. I can only get half the steak into me. And I can only get half the pea soup in. This drug is very powerful.

There are one or two people in senior management in RTÉ who thought that I was being paid by the drug company. Eventually, it got to the point where I was officially reprimanded and asked not to mention it again. But I wasn't getting paid. I was just a fan.

OPERATION TRANSFORMATION

Operation Transformation was not a comfortable experience for our six transformees. It wasn't a comfortable experience to stand beside it.

We spend most of our lives trying to cover our curves and our bumps. The exposure to which our six transformees subjected themselves was almost religious. It was like a baptism, an old-fashioned baptism. They had to prostrate themselves before the Altar of Change. You had to see them in all their frailty. You had to see them in all of their weakness starting from scratch. And that was literally what happened. We had our experts – Karl, Eva and Ian – giving them nutritional, exercise and mental-health advice. But, really, they did it all themselves. They did it themselves because, staring at their bodies in those Lycra suits, there was nowhere to go but forwards. Going back was not an option. Even standing still was not an option.

The main reason *Operation Transformation* was successful was because it provided infrastructural support, a crutch for people to lean on. The *Operation Transformation* experience taught me that an incredibly difficult and somewhat mystical struggle takes place in the minds of women around their bodyweight, their physical appearance and what they want to do to enjoy themselves. It was amazing the number of women we came into contact with who did not seem capable of modifying their daily exercise and food intake without some sort of support. Once they had even the basic support mechanism that the programme provided, they were able to take control of their lives. They were able to lose weight. They were able to modify their eating habits substantially. They were able to start exercising.

And some of the changes were phenomenal. The two guys in particular completely transformed themselves. And they are now not just physically in better shape, they feel better mentally, and their long-term health prospects have improved dramatically. Emotionally, now that they have lost all that baggage, the dynamic is richer and much more exciting. I mean, that's what it is. It's baggage. It's not just extra weight. There are all sorts of issues that go hand in glove with being overweight, right from the moment you get into your underpants and see your Homer Simpson belly sticking over your Hugo Boss waistband.

We are creatures of symmetry. Appearances have a huge effect on us. It's wrong to say that first impressions don't matter. First impressions matter hugely. First impressions can make the difference between getting a shot at a job or a romance. It's perfectly natural to be obsessed with physical appearance, style, and all that surrounds that. As a country, we never worried about that in the past because, number one, we didn't have the money. We were the least stylish people in the world. When I was growing up you were scaling the pinnacles of fashion going to O'Connor's to get your Levis.

Now, people are obsessed with their weight. We may be unhealthy. We may not be as fit as we used to be. We may not eat as well as we used to. But we, and women in particular, are more obsessed with our bodyweight than we ever were before. Yet we're heavier than ever before.

We spend hundreds of euros getting our hair done and buying the best clothes. And yet we can't do the very basic thing – and I include myself in this – of stopping and taking a look at ourselves in the mirror and going, 'What's happening here? What sort of lifestyle has led me to this complete physical collapse when I want to be considered sexually attractive?'

For better or worse, women rely more on their physical appearance than men. Men do rely on their physical appearance, but not to the same extent. I mean, there are some pretty weather-beaten guys out there with some very gorgeous women. (Of course you usually find that those weather-beaten guys have got very flush bank accounts and are driving Maybachs.) It's an aspect of the social revolution that has not been conquered. Because women are meant to be pursued. We are meant to chase them, to have sex with them to make more humans. You can't get away from that.

OK. Some women have become more predatory and more interested in the carnival of sex but, generally, the balance is still pretty much as it was in the cave. Men running after women.

The thing is, you only run after pretty ones. You don't run after ugly ones. It may be a hanging offence to say that, but it's a fact. And I'll tell you this. Every ugly girl would prefer to be pretty.

DON'T PUT GARLIC UP YOUR VAGINA

I've interviewed for the Olympics on homeopathy over the years. Millions and millions of interviews. Siobhan Hough and myself were having lunch one day, and we were talking about some guy who'd been recommending hair of Tunisian rabbit or something for cancer. 'Really, we shouldn't,' she said. 'This should stop.'

I do have deep suspicions about a lot of the flower remedies, and HUGE suspicions about some of the hands-off therapies. I think Reiki is complete bullshit. But some of the loveliest people I've ever interviewed are exponents of the art.

And so, look, if it makes you more comfortable, if it makes you more relaxed, if it seems to be assisting you, then do it. Whatever it is. But I have been deeply concerned by a number of stories that came to us as a result of interviews we'd done, in particular one in which it was suggested that some sort of super-ingestion of garlic could help cure cancer. It's a huge tragedy when somebody's fears are manipulated to the point at which they feel the only place they need to go is the garlic shop. I'm quite certain that conventional medical science has a lot more than garlic to offer somebody with cancer. Garlic may be a natural antibacterial but would I advise a woman, as someone on the programme once did, to put cloves into her vagina to get rid of thrush? No!

The radio programme is – was, should I say? – a portal for, I believe, a curious mix of people with wide-ranging ideas and opinions. We had quite a few well-dressed, highly articulate, very charismatic individuals talking absolute freaking horseshit. Not a lot, but a few.

One person gave us a selection of flower remedies for serious psychiatric illness, as well as for eczema, cancer and heart disease. Now, I know that these flower remedies are made with an infinitesimally small amount of whatever flower essence it is mixed with either alcohol or water. In my opinion it's utterly incredible to suggest that these flower remedies can have an impact on anything except your nose. That person was listened to. And people went out and got the stuff and phoned us and told us they were giving up their cancer medication because they were going to go on this stuff. And on that occasion, I had to say, 'You should not do that. You should go to your doctor before you take anything that isn't your recommended medication.'

So there were a couple of experiences like that which . . . I wouldn't say soured us, but were milestones certainly in our growing-up process. You have to be incredibly careful about the welfare of the audience when you're dealing with illness, be it mental or physical. You have to be incredibly sensitive. It's a huge responsibility to have because when people are in trouble, when they've been given bad news, they will often seek out alternative remedies and medicines and can be vulnerable to placing faith in untested methods . . .

There are homeopathic remedies that have worked, and there is anecdotal evidence at least to suggest that they have improved people's well-being. The Udo's Oil stuff really worked for me. My hair thickened up. The arthritis became less pronounced. And also, if you want to know, it makes the passage of compacted stools a less horrendous experience. And I have one or two friends who will testify to that as well. So it's not just me.

The other thing is that we have a wonderful family on the radio show where some people believe implicitly in Reiki, and others don't believe in it at all. And I do try to make sure that that kind of balance is maintained. But the conclusion that we've come to as a group, because of the power that the radio show has, is that we have to be extremely careful about the messages that are sent out.

GERRY RYAN! A MILLION EUROS! ISN'T HE FANTASTIC? HAVE A CIGAR!

When they started publicizing the salaries of the top earners in RTÉ, I didn't give a shit.

I know that some of my colleagues were very sensitive about it. For the most part, I've always been fairly celebratory about how much I earn. In fact, I don't earn enough. I think I should earn at least as much as Pat Kenny.

Bob Collins was the director general at the time and he knew that the Oireachtas committee dealing with the issue was about to insist on the publication of individual salaries. Up to that point, they'd say, 'Well, there's a pool of ten million or something like that.' Now, if you asked anybody in the commercial broadcasting world what they paid their top stars they'd tell you to go fuck yourself. It's commercially sensitive information. Willie O'Reilly's not gonna tell you what Matt Cooper's getting, right? And yet some of the guys in the commercial sector were saying, 'Oh, tut tut tut, RTÉ needs to tell us how much Gay Byrne,

Gerry Ryan, Ryan Tubridy or whoever is getting.' Bob had been sounding out some of the guys on bigger salaries and most were pretty negative about impending publication. They didn't want anybody talking about their salary.

I always worked on the basis that when a record company signed up a big band they always said what they'd given them. The Sex Pistols. Ten million! Virgin says, 'Hurray! We really believe in this band!' So I could never understand why RTÉ, when we were signing a contract, didn't kind of have 'Gerry Ryan! A million euros! Isn't he fantastic? Have a cigar!'

Now, a lot of it, I know, was just political prurience. Exactly what the people of Ireland were going to get out of knowing how much Gay or Gerry earned is beyond me. I mean, what were they going to do? Some kind of cost—benefit analysis? I was mystified but, as I say, I didn't really care.

When the information came out, there were no great shocks. I was surprised that Joe Duffy was getting as little as he was. But what was the point of it? I think it was a wank basically. I think it was a major wank by the Oireachtas committee. I think they wanted to get in there and cause hassle and frighten RTÉ. And they did manage to do that.

PAT KENNY

Well, I've known Pat for many, many years. I don't see him socially as much as I used to when I was younger, but I have great respect for him. He's a tremendous broadcaster, he has a great mind and he's a huge asset to the station.

JOE DUFFY

I get on extremely well with Joe Duffy, and not just because I was in college with him. *Liveline* and the *Ryan Show* are in two parallel universes. Many of the things we talk about have been talked about on Joe's show and vice versa. And certainly a day doesn't go by when Joe doesn't drop by the office to say, 'Hello, anything interesting going on, guys?'

And we keep a very close eye on what Joe's doing in the afternoon. Sometimes out of envy, sometimes to inform us that maybe we should visit that subject the following day. So, there's a lot of interaction between the two.

RYAN TUBRIDY

Ryan Tubridy has recently become a member of the Grumpy Old Men Club, though he's only a tenth the age of the rest of us. That's me, Paul McGuinness, Harry Crosbie and Gay Byrne. Ryan joined us on our last monthly luncheon. He was extremely well behaved, of course, and brought presents for everybody. Hillary Clinton's autobiography. Gay was extremely impressed because he got something for free.

I enjoy these kinds of gatherings, sitting down with fellas who have done exceedingly well in their own fields and who have had tremendous influence on Irish society and thinking. I don't get to hear Ryan because he's on at the same time as I am, but he does come on to my programme quite frequently. And that's always good fun. His opinions are as varied and as passionately held as any I have. It's great fun to have him on just to prod him a bit and get him to say something bold.

MARIAN FINUCANE

Marian's a real soldier when it comes to broadcasting. She's been at the coal face, she's done her time and she's an absolute natural. She's made that choice to curtail what she's doing, *and* she gets paid the same amount for only coming in at the weekend. On Saturday and Sunday Marian's is the programme I switch on. That says everything in my opinion.

RAY D'ARCY

Ray's a bit of a conundrum. He's a very successful broadcaster first of all. You have to accept that. But I often wonder, like, what is Ray doing? I think that Ray doesn't like to offend people and yet he's under a lot of pressure, I believe, to be more aggressive than he really wants to be when he's on the radio.

He has been tremendously successful in terms of television too.

I was out for dinner one night with Willie O'Reilly and Ray showed up. He was sitting there and you could tell he was quite uncomfortable in my company. I could see him thinking, I don't need fucking Ryan. What's he gonna say now? He's gonna be At Me. That's the sort of feeling I got from him.

Willie and I were pissed, and we were talking about doing a charity simulcast with Ray and 2FM. It seemed a great idea for the ten minutes we were discussing it. Ray, I believe, was completely appalled by the idea.

One of the *Ryan Show* researchers did her thesis on 'Ray D'Arcy and Gerry Ryan: The Pepsi-Cola and Coca-Cola of Irish Broadcasting'. I really don't accept that at all. I don't think Ray D'Arcy bears any resemblance to me whatsoever. Ray has a substantial audience, but he's also part of a very well-oiled machine. He's following Ian Dempsey's very successful and well-crafted breakfast programme. Willie O'Reilly is an absolute genius when it comes to presenting and promoting his radio programmes. The advertising campaigns are, without doubt, the best in the history of Irish broadcasting and so before Ray even opens his mouth he's a serious competitor . . . but I just cannot accept that we are comparable in any way, shape or form.

For a start, Ray's a much nicer person than I am.

INSTANT SEARING BLACK GLOOM

There is no point in doing programmes unless people are watching or listening to them. Now, we can't be completely ratings driven. We can't have just one *Sex and the City* after another, one *Big Brother* after another, one blockbuster movie after another, in the coarse pursuit of ratings. We do have a legal remit at RTÉ, which obliges us to educate, entertain and inform, and there are parameters within which we are meant to behave when we are doing that. BUT: we are, by the very nature of the medium and the marketplace, driven by ratings.

I have never been at a meeting where I was congratulated for having a small audience. I've never been at a meeting where somebody went, 'Well, that was really relevant and very significant from a social point of view. We're so glad that you did that programme, even though only twenty people listened to it.'

The only time I've ever been congratulated was when we were successful. *Operation Transformation*, for instance, had absolutely enormous market share. In radio everyone watches the quarterly Joint National Listenership Survey (JNRL books, as they're called), which tells you whether or not your audience is growing. In the recent past, following a period of some uncertainty, we've had four successive positive books. These increases were greeted with champagne pops in the radio centre – and enormous relief on the part not only of myself and my team, but on that of everyone else as well. 'Great, the *Ryan Show* is doing well. That's really, really important.'

I have a bonus in my contract tied into maintaining audience. There are certain targets and, if they are met, I get an extra amount of money every year.

Conversely, an incredible gloom will settle over the station when ratings fall. I'm talking about instant searing black *gloom* . . . People become filled with self-doubt and the finger of blame gets pointed in all directions. Very few, in my experience, point it at themselves. And if it goes on and a pattern develops, well . . .

Willie O'Reilly, at Today FM, says that one bad book is interesting. Two is not good news, but let's not get too excited. Three, however, is a pattern, and may indicate that the brand or the product or the plan has come to its natural conclusion. Now, in the past *The Gerry Ryan Show* has sustained three books down in a row. I believe that if we had been in the commercial world the programme would have been either taken off the air or radically modified. Then, suddenly, the fourth book came along, and we had a huge increase in audience. And, of course, with *The Gerry Ryan Show*, because we're dealing with a large listenership, even a small percentile increase or decrease amounts to a very big slice of audience. So ratings are a huge issue.

Shortly before the publication of a book, people can become consumed and transfixed by what it might contain. Siobhan Hough is the producer in charge of the radio programme. I see a physical change in her coming up to the JNLR survey news. Which is not to say that everyone shits themselves. You'll find in every office, for every programme, there'll be people who feel it's nothing to do with them. And those people are the nine-to-fivers. They go home and they don't think about work. They play golf or whatever. And then there's a bunch of people, and I have to say that they are the people I work with, who live, breathe, eat, drink, shit and fuck ratings. Their lives are utterly consumed by the show.

In television there's more of an obsession with what they call market share, which is basically looking to see how much of the available audience you captured with your programme. So while it's nice to see six or seven hundred thousand, possibly even a million people watching a television programme, the question in Ireland is did you get 40–45 per cent of the available audience that night? Because if you did, then you're a friggin' genius. And I've managed that in recent times with some of the programmes I've done.

When we get bad news on the ratings front my first reaction is always selfish. How long have I got left in my contract? If I've got three, four or five years, I'll go, 'Well, tomorrow's another day. We'll just examine the situation.' Sometimes it's the vagaries of the audience and there's very little you can do about it. Certainly, what I've found in the last five years, with the radio anyway, is that you can reinvigorate. You can reinvent. You can do things that you never dreamed were possible in terms of upping your game, injecting more oxygen, more potency and vibrancy into the broadcast. A lot of it is just bringing a different head to work. As you walk up the steps you say to yourself, 'I'm going to rock the shop today. I'm going to leave all my personal baggage at the door, or if I bring the baggage on-air, I'm going to get out a can of petrol and set fire to it in public.'

You cannot coast. You cannot coast, even during difficult personal times. I've never coasted. I believe that I give 110 per cent on-air. There are times when you may come away from a week of OK broadcasting, and you say to yourself, 'Well, what was happening there? I was kind of marking time.'

And you'll usually find there's an explanation. You've had a row with someone, your health isn't great. Maybe you're tired. Maybe you're exhausted. There's usually a physical reason for it. You can also examine the formatting of the programme. You can employ the so-called radio or TV doctors to tinker with what you've got, to try to make it more audience-friendly. You can reassess the elements of the programme on an ongoing basis. But you know something? If it worked yesterday, it should work today, and it should work tomorrow. A lot of it has to do with how fresh and how vibrant you can keep it.

WHY DON'T YOU FUCKERS JUST STAY DOING WHAT YOU DO BEST?

To this day, I think it was a gigantic act of folly for Ryan Tubridy to go to Radio 1.

When Ryan was doing *The Full Irish*, it was the most exciting broadcast at that hour of the morning since Ian Dempsey started on Today FM. Ian has this really gentle delivery style, with a stellar cast of characters, courtesy of Mario Rosenstock . . . It's still there and it's a great programme.

Ryan Tubridy started his broadcasting career with us on the *Ryan Show*, working literally as a tea boy. I know he hates me saying this, but here was this highly educated guy who decided that he was going to come in and basically do anything in the *Ryan Show* office. Within a few days, I'd realized he was brilliant. I would come in in the morning, and if I wanted to talk about Vietnam, the Kennedys, whatever, Ryan was the man. He was kind of like a son. And, God help him, I used to lecture him all the time. And I still lecture. I hector him because I believe he needs to get his cock out a bit more. Because he can. Everyone thinks he's the best boy in the class but he's not. Not at all.

Anyway, when John McMahon was producing *The Full Irish* and Shane was doing the sports news with his own kind of Nob Nation, what you had was a splendido team. I mean, this was a team of guys that was very, very cool. Ryan brought a kind of effortless ease to the broadcast, which was hugely attractive to a massively wide audience. So along comes Bloody Radio 1. I was utterly appalled that, without any consultation, they took this guy out of our schedule. OK, he did have a part to play himself. He could have said, 'No, I'm not going . . .'

Part of me was kind of impressed that he was willing to go up against me. But another part thought, Well, fuck this. This is working so well. His show feeds so well into my show. And it was a bit like 'the fans not wanting the band to break up.' John

McMahon is married to Evelyn O'Rourke, our reporter. John was a guitar player in a band that was coming to the end of its life. It was Oasis's final tour, that sort of stuff. And John wanted to go for bigger things. He wanted to be In Management. He wanted to be Grown Up. So Bloody John and Bloody Ryan wanted to be Grown-Ups. That's what it amounted to, and I really – I mean, if I didn't beg them on bended knees, I begged them over whiskey. 'Why don't you fuckers just stay doing what you do best, and that's making this programme?'

I really didn't think that it had been on long enough. I thought that there was another two or three years in it. THEN go and become the editor of Radio 1, which John did do, eventually. He's now in a senior position in television scheduling.

But both John and Ryan wanted to be grown-ups. I mean, I really love both of them, and they're still friggin' kids. They still love gadgets. They still love having a good time. They love all the right films. They love all the right books. They're the two brightest boys on the block, John McMahon and Ryan Tubridy. But the fuckers broke up the band. John became a fully fledged adult and put on a tie and got a real office. And took up residence at Radio 1 as a Serious Broadcaster.

OK, Ryan's programme has done really well. I mean, Ryan has valiantly battled against what happens to you when you go to Radio 1. And what happens to you when you go to Radio 1? Well, no disrespect to the holders of great office over there, but it's like you get covered in treacle. It's a much more difficult place to work because they have very, very strict editorial controls. Their procedures and protocols are strictly enforced. Ryan went into a world where the senior producer is God, and you can't be stepping out of line, and you can't say, 'Fuck,' and you can't say, 'I farted,' and was that a good idea for the brightest boy in the class? I don't think so.

But now he's made his bed he has to lie in it.

So he's done really well, and he's great on the TV. If they wanted to emulate a *Conan O'Brien* or *Letterman*, it's certainly happening in spades now. As a guest, it's a hugely comfortable place to be. I love the Camembert Quartet . . .

But I was just so upset when he left 2FM. I had huge arguments with the head of 2FM, John Clarke, because at the time I had a bigger editorial role in my contract. They were obliged to consult me about schedule changes, in particular about those across the radio division that might affect *The Gerry Ryan Show*.

I don't have that now, and I'm delighted, to be honest, because nobody ever listened to me anyway. We used to have these long, meaningful arguments and discussions, during which they would listen politely to everything I said, then go away and ignore me. So besides being completely pointless, it was also quite hurtful. I remember arguing with poor John Clarke. Poor, beleaguered John Clarke. John is so patient, and he's so supportive of the *Ryan Show*, and I always can see it on his face when I come rocking into the office. *Gerry Ryan. Ah, fuck. One more minute and I'd have been out of here.*

And I'd sit there, and I'd go on and on. Eventually, one day, John just said, 'You know, Gerry, the guys at the top want Tubridy on Radio 1, so just fucking stop talking about it. OK? Get a life.'

So then we went through all sorts of gymnastics trying to replace him.

And nothing worked.

And everyone involved in those experiments was, I think, damaged by the experience.

This is a cut-throat business, and there was a period when we were going through absolute hell in trying to deal with our nine a.m. start because we were taking delivery of only 150,000 people. Ryan Tubridy would be getting close on 600,000 from *Morning Ireland*. And let me tell you this: by ten o'clock, that account would have been balanced. But to achieve that, the effort involved was absolutely phenomenal. I don't believe RTÉ recognized that. They got very upset about my ranting and raving about it, first in meetings and then, understandably, when I went public. I said I felt it had been a bad decision to put Rick and Ruth, two otherwise very talented broadcasters, into the breakfast slot. Adrian Moynes, the head of the radio division, got so upset about that he sent me a handwritten letter of complaint, and he was completely right to do so.

So then what did I do? I bullied RTÉ into giving Marty Whelan the job, and Marty's thing didn't work out much better. However, Colm and Jim-Jim are a breath of fresh air, and an enormous relief.

But I will always feel that John and Ryan are like members of some great rock band that broke up too soon.

GERRY RYAN, GERRY RYAN, GERRY RYAN, GERRY RYAN, GERRY RYAN . . .

I've grown up being famous. I've been on television since my twenties. It's a weird, Olsen twins thing, and it means there are elements of it I don't notice any more. I mean, as I'm walking along, just about seven or eight paces behind me I hear my name. My whole life I've heard this whispered Gerry Ryan, Gerry Ryan, Gerry Ryan, Gerry Ryan, Gerry Ryan fading into the distance.

I understand the process of pressing the flesh and I do it automatically.

I do it in my sleep.

Since my wife and I split up, there's been a different dimension for me when I'm out in public. All these old ladies come up to me in the supermarket and start touching me. It's like that scene in *Close Encounters* when they're all coming out of the spaceship and touching Richard Dreyfuss . . . I've spent my life being stopped by people and told things. I get 'My-wife-thinks-you're-great-but-I-think-you're-a-fucking-queer'; those guys are always available for comment. But more often than not it's very positive. I've spent most of my life walking in the gaze of affection. I get people thanking me the whole time. It's been an incredible experience.

Irish people can take the piss out of you very efficiently. They're very good at grounding you. And Irish people are fantastic at bigging you up as well. I've felt huge support from people publicly several times in my life, and that has been very life-affirming and enriching. I defy anybody to say it isn't a good feeling to have a teenager or a child or an old woman come up to you and say, 'Thank you, I like what you do.'

My kids have grown up with *Gerry Ryan*. That's all they know. I remember watching *The School Around the Corner* with my eldest daughter and eldest son, Charlotte and Rex, when they were very young. One of them turned round and said, 'Look, Daddy, there's Gerry Ryan on the television.' They were actually able to differentiate between my TV persona and me at home.

My children have seen their father in his underpants, drunk, besuited and fêted, celebrated, falling down and getting back up again. By and large they have a positive reaction to me as a public figure. They're entertained sometimes by the way that the outside world reacts to their father. They get a giggle out of it. They've always understood that it will get you a good restaurant seat, those first-class seats on a plane. They love the private knowledge, the sacred knowledge, the inner-sanctum knowledge; yeah, well, he farts and looks ridiculous in the mornings with all his hair sticking up. They're proud of me and they're protective of me. Now, I'm quite sure at school they've often heard, 'He's a wanker,' though they've never come home and said that to me. I don't know how they deal with it. As I always said to them, 'If you're getting that, you'll get over it in the five-star hotel when you're on holidays with me.'

My boys are more reticent about the showbiz stuff. They will be less likely to stand for the photograph at a public event. They usually scatter. You won't see them doing it. You'll look around and you'll go, 'Where's Rex? Where's Eliot?' If you ask them, if you say, 'Lads, I really need you to stand in this photograph with me,' they will do it.

The girls on the other hand are very showbiz. They'll stand and they'll pose and they'll give good copy.

But they're all good ambassadors for me. They have impeccable manners. They're very articulate. They know how to speak up when it's appropriate. They're not imperious in the way they behave. They don't appear to be spoiled. They're generous. They're complimentary to people and they give up their time when they see, oh, it's people who want to speak to Gerry's children. They're very good like that. I mean, they remind me of the Royal Family.

They know that there's this burden and they've accepted it.

GOD, DEATH, ET CETERA

One morning my wife got a phone call from my mum, who was in a bit of a state. She said that my father hadn't been to the toilet for a couple of weeks. A couple of *weeks*! I had to go to work, so Morah went down to the house and took him to the Bon Secours. When I got to the hospital later that day, he was in very cheerful humour. A catheter had been inserted and that had given him tremendous relief. But I knew.

One of the most common symptoms of prostate cancer is not being able to go to the toilet. I got everybody out of the room and I asked him how long this had been going on. And I knew, I just knew, without him uttering a word, that there was a serious problem here. Like so many men, like with that tax issue years before, he had just ignored the problem.

'Well,' he said, 'a good while.'

'Like six months?'

'No. Longer.'

'Well,' I said, 'you're fucked, Sunshine.'

'Don't say that to the women. Don't say that to anybody outside.'

'Don't worry, I won't.'

He was very enthusiastic about getting treatment, and a very fine surgeon, an expert in the area of prostate, operated on him. I remember taking the call from the surgeon while I was sitting at my desk in RTÉ. 'We just did the operation on your dad,' he said, 'and he's going to be much relieved after this. We've sent off the tumour . . .' Here, again, I just knew there was more information on the way.

'Well,' I said, 'what do you think?'

'We'll know when we get the results from the biopsy.'

'Come on,' I said, 'you've been doing this for years.'

There was a pause.

'OK,' he said eventually, 'I'll be straight with you. I know instantly, by handling the tumour, by the very texture of it. On a scale of one to ten, it's a ten.'

I went to see my father in hospital when he was recuperating and he was in absolutely flying form. There was a guy beside him who was in a much more advanced state of cancer, who was close to dying and had only days, literally, to live. My father was counselling him, bucking him up, telling him stories. He was a real fighter, my dad. He walked up and down the hospital wards, trying to get himself back into some sort of physical shape, and there was a substantial improvement in him in the short term. But when he came home, he just wasn't the same. He never really regained his full physical articulation again.

My mother started making these whispered phone calls in the dead of night, saying that he was up at all hours, that he was in pain, that he was uncomfortable. I realized there was more going on than just the prostate cancer. Finally, one night I went down home to see him and he was so bad, he was almost crying in agony.

'You have to ring the surgeon,' I told him. 'You've got to find out what else is happening here.'

So he rang him and, without my father knowing, I listened on the extension. I heard the doctor saying, 'Well, it could have gone into your bowel or some of your other organs, or maybe your spine.'

I just remember my father saying, 'Oh dear.'

'You know, Vincent,' the surgeon went on, 'we'll bring you in to have you checked out further and maybe we'll consider chemotherapy.'

He had already undergone some chemotherapy, but it was the kind that should have been applied early on and was probably pointless at that stage.

I remember going in to him after he finished on the phone. 'What did he say?'

'Oh,' he said, 'everything's fine. It's grand.'

We got him into hospital and he went downhill pretty quickly. I was due to go on holiday. I remember asking him, 'Do you think it's safe for me to go?'

We went.

Sanibel Island, one of the most beautiful places in the world. While I was out there, I got a phone call from John Clarke in 2FM, saying that the audience figures had just come out and we'd shot up. 'Get a cigar. Buy a bottle of champagne on me.' Then he said, 'By the way, I think there's some news on your dad. Maybe you should phone home.'

So I got in touch with my brother, Mano. 'He's not good,' said Mano.

'Well, should I come home now?'

'No,' he said, 'I don't think so.'

It was one of the most difficult decisions ever. I walked down to the beach at sunset and I remember looking out across the ocean and thinking how much my father would have loved to be there. I thought, Well, OK, on the balance of probabilities, he'll last another few days. So I didn't go.

When we got back and I called up to see him, I remember thinking, *Oh, Jesus, this guy is really bad.* He had got to a point where the cancer had spread quite extensively.

One evening, I was visiting him in the hospital with my two brothers. I had sent Mum home. He was very, very bad, very close to death but aware, I believe, of what was ahead of him. He was terrified of death, I think; absolutely terrified. I don't know why. It's easy for me to say, but I think when my time comes I just want to be really, really comfortable. My father, on the other hand, just didn't want to die.

Not long after my mum had gone home, the nurse said to me, 'Look. He's going now.'

We gathered around the bed, the three of us, and listened to his breathing begin to change. And there is a death-rattle noise, a kind of breathing that develops when the system is closing down. The nurse was wonderful. She said, 'Speak to him, speak to him. He can still hear.'

And I remember thinking, *Wow, what must this be like? For a man who's frightened of dying? Who physically cannot sit up any more? How terrifying would that be?* And I remember leaning down and telling him we were there. I remember saying, 'It's OK now. You can go to sleep. It's all right to do that now.'

And he just stopped breathing.

It was incredible, the closest thing to being present at the birth of my children that I've ever experienced. My two brothers were absolutely devastated. I remember holding their hands and realizing that I was now in charge.

ANTONY AND CLEOPATRA

My mum had been called and, God help her, always the drama queen, she arrives in wailing, 'Is he gone? Is he gone?'

One of the medical staff there started to say, 'Yes, he's —'

I looked at her and shook my head briskly. 'No, no,' I said.

'He's not gone yet . . . He's just, ah, slipping away. You're just in time.'

So in she came in and, in a theatrical flourish, leaned over the bed: 'Vincent! Don't go!'

I don't know whether she knew he was dead or not but, certainly, her final goodbyes were spectacular. And I had to smile. *Whoa*, I thought, *good girl. Well done. This is the way to handle it.* She threw herself on him like Cleopatra on Antony. It was sad, of course, but I think she was also tremendously relieved because he'd been in such pain.

Like my mother, I was relieved. It was about two days before I cried. Then I cried a lot, which was good. And that was it. He was gone.

My dad's father, Stephen Ryan, had come from your typical Irish Catholic background, but his mother, Charlotte McKenzie, was of Scottish Protestant stock. Though my father was raised as a Catholic, that Protestant tradition remained in the family. It was in the atmosphere. I remember visiting the house as a child, and it wasn't like a conventional Catholic home. It had more of an Anglicized feel to it. There were pictures on the mantelpiece of people in British servicemen's uniforms. That side of the family, who visited us less frequently than my mother's, could hardly have been more different. But that tradition survived in our own house, and my father frequently reminded us that in this respect, as in so many others, We Were Different.

I remember once arriving back from primary school full of Catholic piety. We were getting ready to go on retreat, or there was a sodality coming up in St John's Church, and I was all fire and brimstone and Down With The Protestants. And my father said, very gently, that we had to respect all other churches. And I would say no, the only way into Heaven was through the Catholic eye of a needle, and he said, 'You must recall that there is Protestant blood flowing through your veins as well.'

That tradition has survived into my own family. We ended up sending my children to the Presbyterian school in Clontarf. This was a great moment for my dad, seeing an aspect of his history now openly reflected. I spoke about it on the radio quite a bit. I'd talk about my background and where I'd come from, and that I wasn't just a Catholic or just a Protestant, that I came from this uniquely Irish mix of two very separate Christian communities.

The older my father got, the more he seemed to place his trust in God. And I think the older he got as well – I don't think this is untypical – he found a great comfort in the mysticism of the Catholic mass. He always liked things on a grand scale. When we were children, we stopped attending mass in our local parish church and went instead to high mass in the Pro-cathedral. We'd get dressed up and be driven into town, into the Proger, as we used to call it, where mass was a Major Production. You had a couple of priests on the altar, there was incense, millions of candles, and they were all speaking this weird Klingon language, otherwise known as Latin.

He was perpetually searching, my father. When I think back to the time of his death, I believe this was a man who really hoped for an afterlife, who hoped that there would be something in the Christian message of salvation. I'm not so sure whether he completely believed it. It wasn't that he was an atheist or anything, but I think he had his doubts. I think he would have been much happier to have had a very simple faith. This search of his led him sometimes into some pretty ludicrous fixations. One of these was Erich von Daniken's *Chariots of the Gods*. This guy's contention was that ancient civilizations were in communication with space travellers, who they more or less believed were gods. This notion really appealed to my father. And it was just utter shite – absolute and utter shite. Dad used to get quite upset when I tried to point out how utterly nonsensical it was.

When he died I went to the Protestant pastor, the Reverend Jim Brogan, in Clontarf, and asked him to participate in the service at my father's funeral in St John's. My mum was Catholic, so he was always going to have a predominately Catholic funeral, but James Brogan, with the parish priest in St John's, did something that I think was very brave. They shared the one altar.

The two traditions came together really well. James contributed substantially to a very moving service. I was really impressed by and found great comfort in the fact that these two sometimes polarized churches were coming together to serve their community. These guys were doing what priests *should* do: administering comfort and easing the passing of this man. It was a great moment for my family.

CHRISTMAS IS NOT OVER

My mother died on Christmas Day 2006. Christmas Day. Could it have been on any other? She died suddenly, which was as it should have been. She could not have handled anything like my father's ordeal. I mean, if he was frightened, she would have been utterly terrified. As far as my mother was concerned, all of my father's pronouncements on technology, science, medicine, literature and art were gospel. If he'd said, 'Don't take aspirin, it's bad for you,' she'd have gone along with him.

We had just finished looking at the presents Santa Claus had left for the children and the phone rang. Once again, I knew. I knew the second my brother Michael said, 'Ger.' I just knew he was going to tell me that Mum was dead.

'Ger,' he said, 'she's gone.'

'Gone where?'

'Gone,' he said. 'She's gone. She's dead.'

And, God help him, it must have been awful for him because he was still living with her. He went in to say, 'Happy Christmas,' to his mum on Christmas morning, and she was dead in bed.

When I got down to the house, she was lying there, looking as if she was fast asleep. I know people often say that, that the dead person looked like they were about to sit up and start talking to you, but it's true. It was uncanny. I now know from talking to our doctor that in all likelihood she had died peacefully in her sleep.

When the undertakers had removed her body in the black ambulance, I went back to my family. There they sat, all looking up at me. I remember thinking, This is a time for strength. I could sense what they were saying: Is Christmas over? And I knew that if I fell apart and didn't continue with the day, Christmas would be ruined for ever. So I said to myself, No, Christmas is not over.

I made the Christmas lunch and served it up.

My mum had wrapped most of her presents the night before and I brought them up from Clontarf Road to our house in Castle Avenue and we sat down with the children. That was absolutely incredible. The experience of reading the Christmas messages, these notes in her almost indecipherable writing, as we opened the gifts that night, knowing this was the last thing she had done. It's impossible to describe how powerful and valuable that experience was. I really felt she was reaching out to us through those little cards.

I'd gone to see her on Christmas Eve. She was very ill, I now realize, and I have some guilt around that. I do wonder was there anything more I could have done.

She told me she was dying.

I thought it was bullshit. She'd said it several times before. She was a robust, healthy woman. I mean, she'd never died before, so I didn't see why she was going to die then. But that night she'd insisted that I take my wife's Christmas present and give it to her. I just wonder, did she *really know* that she was dying?

But I do believe that continuing with Christmas was the right thing to do. The children will never look back on Christmas and say, 'Well, that's the day when Dad was banging his head off the wall because his mother died.' It's a test that I feel I passed.

It was a big show, the funeral. Bono was there. Colin Farrell was there. My mum would have been absolutely delighted that so many of the showbiz élite turned up. Guys like Colin and Bono, I don't know whether it's because of the line of business they're in, but they always seem to know the right thing to say and the right embrace to give. And they always, in all circumstances, get the right side to the cameras.

I was delighted that so many people turned up. The church was absolutely bursting at the gills. OK, one or two unseemly things happened – the press photographers in the porch was wrong. But you know something? A story's a story. My son carried the coffin with me, my eldest son. There was a photograph on the front page of the *Daily Mail*. One half of me was going, 'That's a very inappropriate photograph,' and the other half of me was going, 'Yeah, bloody great photo.'

It was also an occasion for me, once again, to test my skills as an orator. I'm looking at the two brothers and they're going, 'Well, this is what you do . . .'

But I really enjoyed speaking about Mum. I mean, it had been very moving to give the oration at my father's funeral and it was from the heart. But he was a difficult man to capture. I hope I did him justice. I think I did. But my mother was so much easier because she had such a flamboyant personality. There were great stories to tell. I talked about lying in bed when I was eleven years old, with a cocktail party going on downstairs and these women with their Elizabeth Taylor hairstyles and little black dresses arriving up to kiss me good night. I remember being transfixed by heaving bosoms spilling out when they leaned over me, and the unique smell of Chanel No. 5 and Martini mingled together. This was the superchick generation my mother belonged to.

Mindful of what my mum would have wanted, I did my best to give her crying, laughing and clapping, and she got all three.

A year later, when I stood in the Odyssey Arena in Belfast and watched my fourteen-year-old daughter on stage with her band, Lady Nada, supporting Westlife in front of a crowd of ten thousand, I could feel my mother everywhere. In the gods, in the wings, on the sound-desk. I think my mother was more proud of the fact that her granddaughters had become dancers than of anything that happened in my career, because all three, Lottie, Bonnie and Babs, are dance obsessed; they're great instinctive dancers. Watching Bonnie dance, watching her move that night, I could sense my mother in every step.

GHOSTS

We haven't got around to selling my parents' home on Clontarf Avenue yet. This home was originally my grandparents'. My father ran his dental practice out of what was his old bedroom, and we left Kincora Avenue to move back there when I was in college. These days, I try to visit as little as possible, because there are too many ghosts. I find it very uncomfortable.

I can still smell my mother. I look out the back window and I can see my father's workbench. I can see myself, my two sons, one or two of their pals and my dad working on a model-aircraft engine, getting it ready for flight. We spent an entire summer doing that. Then, behind him, I can see my grandfather with his patch on, from the time he damaged his eye burning twigs in the backyard. And then I go back even further to when I was very young and I can see the tennis court that used to be there. I can almost hear voices from a time long, long gone. I remember visiting there as a very young child, when my grandparents lived there. I remember going down to see my father when he had his dental practice there. Walking into the packed waiting room, which is now the living room, and seeing all those people fidgeting and nervously reading their papers before going in to see the dentist . . .

It's been through so many different incarnations, that house. I have very powerful memories, and I can experience them quite efficiently and faithfully now, here, thinking back. I don't know whether I really want to spend any more time roaming around inside the tomb.

GOD

I do believe that without religious belief you are a little lonelier than everyone else. And I think that the Christian faith has been a pretty good moral compass in its pure form. I mean, obviously there are aberrant forms of it, and we've seen terrible examples of that in this country. But if you take the basic Christian message, which is one of mercy and compassion, love and understanding – Christ as a sort of revolutionary hippie – if you stick with that aspect of the faith, it has an awful lot of positive things to offer.

BEING DAD

We didn't plan to have a big family. We never really talked about having children at all. All of our children materialized pretty much as a surprise to me.

I think that was kind of good.

When my eldest daughter was born, I remember everybody saying, oh, she looks so like this person, she looks so like that person. I just remember thinking, She looks like Yoda from *Star Wars*. Women have a fantastic capacity to see likenesses that I would need some sort of cosmic microscope to discover. Maybe there's a Darwinian explanation for that, you know, to stop us throwing the baby who looks like Yoda into the hole in the ground. But, of course, they do blossom later in life.

I was there for the births of my children and I remember them all individually. They were unique experiences. The thing that I have always found fascinating is how it actually works out. Through the drama and the physicality of it, a child comes into the world and that child is OK: it's living and breathing. Women become emotionally entangled with it much more quickly than men do. Men certainly develop an equally powerful attachment to their offspring, but I think nature has designed it very cleverly so that women become *instantly* attached, even to the most hideous baby imaginable. That bit fascinates me: the power of nature to protect the species in the post-reproductive moments.

Some guys I know were hugely involved in antenatal classes. I never went to one. Also they engaged in the process of giving birth to the extent that they were almost doing it simultaneously with their wife. I never bought into that at all. I was more or less a bystander. Obviously if there's love and trust between the couple, the guy's presence can certainly make the woman feel a bit more comfortable, but I'm not really into becoming part and parcel of the birth process. Women do that on their own with the assistance of midwives. Some of the stories I've heard of women trying to take care of their partner while simultaneously giving birth are bewildering. He's fainting, he's crying or confused – or suddenly he wants to be an obstetrician. My attitude was to stand back a bit and basically marvel at what was happening. It still astonishes me that out of another body can come another human being, perfectly formed.

I don't believe either that men *have* to be there at the birth. I think there are some guys who just can't handle it. They get in the way. And others become an absolute burden. Some women would be much better off with their mother or a girlfriend, and if that's the case, they should be able to go for it without being afraid of upsetting anyone.

Guys do take a while to come to terms with what's happened. It's quite a shock to the male system to suddenly have to deal with something that renders you less significant in your partner's life – for the time being at least – than you were before. And I don't care what anybody says, in those early stages, women tend to carry the main burden. It's not so much that guys are unwilling to contribute but, basically, establishing the bond between mother and child is essential to the child's physical and emotional safety. Guys tend to adopt a satellite existence around them, and I think fellas who take that too seriously or who take umbrage over their partner not responding to them in the same way really need to take themselves aside. You just have to accept that that's the way it's going to be for a while. Slowly but surely, the male role begins to re-emerge, which is as it should be.

When the baby arrives, you have no idea what you're doing. I mean, I remember waking up our children all the time, particularly the first two, because we constantly thought they were dead. Over time, you do become more comfortable and confident about simple things like holding a child, bathing a child, feeding a child. I remember men of my father's generation. Some guys didn't hold their sons or daughters for the first year of the child's life because they didn't know how to. But the emotional bond that men can forge with an infant is underestimated. It can be very, very strong. Most of our children ending up sleeping in the bed with us. I know some child psychologists will say that that's a recipe for disaster, that you'll never get them out, but it gives a man an opportunity to get to know his child very well. Certainly it worked for me.

When work would ramp up – and I did a lot of travelling in the early days of my career – the lion's share of the childcare was left to my wife. But I think in the final analysis I've been more engaged than a lot of other guys of my generation. I am proactive in what I do with my children, and I worry a lot about their connection with both of their parents. I believe I have that connection, not necessarily by instinct but because I've worked at it.

ANYBODY CAN PARENT

Anybody can parent. I've been very lucky for the last twenty years. I've grown up on a continuous parenting course with the radio programme. I'm constantly being challenged by people whose livelihood is based on understanding parenting. I've learned a lot about myself, about my shortcomings and the good things I bring to parenting.

There's so much more to it, these days, than there seems to have been in our parents' time. When I was a child, the idea of a child psychologist becoming involved in your life would have been bizarre. If my parents had had to resort to counselling or therapy they would have been seen as freaks at best and failures at worst. That has changed dramatically. My parents never attended a parent–teacher meeting in their lives and were never phoned up by the school to discuss poor behaviour at break time, but that seems to be part and parcel of any parent's life now – mine included, and my kids are no more or less wild than any others. I sometimes think the level of involvement that we have in their education is a bit unnecessary. Parents on the one hand demand to be consulted on how their children are educated, yet when the school rings up we say, 'Well, could you not deal with that? Why have I got to be involved?'

These days, you have to understand the child's curriculum. You have to understand the subject choices. You have to understand the implications of the results they get in the Junior Cert in terms of what they're going to be doing in the Leaving. You have to understand how the points system works. You have to understand how the CAO form is filled out. You have to intervene at moments of indecision and moments of misinformed decision. I have certainly been involved in every one of those things. I can't say I've enjoyed it all, but a lot of the time, I've seen a positive result. In other areas I was hopelessly out of my depth and I was probably more an interference than anything else.

YOU'LL NEVER GO TO THE SPAR AGAIN

I understand why parents might be reluctant about allowing a child to walk to school. At one stage for nearly an entire year, we had Madeleine McCann peering out the front page of every single newspaper. For nearly a year! If that isn't going to put the wind up any parent I don't know what is. But maybe a little bit of risk is OK, because I do not believe that the threat is as pernicious as some of us seem to think. Which is not to say that I don't worry about it. I do. Following the Madeleine McCann abduction, my youngest daughter asked could she go to the local Spar – and suddenly this was a massive issue.

'No, no. You'll never go to the Spar again.'

'Well, can I go round to the side of the house to play with my friend?'

'No. No. Too dangerous.'

So we talked about it. I said, 'What are we going to do here? The poor child can't stay in the house the whole time.'

So we decided she could go to the shop, with a mobile phone and preferably using her bike. It's taking a bit of a risk, but she's probably a lot better off than some of her peers who aren't allowed outside the front door at all, simply because their parents are terrified. It leads to indolence and a completely sedentary way of life. I mean, my father drove me to school five or six times in my entire school career, while my children are driven by their mother every day. For several years, I brought my oldest son to school across the city. We're lucky that our kids are very active. They're sporty. My girls dance. They teach choreography. They perform in shows. My boys are very athletic and play a lot of games. That's quite unusual. These days, you have obese nine- and ten-year-olds who are driven home from school, have the big feed and then plant themselves in front of either the video or the PlayStation. And the most active thing they do all day is go to the fridge. And these are the very same ones who want to emulate the various icons. And all of these icons, be they male or female, tend to be pretty skinny.

I'm glad I'm not a teenager.

The other thing is, we didn't eat like kids do now. We used to have a lot more home-cooked meals, so our diet was more regulated and balanced. And we didn't have pocket money so we couldn't pile in the super-processed high-carb confectionary. The first time I went to McDonald's, I was in university. The local chipper was an occasional treat. Most of the time, your mother was making your meat and two veg for you. And we were much more active. I mean, when I was a child, we played out in the streets. If it wasn't three-and-in football, we were riding up and down on the bicycle or playing cowboys and Indians and chasing. Now, a lot of these quaint little games have faded into obscurity behind Grand Theft Auto IV on the Xbox. And I celebrate the Xbox. The Xbox is great, but there's no denying the simple fact that you don't do much running around when you're playing a video game.

CREATING WEAPONS FROM FRUIT

Girls and boys are so utterly different. I've been through so many arguments with other parents about gender conditioning and the impact of environment on boys, and how boys would be exactly the same as girls if only we didn't force them to play with guns. I just don't buy this. I'm mindful of the son of a friend of mine. His mother was determined he would not play with toy guns. She became fanatical about it and would ring ahead to any house she intended visiting to say that all weaponry must be hidden away. Then one day this child was in our house and he ran into the room chasing one of my children with a banana in his hand.

He'd figured out how to create a gun out of fruit. This guy came from the most politically correct home you could possibly imagine. There had been no stereotyping whatsoever. His mum gave him Barbies for Christmas. Yet he found a gun in the fruit bowl.

I think you just have to accept that a huge amount of male development is based on physical activity. Rough-and-tumble is extremely important for boys. You have to allow it. This must be a huge challenge, especially for a single-parent family. The mother is looking at this creature smashing up the place and himself. If she has no man in her life and there's no male input, she could be forgiven for thinking there's something utterly dysfunctional about this child. But boys act out part of their development in a very physical way. You've got to accept that some things are going to be knocked over and broken. Black eyes will ensue, fellas will fall downstairs. They will play violent video games and they will want to play shoot 'em up. They will want to have gunfights at several corrals, OK or otherwise. That's just the way it is.

The trick is to figure out when that particular dimension of the young male psyche is going into territory that maybe it shouldn't. This is when you have to start being very careful about, for instance, the sort of video games they play. You have to make sure that the violence isn't gratuitous, that it isn't celebratory, that the good guy wins, that there isn't any positive message in relation to the physical domination of women, or that torture is entertainment. You have to be incredibly vigilant around that. You have to sit on the shoulders of your boys. I mean, you can't say, 'I'm going to create a little Gandhi out of young Tommy,' but you can make bloody sure that you don't create a serial killer.

When something goes wrong, boys often find it difficult to articulate what it is. When a girl mopes around, it usually doesn't take long to badger her into telling you what's upset her. The boy, even if he wants to speak, may not be able to find the language to say what he needs to say. One of the big, big problems at the moment is young-male suicide. Some of these boys have killed themselves in a sort of ludicrous recreational way, and then there are others who I firmly believe that if somebody had spotted they were becoming disengaged from their friends and family and their own reality, they would have been able to deliver the language to them to allow them to articulate the problem.

From the get-go, girls are incredibly sophisticated and very, very complex, and I think any father will find them difficult to second-guess. All girls become sort of mini-wives at some stage in your relationship with them.

Girls look to their fathers for strong male direction. Consistency and reliability with daughters is hugely important. They must know that you will deliver because that is what they're going to look for in a man. It will enable them to be happy. Something similar happens with boys. I think it's a marker for women that they should try and be as calm as humanly possible with boys. They should try and be as reasonable and logical as it's possible for a woman to be. What you don't want is a boy hooking up with somebody who cannot control their emotions and cannot make a logical decision because they are utterly hormone-driven.

BOYFRIENDS AND GIRLFRIENDS

My mother and I used to argue over girlfriends. She did not like her boys hanging around with other women. I actually think we could have killed our partners stone dead, and our mother would have said they deserved it. There were plenty of harsh words exchanged when I arrived at the point where I could persuade whoever the current girlfriend was to come up to the bedroom to listen to the latest Joni Mitchell album, in the unfailing hope that she might take her top off. This never happened, of course. And my mother had a great habit of bursting into the room at the most inopportune time. Getting the name wrong seemed to be the most efficient weapon of choice. Nothing so off-putting for Maeve as to be called Mary, or vice versa.

First of all, you've got to accept that your children are making their own choices. You can't pick boyfriends or girlfriends for them. Now, obviously, if there's something that's so toxic as to be an actual threat to their physical or emotional well-being, you have to step in and separate them from that threat. Most of the time you'll just advise or guide them – but remember that when you say, 'You shouldn't be going out with him,' that's exactly who your daughter will want to go out with. You'll always hope that the young man who comes into her life will treat her well and take care of her, and not lie to her or cheat on her. And you know what? At the end of the day you're just going to have to accept that maybe that's what will happen. Certainly taking the boyfriend aside and giving him a good talking-to is utter bollocks.

My eldest son belongs to a generation of boys who have loads of girlfriends. It's not like when I was eighteen and most of my generation were in sort of mini-marriages. Thinking back, that's not really a healthy situation. Hooking up with one person for two or three years and going through all the dysfunctionality that you go through with a failed marriage, because at eighteen, you're completely incapable of forming a sophisticated adult relationship, despite what the law may say. But you can't step in: when you do try to influence things, you're ignored and rejected.

There are, however, certain situations where you have to say no.

When your child is under eighteen and they're involved with the wrong company, such as criminals or people using drugs, you have no other option but to get in there and separate your child from those pernicious influences. I haven't always held that opinion, but I do now. You have to do that. You have to lay down the law and you have to say, 'You're not going out with these people any more and if you try to do that I'm going to keep you locked in.'

If you believe your child is under threat, if you believe that they're going to get into trouble with the law, or that their health, well-being or sanity may be at risk, you must step in and do the unpalatable thing. And at that moment you will not be your child's friend, but you will be their parent. I didn't always think that way, but I've seen so many things happen not just to my own children but to all the children who have been in my life. I've seen a lot of things happen that could have been stopped by parents taking more robust action and being unpopular for a while. It took me a long time to learn that being unpopular at home wasn't the end of the world. It passes.

COOKING DEALS AND WEARING STUPID CLOTHES

It's not easy when your kids go from idolizing you to thinking you're a moron. The trick is not to take it too personally. I think the first time your child, now a teenager, looks askance at you, you've got to have a sense of humour about it. You've got to understand that this is just a period in your relationship; it's not that significant. You can make it more significant than it needs to be by taking it personally.

Women can find it very, very difficult. The little boy who was so dependent on his mother, so loving towards her, suddenly turns into a monster with a much deeper voice who grunts and can't be got out of bed and won't look her in the eye. That can be a very disturbing experience for a woman. Less so for a man. I think men tend to be less engaged with the issue. But, from my experience, you just have to have a sense of humour about it. Deliver yourself to their ridicule. Say stupid things that you know they're going to pick up on. Wear stupid clothes. Comb your hair in a silly way. Give them reason to laugh at you and it'll defuse things much more quickly.

The most difficult stage, for them and for you, is when they're in their mid-teens. At fourteen, fifteen and sixteen, they're becoming adult, with all the same desires and ambitions and hopes and angst that we once had. Young men of sixteen have died, and still do die, in war, and young women have had children and brought them up successfully. But they're not complete adults at that stage. There are still huge growth spurts to come, emotionally and physically. And they have no adult rights. They can't say, 'I'm not doing that,' or 'I'm going to go out' or 'I'm definitely doing this or that.'

They have none of the normal privileges that adults take for granted, and they're expected to be responsive to adult demands. And, of course, they've all those hormones coursing through them. It's terrible being that age. Consequently it can frame pretty challenging experiences for the parent.

This is when you stop being your child's friend. And I think this is where both parents need to be seen to be singing from the same hymn-sheet. It's very tempting to go, 'Your mother doesn't know what she's talking about. Don't worry about that. You go out and do it anyway. Be grand.' Immensely tempting, but a recipe for disaster. So, I think what you really need to do when you see that moment arriving in a child's life is to sit down with your partner and acknowledge what's happening and what's ahead of you both and agree that you'll go through this period together. And that you're not going to try to cook deals behind one another's backs. No matter how much the woman may think the man is being too easygoing, no matter how much the man may think the woman is too psychotic, you've got to accept that you must support each other during a potentially explosive period in the child's life. And you will get a good result out of doing that. I can't say I always managed to come up to the mark on that, but certainly in later years I've tried to.

One other thing. Not cooking deals behind one partner's back doesn't mean you can't cook deals. Deal cooking is an absolute essential with boys. Men understand negotiation. It's no harm to bribe a male child to do something. I certainly bribed my boys to do things and negotiated with them for school goals versus social aspirations. I promised them things depending on how they behaved at home or performed at school. With girls, I think you have to appeal to their sense of justice and their sense of propriety. If they believe the right thing is being done, they'll step up to the plate. This all comes back to women having a better relationship with the whole concept of truth. If you can show your daughter that what you're asking her to do is reasonable, and that only a very unreasonable person would not acquiesce, more often than not you will get a positive result.

With boys, you say, 'Look I'm going to get you the PlayStation game, but you have to promise me that you're going to turn up for supervised study for the next month, OK?'

The boy will NOT say, 'Hmm, that sounds like the right strategy for the Junior Cert.' He'll go: Supervised study = PlayStation game.

I've had arguments with some of my friends because they say it's teaching boys all the wrong things. It's not. It's getting a result. That's really what matters at the end of the day. Through the rest of a fella's life, hopefully, he'll develop a moral code, but in the meantime there are certain things that just have to be done and if the only way to do them is through bribery, well, so be it.

None of which is to say you can't negotiate with girls. When you've negotiated with the girl over whatever the issue is – going out or what she's wearing, or study – and it's been established that this is where we're going on this issue, I think you get quite a positive and long-term result. You frequently find that boys have to be reminded. There's no let-up really with boys. You're only fooling yourself if you think you're going to be able to lay down the law, make the pronouncement, issue some sort of threat and everything's going to be fine and it's all rock on regardless for the next year. You'll constantly be revisiting these arrangements. Constantly. You'll also find down the line that whatever you came up with is utter balderdash and at that point you have to decide how to say, 'This is stupid, this plan didn't work out.'

It's not about saving face. It's about continuing the forward momentum of the child's development. I think when that happens you're better off going to the child and saying, 'Look, I don't know what I was thinking when I came up with that plan. Give me a day and I'll rethink the whole thing.'

WAIT TILL YOUR FATHER GETS HOME

My eldest daughter would say that I was always hard line on discipline. Not that I ever slapped her, but she will tell the story that when she was a teenager, she would run home from the bus to be in on time. From the word go, we impressed on our children that rules and regulations were to be taken seriously. I think you have to deliver that message as a couple. And this goes for people who are separated as well. You need to shelve your own animosities, issues and problems and unite on this. If you don't do that the shit's going to hit the fan.

Men, I believe, have a very vital role to play in discipline. They can deliver authority. There's a selection of reasons why. They have deeper voices than women. They're physically more imposing. They are much more economical when it comes to expressing themselves so there's less room for debate over an issue. These are important factors when you're trying to lay down the law. And it's not by accident that an entire television series was called *Wait Till Your Father Gets Home*. I mean, I don't think you can rely exclusively on waiting till Dad gets home to deal with a problem, but men have a key role in enforcing sanctions when things have gone wrong – but that's hugely dependent on the way both partners treat each other. If you're demeaned by your wife in front of your children, you're going to be hugely compromised in the way that you maintain discipline, and vice versa. When the children see that Mum has him on her side, they're much less likely to fuck around with her. Mum's reasoned with, she's cajoled, she's massaged, she's loved, she's embraced, she's hugged. That didn't work. Now Dad's coming in with a half-sentence and a threat.

I think everybody will find at some stage, probably not with girls but with boys, that you end up slapping them. Usually it's when you've lost your temper and you're out of control. And at the end of the day, an act of violence against a child is an act of violence against a child. When you slap the child, you'll get results, but the reality of it is you've assaulted a human being who is not able to defend themselves. It is not a long-term solution. You can make a physical presence potent by just standing there, but when you hit your child, you cross a line and you're in trouble because what are you? You're an ogre. You're a bully. What's the next thing? What do you do after that? Hit them harder? Corporal punishment has diminishing returns.

I think you have to be realistic about what you can do when it comes to discipline. You have to accept that grounding somebody for two weeks or for a year is utter nonsense. I now believe the best thing to do is ground the person for an hour, then it's all over and you're not made a fool of by having to give in a day or two later because Johnny has to go to hurling. Taking away the mobile phone is a very powerful sanction, but not for a month or something. That's ludicrous. It's going to backfire because you need them to have it when they go to the chemist and you want to tell them they forgot to bring the money with them. Or if they're in trouble – somebody's attacking them and you've got their mobile. Keep it for a night. Video games are now a hugely powerful sanction for boys: no video games, no Xbox, no PlayStation for one or two nights is workable. With sanctions it's go to your room. It's a denial of luxury, but only for a short time because you can enforce it. Anything beyond twenty-four hours is basically unenforceable. Uttering the immortal words, 'You're not going out until after your Leaving Certificate,' is ridiculous. It's unenforceable and counter-productive.

WHAT THE HELL IS THAT EEJIT TALKING ABOUT?

What I did with ecstasy was this.

'Listen,' I said, 'you will probably have a good time. You'll feel great, though maybe a bit knackered tomorrow. But, in all likelihood, if you take this drug, and if you take it regularly, you will find yourself in a scenario where you cannot be naturally happy. In a couple of years' time, you'll be depressed.'

That is a fact. And it will happen to an awfully large number of people who took the drug. That's as far as you can go. You've got to hope that they'll be able to see into the future, which is not something young people are renowned for. But it's nonsense to do the 'Just Say No' thing.

I find that teenagers are much more receptive if you say, 'Well, the reason they're taking those drugs is because they feel fantastic when they do.'

But if you tell somebody, 'Do not take ecstasy. You will die immediately, and you will go to hell,' then the child goes out and takes it, has a fantastic night, loves everybody, dances for Ireland and the next morning wakes up feeling pretty good, because they've got fresh young bodies . . . they're just going to go, 'What the hell was that eejit talking about?'

SHOW ME THE MONEY

My kids don't get regular pocket money – or salaries, as some children seem to get nowadays – but they do OK on the money side of things. It's just not possible not to give your children money now because, at a very basic level, they need cash for phone credit. I find myself going into shops and buying credit all the time. I'm fascinated by how much it seems to cost a teenager to go out on the town. They'll laugh at you when you give them twenty euros. I'm intrigued by how upset and hurt and slighted children can feel if you don't step up to the mark with the dough, or even jokingly suggest they should try going out tonight with no money. I certainly did that a lot. If I suggested that to my children, they would think I was in deep need of psychiatric evaluation.

I encourage them to try and come up with schemes to earn money and they're pretty good at that. My eldest daughter teaches choreography. She's still in college, so her wage pays her student bills. That's fairly impressive. The rest of them are entrepreneurial in their own way. They seem able to generate cash by babysitting and that kind of thing. Once you see them making some attempt, I think it's a good idea to reward them – if you have the capacity to do so.

I have no favourites among my five children. What else would I say? They're all radically different. They present completely different challenges, trials, tribulations and joys. And I think, really, what I try to do is just be there for them. I've tried to recognize that the best thing I can do is be available, whether it's driving them to drama, organizing a sleepover or going down to sort out something at the local police station. Just being there.

You'll really find that the best thing you can do is just accept that you are your child's servant.

My kids are – and I would say this, too – super-overachievers. They're fantastic. I mean, all the singing, all the dancing, all the kicking and running . . . These are well worth celebrating and I've got a big microphone so of course I'm going say that sometimes. I mean, it's my ball and I decide who'll score the goals. The world of show business has embraced my two eldest daughters and I certainly would celebrate that publicly. They've never come to me and said, 'Don't talk about us,' though as they get older I'll be very careful not to intrude on their privacy.

I enjoy my children hugely. I celebrate them. They're wonderful. They advise me a lot. They're very informed, right down to my eight-year-old, Babette. They're all very switched on and very outspoken. And they get on very well together. They're incredibly close-knit. They're an amazing bunch, and a formidable bunch as well. And they can speak as one. If they think there's a problem, they'll walk up to their parents and they'll say it.

LEAVING RTÉ

Last year I came very close to signing a deal with Denis O'Brien. He wanted me to come to Newstalk and do a daytime programme there. The station was about to go national and its owner, Denis's company Communicorp, was ramping up to become a very big player. There was a shareholding potential. He was hoping I would take a role in building the station, and maybe get involved in Communicorp's stable of stations. Altogether, the package was worth several millions more than RTÉ was offering. One of my best friends, Willie O'Reilly, is head of Today FM, another Communicorp station, and is heavily involved with the other stations. I was really quite excited by that. Certainly I was very excited by the amount of money we were talking about.

But the negotiations fell apart, and I suppose they fell apart because I was too cautious. I'm sure Denis would say I was too greedy, but I think probably I was too cautious. This was one of the most dangerous moments in my career, because RTÉ were looking at my contract and deciding whether I was of value to them any more. Despite the public-service remit, RTÉ is a much more commercially run organization than ever before, and those who run it are now responsible for the performance of their own individual sections. RTÉ Radio, for example, would have been looking at what it cost them to employ me and how much trouble it was to have me around . . . Anyway, I got to the point at which I'd begun to sort of think, Well, maybe it is time for me to go. Maybe it is time for me to leave RTÉ and do something to reinvent and reinvigorate myself . . .

I was getting ready to tell RTÉ to shove it when Denis disappeared. He was out of coverage, I was told. This was pretty incredible for a guy who owns most of the mobile telephones in the world. Obviously he had just got fed up with the negotiations. I'm mad about Denis, I think he's a genius, so when he came back, he called me up and said, 'Have you signed back up with RTÉ yet?'

'Of course I fucking signed,' I told him. 'I had to sign. I nearly lost everything. I nearly didn't have an RTÉ contract.' And the two of us just laughed.

Denis said, 'Well, maybe next time . . .'

Our friendship was not affected by it.

Negotiating with him was certainly an experience. His idea is that a deal can be done on a child's copybook with a crayon. Keep the lawyers away from it. Get the essence of the deal together, understand what you want from the other guy and what he wants from you, then bring in the lawyers to pull it together. I work on the basis of dotting *i*s, crossing *t*s and parsing sentences right from the word go.

That's not to say Denis is anything other than a highly sophisticated practitioner. His way of conducting business is highly challenging. 'Look,' he said, 'you have to take a risk. This is a baseline income here, and if it works, you've earned an awful lot of money. If it doesn't, you've earned not so much money . . .'

I was too afraid to do that. I mean, it seemed hugely attractive over loin of rabbit in Patrick Gibaud's, but the reality, as we entered a much more troubled economic climate, was that the commercial world would be much more pressured than the world of the public-service broadcaster.

THERE'S A HELL OF A KICK IN THE TAIL

The same thing happened with Robbie Wootton when he was representing Radio Ireland back in 1997. I was too cautious to leave. I suspect I may be destined to remain with RTÉ for the rest of my life. It's because I'm so familiar with the way the organization works. At the time, Robbie described RTÉ brilliantly. He said, 'People say it's a dinosaur, but be very careful when you wake it up. There's a hell of a kick in the tail.'

I know that dinosaur really well. I know how it works, its colours and moods and tendencies. The commercial world is much more cut-throat: when there's a problem, when there's a hiccup, when there's a fall in the ratings, when there's a shortfall in revenue, you're gone. That doesn't happen at RTÉ. You get breathing space to recover.

Anyway, Robbie was a very significant power broker in Radio Ireland. He was substantially, if not completely, responsible for brokering the deal with RTÉ to have Radio Ireland – now Today FM – transmitted on the RTÉ transmission network. That was a hugely significant deal for them. He knew a lot about broadcasting, and understood that he needed a Beatles or a Stones to make the thing fly. But he took it one step further. His courtship involved taking the whole show, everything, lock, stock, and barrel. And he almost succeeded. He convinced all of the major players to go. He had deals put together for each one of us – researchers, broadcasting assistants, producers. Willie O'Reilly was the series producer at the time. He had just done what he believed to be his deal with Radio Ireland. We were doing a programme live from Dublin Castle. I remember it well because I interviewed US shock-jock Howard Stern on it. Stern was fascinated that we could say 'fuck' on the radio.

So, we were breaking up for the summer season, and I recall sitting in the courtyard in Dublin Castle with Willie O'Reilly and Siobhan Hough, and Willie said, 'Well, what are you going to do?'

I said, 'I don't think I'm going to go.'

He took it well, because I found out subsequently that he was absolutely furious and hugely disappointed. But from that moment on, Willie was gone. He continued to produce the programme, and it wasn't until year or so later that he actually left, but his head was gone. I believe RTÉ made a big mistake in not appointing him head of 2FM when the job came up. I told them, 'This guy has an incredibly astute mind in both broadcasting and business terms. He has that unusual combination of intellect and acumen.'

They should have given him the job because that would have kept him there. Instead he went to Today FM, and I have no doubt that without him Today FM would not be the success it is today.

So I told Robbie, 'I'm not going.'

He then had to go back to his board and tell them that the thing he had promised, *The Gerry Ryan Show*, was not going to happen. That was not a good moment in his week. But that night he rang me up and he said, 'I'm coming over to you. I'll bring a bottle of whiskey and we'll get drunk.'

He didn't mention it once that night. We just talked as friends. And the next day I drove to work and he came with me. We both had pretty substantial hangovers. I remember dropping him at Sandymount. As he got out of the car, he said the only thing he's ever said to me about it, before or since. 'Pity.'

The courtship of somebody like me in that sort of scenario is very difficult. But, really, the one thing I now know, the one thing that would have worked in all of those situations, would have been if somebody had just got a cheque for a million and put it on the table in front of me and said, 'Can we go from here?'

That would have worked.

INDISPENSABLE? ME?

The radio show brings in a huge amount of 2FM's revenue. Without that money, I think that 2FM, if not the entire radio division, would be in very serious difficulties. So, yes, it's a powerful position to be in. But the one thing people take too long to learn is that RTÉ is capable of turning round and going, 'Well, OK, we'll take the hit for a couple of years. Something will come along and the figures will balance out.'

I'd be a fool to think they were incapable of making such a dramatic decision. Am I that indispensable? I think probably I am. But I'm not so sure whether I have the *cojones* to push it.

THE FUTURE

'*Happiness is being able to smile, laugh and treat other people nice when I, myself, am feeling really bad.*' Gerard Ryan, third-year religion exam, St Paul's College

I saw my wife before I met her, this extraordinarily radiant woman. Probably the most beautiful creature I'd ever seen. I can remember it quite clearly. She came up to Trinity College with the girl I was actually going out with at the time. She was a pal of hers. I was organizing something for the Law Society during freshers' week and I was looking for stuff to decorate the front square. My then girlfriend, Maria, was a fine arts student in the National College of Art and Design. She said she had a pal who was good at that sort of thing. They'd bring some 'soft sculptures'. I didn't know what that meant, but it turned out to mean pillows, sort of. So, she arrived with this girl who, as I recall, was wearing a bib and braces. She had this kind of *kabuki* white makeup on, short hair.

Incredibly striking. Luminous cherry lips, huge eyes like an antelope's. Just radiant. And I remember thinking, My God, she's something else. And, of course, it's always a bit difficult when you're going out with somebody else but, really, that's what's meant to happen when you're that age.

That was that for the moment. I didn't see her for a while. At the time I had a bit of a nomadic existence. I was living part of the time with my girlfriend and part of the time with a pal of mine, Mark, who had one of the old soldiers' cottages in Killester. There was a dinner party, someone had a dinner party, and this girl, Morah Brennan, showed up again. I remember holding her hand underneath the table and it was just like touching a high-voltage cable. It was nothing to do with sex. It was instant falling in love. I remember she was wearing a flowing white muslin dress. She didn't look like any woman I had ever met or even seen before. I held her hand under the table and I remember thinking, This. Is. It.

But I had no idea, no idea, what to do next. I didn't know what I was supposed to be doing about these feelings. Do I say something to her? Do I make a date? When I think back on my generation, we boys had no ability to articulate what we felt, no idea how to act upon these feelings. There was something staring you in the face that you had to do. You had to say privately, in the kitchen, wherever, 'I really want to meet you again,' but I couldn't get that out. Instead I was talking about Nietzsche, or some bolloxology, trying to impress her instead of getting a plan together. I made a complete cock-up of the thing, and all I achieved was a lot of staring at her. It probably made her a bit uneasy. Maybe this guy is a bit peculiar . . .

So she disappeared again.

Next time I saw her she was with her mum, just outside the Central Remedial Clinic in Clontarf, and once again I was thunderstruck. So vibrant. Shining in her difference. I've always been like that. I think maybe it's been my downfall in terms of the people I'm interested in. I will always be more interested in someone who's completely different . . . but she was beyond different. She was hugely attractive, and happy and innocent . . .

I'd begun to hang around with a lot of arts students and architects. My rationale was that if there was any free love going on, as they'd called it in the sixties, it was more likely to be going on among an arty set than at a law or engineering party.

So I was at this party, and this wonderful Morah Brennan materialized again. She was always surrounded by men. A whole set of boys was obsessed with her in college. And I remember thinking, I'm going to have a shot at this, I'm going to have a shot at her. So I said to her – the naïvety of it – 'Do you like kittens? Do you like baby kittens?'

And she said, 'Oh, I love baby kittens, I adore kittens.'

'Well,' I said, 'there are newborn baby kittens in the back garden.'

I brought her outside and we were standing there and she said, 'Where are the kittens?'

And I said, 'Ah, there's no kittens.' I just remember saying to myself: Good man! This is the first time you've ever actually got this right. I felt like David Niven . . . Like Errol Flynn, like James Bond. It was the first time I'd ever actually got a line together that actually worked. So we're in the back garden and I'm kissing her and knowing this is the person I'm going to be spending the rest of my life with.

What happened with Maria? She'd broken it off with me before that. I mostly ended up being dumped by women. I think what used to happen was girls would be quite fascinated with me, they'd be attracted to me, then they'd realize, Your man's a complete fabrication. I'm out of here.

THE GIANT GERRY RYAN SATURDAY NIGHT LIGHT ENTERTAINMENT SHOW

RTÉ are constantly in search of *The Giant Gerry Ryan Saturday Night Light Entertainment Show*, and this always amazes me, considering that most of the damage done to me was in *The Giant Gerry Ryan Saturday Night Light Entertainment Show* business, whether it was *Secrets* or *Ryantown*. Today I still sit in meetings – the faces are younger, the names are different – where they're in search of the holy grail, the *Fabulous, Massive, Fuck-off, Giant Gerry Ryan Saturday Night . . .* and so on, despite the success of *Operation Transformation* and *Ryan Confidential . . .*

And I just go, 'Oh, no . . .'

But, of course, inevitably, part of me goes, Well, imagine if we did find it! Wouldn't that be fantastic? Wouldn't it be great at this stage in my career to revisit the stuff that didn't work in the past and, you know, repair it and make it work? The only thing is, I mean, I've had a very good relationship with the media in relation to my television work in the last few years. Most of the time they just couldn't be fucking bothered with it . . . I have some sympathy for television critics on the Gerry Ryan issue, because they must be mesmerized as to why, like, why the fuck is he still on the television? Either that or they've decided that, well, you know what? He seems to have found a level at which the world can live with him. I'm very proud of what I've done with *Ryan Confidential*, and I was hugely proud of *Operation Transformation*.

So I'm torn. Would I like to do a big light-entertainment show? One part of me goes, 'Absolutely not.' I couldn't face the cartoons with the turkey's body and my head on it. But you know something? Never say never, because imagine sitting down some Saturday night, having rejected a plan out of hand, and watching a television programme take shape before you. This is one of my nightmares: watching a television programme unfolding, say, before Tubridy, right? Because that's where it would go. Watching it unfolding and going, 'Fuck, that's good. Wow, that's good. It's fun . . . Shit, I should have done that.'

Eddie Doyle is the new head of entertainment, and Eddie's a very experienced guy. Eddie, God love him, has to sit and listen to me talking about My Credibility and about how it's taken so long for me to do programmes that the radio team aren't embarrassed by. And I can see his eyes glazing over, and he's going, 'Oh, yeah, yeah . . .'

And he goes, 'Yeah, OK, you can do *Ryan Confidential*, that's fine, you know. We're really looking forward to it.' (Coughs.)

I said to him recently at a meeting, 'You know, Eddie, what you really want is a *Giant Gerry Ryan Saturday Night Light Entertainment Show*.'

'Yeah,' says Eddie, his face lighting up.

It's kind of flattering that they still think of my name in relation to it.

I'm the flavour of the month at the moment, so a lot of people have been ringing up, saying, 'Oh, we'd love you to do this thing – it's a gardening programme.' Or 'We'd love you to do this – it's judging children doing Irish dancing. Would you like to do that?' I've had a lot of those conversations. And you know what? I'm super-practised in saying no. There's a lot going on at the moment, so I think maintaining an even keel is the thing. I really believe that the radio programme has been reinvigorated to an enormous extent. I'm really looking forward to bringing the same level of excitement to the next series of *Confidential*. There's a new series of *Operation Transformation* in the pipeline.

That's enough to be going on with at the moment.

I'M NOT TOO BAD IN MY OWN COMPANY EITHER

I'm not removed from my family. They are still my life. When you've got five kids, you've got to look at it like that. That's your life until the tomb, and the rest is just a satellite round it. I think it's incumbent on somebody like me to make sure that I am committed to that completely, and that I can get something out of it that's positive for me. It has to be a two-way street. I've a tremendous relationship with my children. Privately you hope you're needed, publicly you're united. I'm travelling on holidays with the kids very soon, so I'm looking forward to that, and I have daily contact with them. That's really at the heart of my life, so in my present circumstances, I've just had to redefine myself in practical terms. Geography changes a bit, your emphasis changes a bit, your daily structure isn't as it was before. What I'm surprised by is that at the heart of it is the same thing that was always there, and that's my complete commitment to and fascination with my children.

If you haven't got children, it's really hard to understand this, but you draw on that relationship so much. It's the most appropriate relationship you're ever going to have. It gives me strength, it entertains me, and it also empowers me because I'm guiding them. I'm providing the simple material things that they need: money, assistance . . . more money.

And I'm watching them becoming adults as well, so they're not just my children any more, they're my friends too. I socialize with them, and I enjoy their company tremendously. I remember once saying to Ryan Tubridy that I didn't understand why he had his children over to stay with him at the weekend. I thought, Surely when you're separated, would you not be better off trying to make an arrangement that was a bit more flexible so you could go out on the town at the weekends? It's not until you're actually in the situation that you discover you'd prefer to be with the kids. None of which is to say that I don't have a social life. The truth is I've never had a particularly extensive social life. I've always been a very private person, so a lot of my life was spent reading and watching movies, sometimes going to pals' homes for drinks or meals. A lot of that hasn't changed. And if the truth be known, I'm not too bad in my own company either.

Now I do find myself sometimes going, 'I gotta get out of here . . . now!' simply because it's too quiet. More than a quarter of a century of noise is hard to get over. It's hard not to feel some withdrawal symptoms. But you find an accommodation with your new life and, contrary to what I'd thought, there's a lot of my old life in my new life. And at the end of the day, the children will grow up, find their own lives, their own partners. They'll seek their own happiness, they will become less and less reflected in me and their mother. You've got to be careful not to think, Well, if I'm not living permanently with my children, there's no point to my life. Hopefully your children are not going to live with you permanently. I'm just enjoying what's offered to me, and I've been very lucky. I have their company often, they're healthy, they're not in trouble. And I suppose you could say the same about me.